Kathleen

The War Years

By

G.A.Chamberlin

Crown Eagle Publishing

Copyright © 2014 by G.A.Chamberlin
All rights reserved

First Edition, 2014

Printed in the United States

ISBN 978-0-615-97091-2

Crown Eagle Publishing

Cover: Close up of Kathleen, daughter of U.S. Ambassador
Harriman to Moscow, 1943-1946

Book Cover Production by Jennifer Chamberlin

The documents used in *Kathleen The War Years* are declassified by the State Department by Executive Order 12356, Section 3 (a) They were initially declassified on or about 1986. These documents certify their Declassification Status at the start of each segment of documents.

~

Documents imaged, used or cited are from the Averell Harriman papers in the US Library of Congress, Special Collections.

It should also be noted that Averell Harriman donated all his papers to the US Library of Congress long before the declassification assignments were given: There, they have remained under the curatorship of the Manuscripts, Special Collection.

The US Library of Congress at its discretion allows viewing. Also included in that collection are the approved records and writings made by others related to his mission and work.

*

All images Courtesy of the Library of Congress, Special Collections

All official documents originally generated by the US government. Section 105 of the Copyright Act.

This publication was arranged by the Editors and Author citing official source material. Any digital images made, and those resulting images and content produced is Copyright protected as presented herein.

This is an original creative work based on sources found in the public record. The names, characters, places and incidents are those found within the public record and based on original and declassified documents authorized for public viewing by the US Library of Congress and other recognized public repositories.

The publisher does not have any control over and does not assume any responsibility, or any results, or third party uses of this content. Nor does the publisher assume any responsibility for activities that might have been published as source material.

Averell Harriman, 1937, Sun Valley.
Courtesy U.S. Library of Congress.

Foreword

Prior to America's official engagement in WWII, and during the war, President Roosevelt utilized a Lend-Lease Program to supply and provision the Allies in Europe. He chose the chief executive of Union Pacific Railroad, Averell Harriman as his Special Envoy to head the Lend-Lease mission as his "expediter."
In London, the effort was known as the Harriman Mission before attaching to the US Embassy as office of Economic Affairs.

After two years in London, Harriman was appointed US Ambassador to Russia 1943-1945. As his only accompanying family, Averell Harriman took his daughter, Kathleen Harriman.

Kathleen was 23 when she landed in London. Employed as a member of the American Press Corps, she worked amongst the American staff. As a family member, she was the only American woman on mission during the war.

The story of Kathleen Harriman is the account of American leadership during WWII as she accompanied her father. She interacted with Churchill; Eleanor Roosevelt; Hopkins; Winant and countless staffs; mission leaders and military chiefs. In London there were Sovereigns; celebrities; head of states; executives of industry, directors of treasure, custodians of resources, specialists for intellect and expertise. In the field there were battle-group commanders, post leaders and strategists; at the Allied Conferences Kathleen mixed with Marshalls, Generals and Policy leaders. At Moscow, as consort to the Ambassador, Kathleen was the diplomatic hostess of the American Embassy if not for the diplomatic colony congregating at Spaso House, the official Residence and headquarters for Harriman's missions as both US Ambassador and Special Envoy to Churchill and Stalin...

Most of all, Kathleen enjoyed the young at heart - all those willing to throw themselves into a just cause. And she loved to ski.

The US Library of Congress holds the papers of the Harriman missions. It is known that he donated much of his papers to the Library several years ago. Also included in his archived papers are the letters written, later retyped, by Kathleen. Using her own correspondence, censored as it was, this book shows the events of the war unfolding around them, beginning with Harriman setting up No. 3 Grosvenor Square in London.

Source material for this work come from the official Reports of the Harriman Mission; the daily office log of his Aide Robert Meiklejohn (later compiled as a Diary and copyrighted); Memoires of other officials, and secondary analysis of the era. It is known that official records were continuously kept in secured quarters and subsequently curated at repositories holding our nation's manuscript collections. The US Library of Congress compiled all attending documentation into the archive of the Harriman papers. By the time of this writing, all were officially declassified, and accessible for review.

Kathleen herself faced personal challenges. As both daughter of a high official with sensitive information, and reporter for the dissemination of information, Kathleen walked a fine line: Neither did Americans have reliable information, nor did the interests of national security serve them at arms length. Harriman saw the gap, and he pressed her to remain undaunted, if discrete. Thus, as a reporter, she faced daily questioning of confidence about her editorial abilities, propaganda writing, inexperience, depth of understanding ...often finding her work squashed or marginalized. Much of it might well have been professional envy by her colleagues and superiors. But in fact there were real obstacles to the free flow of public information including censorship; security; fierce media brazenness; misinformation; sensationalism - such that Harriman would employ his own media to aid the President. Kathleen understood the gravity of the situation. For one so young she demonstrated remarkable perspicuity in her observations.

Kathleen, in her subtle way, would have an impact on this war:
If her position as the daughter of an American diplomat went unnoticed on a stage of world leaders, it was her bright appearance that reminded Churchill to aspire to global economic opportunities

as well as military liberation as early as August 1941 at the First Atlantic Conference when addressing Roosevelt.

As a member of the American Press Corps, Kathleen's dilemma opened up new media venues for Americans to make better informed decisions...

When insular isolationism closed American eyes, Kathleen focused on the youthful troops coming to Europe with hope in their hearts.

In was Kathleen's image that prevailed upon the world to enjoin the Russians to tell the truths about the Katyn Forest...the subject of investigation that would continue through 1956 in US Senate Hearings.

Finally, it was Kathleen's visage of dignity, loyalty and high spirits that saw the Moscow mission through disparagement and neglect in the months of transition following Roosevelt's death.

As the allied era gave way to a cold war in Moscow, it was because of Kathleen's fresh and sunny disposition that Stalin gave to the Harrimans a parting gift of two prize stallions to bring to the United States in 1945...

Averell Harriman, a "dollar-a-year man" was a political executive. After a year of preparations in Washington DC., he was the man sent to administer the writings of the Conferences, the Agreements, the Protocols, the re-mapping of Europe, the strategic affairs that would linger far beyond the war, using his staff, his pen and his personal brand of patience and perspective to give us a post war world. Without Kathleen at his side, his diplomatic disposition would have been altered, if not disfigured. Kathleen gave him the grace to write in American, even as he would go on to serve in Washington for decades after the war. This book shows the records of those involved with the decisions of the war.

Primary acknowledgements for source material must go to the US National Archives; the Roosevelt Library; official US Government policy papers; US Library of Congress in Washington DC; numerous

Banks' Archives, and the Public Records Office, Kew Gardens, London UK.

With unbelievable intensity, the first year of the war fell upon the Harrimans: We see Harriman with his Aide Meiklejohn saying farewell to friends and family at La Guardia before a harrowing flight across the Atlantic. It is early, still dark, foreboding, the war in Europe perilous in March, 1941.

Immediately, Harriman is being shown the ruins of England by Winston Churchill -- his own Mission quarters set up entirely by his able Aide, Robert Meiklejohn who keeps the official daily log, like a diary...

Mid-May, a young American Kathleen arrives in London during a bombing blitz, having crossed the Atlantic as dangerously as her father. Accommodated in a Hotel, they assume diplomatic life in London where Kathleen also works as a member of the American Press Corps. She is to write about the war.

Kathleen writes letters home. Britain is losing ground in North Africa, center of its colonial and Middle Eastern interests. Harriman, Roosevelt's Special Envoy, is invited to tour North Africa to assess the damage and review performance of the British military there. In Cairo, he meets Randolph, Churchill's son.

It is June. While Harriman is away, Germany turns on Russia: The war is spreading. Roosevelt sends Harry Hopkins to talk to Stalin.

Kathleen is adjusting to London life: She greets her father now returned, and they witness the first US Shipment of American Aid arriving at English docks... Hopkins appears in July with shocking reports from Stalin who desperately needs aid. They can withstand only weeks longer... How can the US help?

Harriman must report to the President with his findings...

Harriman leaves Kathleen in London. She is coping fine, she tells Mary in a letter...

Harriman recommends a Middle East Route for sending supplies to Russia. Roosevelt asks Harriman to arrange for a meeting between himself and Churchill. Japan is now viewed as a threat. Hopkins returns to Stalin.

In an August rendezvous at sea, Harriman has arranged for the meeting between the two leaders off the coast of Newfoundland. It is the First Atlantic Conference, and Harriman shoots off letters to Kathleen from aboard ship. Harriman must return to Washington to prepare for Aid to Russia, Kathleen still in London...

London, under curfew and nightly assault, is in blackout, the American Embassy and Harriman Mission at No 3 Grosvenor still functioning. They have a country retreat for safety, yet Kathleen is busy, entertained, making friends, London has a nightlife for those working on the war efforts...She is observing, writing, reporting, and seeking balance. Is she finding her stride as a London staffer coping with the war?

September 1941, Harriman reappears in London - on his way to Moscow to deliver Aide, Protocols, Agreements to the Soviets, their new ally. Kathleen wants to talk to him about her problems at the Press. He tells her to keep at it.

Kathleen is left at the Embassy Mission staff where sirens send most people fleeing to Air Raid Shelters. In London they are essential, engaged, active without hesitation, if in a stylish kind of way, Kathleen at the center of it all. This is, after all, the epicenter of the war where American Lend Lease Aid is being arranged by the Harriman Mission attached to the Embassy.

October 1941, inside Catherine the Great's Palace at the Kremlin, Stalin meets with British Lord Beaverbrook and American Harriman: They complete the Moscow Conference with Protocols of war deliveries, schedules, payments, Russian assault fronts and military strategies. An opera is scheduled to close the meetings as the city is preparing to evacuate, and they leave Russia in a harrowing journey, the enemy now positioned south of Moscow.

Harriman arrives in London but must report immediately to the President, and Kathleen must stay. Besides, her passport would never allow her to return if she left... She is safe, sheltered amongst the staff of the American mission. Plus, she has friends now, Pam Churchill, Mary Churchill, the wife of the American Ambassador to the Nations in Exile, Mrs. Biddle..

Kathleen misses nothing, she sees everything: When necessary in her father's absence, she is by default representing him in London.

London, officiating in normal tones and dressing up for evening social events in total defiance, then a drink with airmen before a flight raid …. England, strong, so generously human, is in trouble. Kathleen's heart aches, and she writes at night, the curtains drawn "Dear Mary"…

Kathleen is, for the most part, alone. She interviews sovereign leaders-in-exile stranded in London. She writes of their news, opinions, narratives and intelligence. America is badly misinformed about the war. Roosevelt wants to meet with Stalin. Arrangements must be made…

US Congressmen arrive in London balefully uninformed, their political world still divided. The war is worsening. The enemy are downing aircraft; sinking ships of supply to England, to Moscow…

December, Pearl Harbor is attacked. Kathleen in London feels abandoned. "Dear Mary" she writes…The Churchill family try to pick up for her, it is Christmas.

Harriman is sequestered with the President and Prime Minister Churchill in Washington DC. Declarations of War follow. They are meeting as the ARCADIA Conference. For America, this was only the beginning of the war…

Kathleen remained with her father throughout the war, journeying to many destinations and a WWII Conference, stopping in America only twice to restock for their household on mission overseas. Together, with their staff, the Harriman's returned to the United States in 1946 at the completion of their tour of duty.

Kathleen's ultimate success came when she found her own voice, identify and maturity in her unique position as consort to the US Ambassador to Moscow.

"...establish an order of peace in the world, which – after the war was won – would lead to a golden century with prosperity and security undreamed of for all classes of society and all peoples."

Winston Churchill,

HMS PRINCE OF WALES

First Atlantic Conference, 1941.

*

Finally, the book presentation uses Courier type, bold, unspecified justification to resemble the source records. Carbon copies of letters and reports showed black bold ink, struck from keys on manual typewriters, like those that produced the Yalta Agreements requiring eight copies, after the President's top copy. Cables, if typed, were in courier - propelling all necessary responses for decisions. Kathleen's own letters, even if later retyped, were originally from the same type face, her spelling and grammar of secondary importance to the crisis at hand. Above all, this was the look of her day.

* * *

Kathleen

The War Years

1.

Kathleen was excited.

Last January at 6,200 ft. elevation, Sun Valley had accumulated 130 inches of snow, snow that drooped from fir boughs in powdery softness all over the mountain. At dawn, this presented a blushing invitation to test the delights of winter skiing.

It was early in the year still, September and the sun bright. The resort was already filling with people. Moreover, her father was on a train with a private party from New York, all of them arriving later.

Kathleen leaned on her poles, filling her lungs with fresh mountain air, skis firmly beneath her. She glanced uphill and then pushed off, her furry hood feathering as a bird in flight.

In choosing the Lower Olympic run, she would race through a fresh snowfall upon a still verdant Bald Mountain, Ketchum Idaho. Here, the Olympians trained. Suitable for the best of the best, this new winter sports resort was built for the corporate owner of the resort, Averell Harriman.

Once a gold mining town, it was known in the 1880s as the Guyer Hot Springs Camp Resort. Popular for its mineral waters; croquet, tennis and general entertainment, it was later rediscovered by an Austrian scout for the development of a new ski resort.

Success was immediate. By late 1930s, celebrities were popularly photographed at Sun Valley while skiing, fishing in lakes or bathing. It was said that Ernest Hemingway wrote there while staying at a cabin.

Kathleen raced down the ridge knowing that even 10,000 years ago, native American Indians living in the Wood River Valley would have been equally mesmerized by the wonder of these mountains.

* * *

Harriman, chief executive of the Union Pacific Railroad, was on his way to Sun Valley to join his daughter. He and his guests were onboard a special rail car, having travelled from New York where he kept his offices on Wall Street.

Robert Meiklejohn, Harriman's assistant, handed him a note. It was a message from the President. Harriman excused himself from his party.

Harriman had known Roosevelt for a long time and had invested in his political election campaigns of 1932, 1936 and 1940. As a volunteer, he served on Roosevelt's National Recovery Administration and then as transportation advisor to Edward R. Stettinius, head of US Steel.

Harriman looked up, the train crossing landscapes of Fall unfurling along the many miles of track, track built by laborers returning from the civil war; financed by bonds sold overseas, bought out of bankruptcy by his father in 1901, debts and all. Reorganized, the transportation rail cars would span the continent from Omaha Nebraska to the West Coast; from New York City to Washington DC. The Union Pacific Railroad networked the vast territory of the continental United States, giving it the means to become a new world economy.

Averell Harriman looked down at the message in his hand. The world was about to be awoken to a new reality. The Germans had invaded Poland. For America, that meant one thing. Production output.

Within weeks, Harriman was in Washington DC advising on industrial materials; then he sat on the National Defense Advisory commission and Office of Production Management. It took a year.

Roosevelt announced his Lend Lease Program in December, 1940. All American factory productions mobilized for the war effort would be paid for by the British Government facing Nazi Germany in a Lend-leased arrangement.

In January, 1941 Roosevelt's Special Advisor Harry Hopkins returned to Washington from London. His report was not good. Roosevelt invited Harriman to "go over to London and recommend everything we can do, short of war, to keep the British Isles afloat."

By the time Harriman was reading his official Commission papers from the President to "proceed at your early convenience to Great Britain, there to act as my Special Representative, with the rank of Minister, in regard to all matters relating to the facilitation of material aid to the British Empire..." the President had been informed that Czechoslovakia, Poland, Finland, the Baltic States, Norway, Denmark, Belgium, Holland and France were under Nazi domination. Italy had joined the Axis Powers and Dunkirk and Paris fallen. Spain, Portugal, Sweden and Switzerland were still neutral.

Britain stood alone.

Harriman was to present his credentials to Prime Minister Churchill on his arrival in England. "...In this capacity, you will take all appropriate measures to expedite the provision of such assistance by the United States" [1]

* * *

At 8.30 in the morning on March 10, 1941 it was still cold and damp, the sun not yet burning off the ground frost. Averell Harriman stood at the seaplane terminal of New York City's La Guardia Airport surrounded by a small gathering. Marie, his second wife stood with him, his daughter Mary with her husband Shirley Fisk looked on. Mr. Pemberton, manager of his personal and family affairs, stepped forward to shake his hand in farewell.[2]

Forty five minutes later, with only two bags and a diplomatic passport, Averell Harriman stepped onto the Pan American seaplane with his Assistant Robert. With thirty nine passengers on board, the craft YANKEE CLIPPER lifted off for a short duration flight to Bermuda.

The seaplane splashed down at Darrell's Island. From portholes they counted six American bomber seaplanes, several Catalinas with rear turrets and three camouflaged naval planes. The facility was garrisoned by Scottish Highland troops recovering from the battle of Dunkirk.

Harriman stayed at the Belmont Manor Hotel for 24 hours. He met key personnel from both the British and American governments and briefed them on his mission, then embarked on the Clipper seaplane for a transatlantic crossing to Horta in the Azores.

At an altitude of 8,000 ft. over the open sea, they spotted no enemy combatants. However, an issue of fuel combined with foul weather precluded a direct landing at Lisbon. Other venues would have to be found. The flight wore on in cramped quarters. Passengers sought berthing in open bunks, their clothes still on.

Harriman's Assistant Meiklejohn was quiet. He mentioned in his recording that he surrendered his berth to a woman, and that he and Harriman spent most of the flight talking to Anthony Biddle about the Polish offensive. Biddle was the new American Ambassador to the European governments in exile, now stranded in London. Clearly, the situation was very tenuous for an American President operating without a proxy to engage in this war.

At about five o'clock they spotted the Tagus River at Portugal. Lisbon was several miles upriver, the wind persisting and the seaplane had trouble hooking onto a buoy in the fourteen knot tidal current. It took three grappling hooks to come to rest, even as they viewed the wreckage of the sister seaplane CLAIRE, laying on a towline, damaged by a hurricane.

Port of Entry customs behind them, Harriman and Meiklejohn were driven to a resort hotel twenty five miles away next to a gambling casino. They rested as best they could. Harriman met with key personnel and engaged in briefing. Europe was in trouble.

Three days later, under suitable cloud cover, they took off in the dark over the Bay of Biscay to England, dipping low over the water to avoid detection by German patrols.[3]

* * *

Four days after leaving LaGuardia, Harriman touched down at Bristol England. Under cover of darkness, he and Meiklejohn were greeted by Churchill's Naval Aide and a modest escort. A smaller RAF plane flew them directly to Chequers, country home of the British Prime Minister, Winston Churchill.[4]

Harriman was worried. Had he known how perilous the transatlantic crossing was, he might not have consented for Kathleen to come to Britain. He sent a message to the American Legation at Lisbon, "for my twenty two year old daughter Kathleen, due on a Clipper leaving New York." A coded message arrived at Chequers. His daughter had landed safely and would soon be on her way to London.

Harriman turned immediately to become "involved personally with Prime Minister Churchill on matters of the highest policy." Churchill took him on tours to naval facilities, machine shops and factories. Harriman viewed damage inflicted upon Plymouth, Bristol, Cardiff, Swansea and Dover from German air raids and nightly bombing. England's industrial cities and ports were crippled, and Harriman was thrust headlong into the war.

* * *

Robert Pickens Meiklejohn, graduate from Williams College with a degree in economics, had been hired as Harriman's official secretary in 1937. Harriman was Chairman of the Board of Directors of the Union Pacific Railroad and senior partner in the banking firm of Brown Brothers Harriman and Co.

Further, during Harriman's appointments at the National Defense Advisory Commission and Office of Production Management, Meiklejohn was his assistant for all matters of correspondence and administrative support. Meiklejohn claimed that he commuted each week between New York and Washington as a "dollar a year" man on loan from the Union Pacific Railroad. Such was the case for all staff serving Harriman.[5]

Meiklejohn was meticulous. He wrote well, showed discriminating abilities and possessed a strong work ethic. He would generate administrative records, notes, reports, correspondence and type up all official Agreements for Harriman. He would stay at Harriman's side through WWII and accompany him on special assignments; administer his overseas missions and hold the highest security clearances for all strategic documents. Meiklejohn was dedicated to the man most trusted as Advisor to both Presidents Roosevelt and Truman.

Further, Meiklejohn kept an office log of the events of the war during the commission of his daily duties. His accounting would be written while serving the United States government. He referred to Harriman in his notes as "W.A.H."

Meiklejohn had his reasons for keeping a daily office log. His father had been diagnosed with cancer and was given one year to live. Occupied in the service of Harriman, Meiklejohn was overseas and absent for most of that year. The diary was to describe his activities during that year for his father to read when he got back. Neither could such details be disclosed or transmitted for security reasons, nor was the longevity of the war predictable. Thus, while entered as a daily office log of his activities,

Meiklejohn's observations, humor and personal perspectives frame life in the Harriman offices. Or, as their missions required, such that on one flight in a Lockheed bi-motor bomber to Khartoum he wrote "Am writing this with typewriter on a large box of supplies. Very comfortable, and now about half way to Kano travelling along the Niger River. Very yellow and sluggish, winding all over the place like a snake with cramps."

Moreover, it became a source of information since Meiklejohn never left Harriman's side. As his Aide, Harriman's every move, meeting and document was recorded by Meiklejohn.

Also, as a member of Harriman's closest entourage, Kathleen's whereabouts and official activities were fully documented.

* * *

Procuring a passport for Kathleen had not been easy. The United States was not officially at war, but travelling to Europe was banned for most American citizens, including family members, and especially for women. A passport for Kathleen was arranged by Harry Hopkins in Washington and Adolph Berle at the Department of State. The passport was authorized citing "the inability of his [Harriman's] wife to go…" and "in view of Harriman's rank. [6]

Kathleen Harriman's mission was with a job. She was a journalist correspondent, a member of the American Press Corps.

The Harriman Mission staff in London were to set up their quarters at the US Consulate. Administrative affairs fell to his Assistant Robert Meiklejohn since Harriman was cornered by Winston Churchill almost exclusively. He gave particular care to the accounting of the Harriman Mission establishment.[7]

Averell Harriman stayed at Claridges Hotel, an elegant place made popular in the 1930s.

Increasingly, patrons were European officials residing in London as governments- in-exile.

The Harriman offices grew. Cramped in their quarters at 1 Grosvenor Square, sharing space with the American Embassy in London, a decision was made to expand offices. A hole was broken through the wall to the adjoining building of Number 3 Grosvenor Square.

The staff comprised of eight executives; eight secretaries; one Aide; a hall-man, two girl messengers; two chauffeurs and four "charwomen" to clean up. With little direction beyond the President's mandate and a promise of funds to set up, their mission - for the lack of an auspicious title - came to be known simply from its letterhead, Harriman Mission.[8]

London was in danger of destruction. Nightly bombing raids roiled the city with explosions and fire. A bombing blitz of considerable magnitude was delivered on March 16th 1941. One bomb dropped in such proximity to their block that it "scared the living daylight out of us [and sounded] like a freight train pulling into a station."[9]

It was a harrowing start. Harriman himself already showed signs of fatigue and stress. He was treated for "ulcer trouble" [10]

* * *

Kathleen crossed the Atlantic in much the same ways as her father. Two days of travel via Lisbon, arriving in London the night of May 16th, 1941 during the blitz.

They missed. Kathleen's plane landed at Bristol, and her father arrived too late. He proceeded on to Paddington Station at eight thirty that night, and though he did spot her at the station, she climbed into a taxi so fast that he had to follow her to the Dorchester Hotel in his car.

If by morning Kathleen Harriman was rubbing her eyes from a dreamy life in America, Kathleen was facing a new world today. Immediately she absorbed the urgency of the crisis and its impact, reporting to Marie [Harriman's wife] "… already I'm beginning to feel what Ave is. He seems to stand for something secure that people can hang on to and believe in and they have great faith in him…."[11]

According to Meiklejohn, they took a bus tour of the city and saw the bomb damage that hit Big Ben at the Houses of Parliament by Westminster Abbey. The next afternoon Kathleen took the bus to Threadneedle Street, she saw the Bank of England and walked over Tower Bridge and London Bridge.

"Hardly a block has gone unscathed and today I went down to the East End by the docks. I've read about the block-on-end of flattened houses but it's something quite different to actually see it.[12]

Kathleen entered the world of her father populated by officials, and she became one of them. She was known to them all as a friend, especially the original staff. From the United States to assist her father was Colonel George Alan Green, Australian born VP of General Motors Yellow Truck - a man also serving as Vice Chairman of the Advisory Committee of Ordnance in Washington DC; Edward P. Warner, Vice Chair of the Civil Aeronautics Board; Russell Nichols, statistician from Production Management; and Bob Meiklejohn, Harriman's Assistant.

To provide Aid from the Americans, the Harriman Mission absorbed USN Commander Paul Lee from the Naval Attaché Office, specialist on Naval and Ship Repair matters; US Brigadier General Millard Harmon for Air matters; Lt Hatcher for Production and Engineering; Harvey Klemmer and Mr. Spencer, experts on shipping (US Maritime Commission) and Mr. Thomas Monroe, VP of the US Lines.

British personnel included Mr. Whitney, a Major in the Scots Guards assigned as Executive Assistant; William Batt Jr. for assistance with Food and Agricultural deliveries; C.J. Hitch, economist. Others arrived and soon they were once again "chronically short of office space." [13]

Kathleen and her father allowed for a less frenetic pace and embraced diplomatic life. London's hospitality picked up when they were invited to a cocktail party hosted by the de Havilland Airplane Group. They noted that "American Ham" was served as a buffet, "fresh vegetables" and "chocolate dessert". These were relished treats in a world of food rations and fuel conservation. Dancing followed, Kathleen doubtless at the center of it. Kathleen noticed how the occasion lifted up everyone's spirits…

On May 27th, 1941 the German battleship BISMARK was sunk. The news was cause for celebration. Notorious for its escape into the North Atlantic after sinking the British battle Cruiser HOOD, the sinking was demonstrating a war now turning lethal at sea – a sea across which Harriman aimed to deliver American …

Meantime, sovereign states hung in the balance, they all knew.

Kathleen wrote home at the end of May. Less than a week in England, she noted a clear contrast between the United States and a Britain. Her father, she observed, was "really terrific. …people have come up to me and said Thank God for your father. It's kind of nice, being here and seeing it all go on"[14]

But at the Harriman Mission, a growing sense of urgency seized them. The President of the United States had just signed an official Executive Order in Washington for a Lend-Lease Program on May 2nd, 1941. Harriman recommended it. The program was to be administered within the U.S. Division of Defense Aide with James Burns as Executive Director, and Harry Hopkins as head of the program.

* * *

The German-Russian alliance in Europe was collapsing.

In London, it became increasingly obvious that the enemy was reshaping itself. Together as allies, Russia and Germany had invaded Poland just two years before. On June 22, 1941 however, Germany officially declared war on Russia.

Almost immediately, Churchill realized he must bring Russia to the side of the Allies. This, after years of viewing Russia as an enemy. He would have to reconcile with a nation whose socialism had swept through Europe; overturned free-state monarchies and installed dictatorships. WWI had taken its toll on the English, and they were barely recovering from it. Yet Russia knew much about the German Army.

Roosevelt sent Harry Hopkins to Moscow. Harriman's report "Special Envoy to Churchill and Stalin" uncovered the truth.

In Washington, Stettinius took over the supervision of the Lend Lease program from Hopkins. Thus, by early Fall of 1941, with Russia now on the side of the Allies, the President of the United States was setting up the appropriation of funds from Congress for the Office of Lend-Lease Administration.

Congress, with the influence of powerful Southern Congressmen like Cotton Ed Smith and Theodore Bilbo supported the President. But disaffected followers claimed Union activity induced by the Wagner Act of 1935 was pushing the Democratic coalition into Republican arms.[15]

At the Harriman Mission in London, Lend-Lease was viewed as essential to succeed, even if America was not yet at war.[16]

Britain did have some misgivings. With the war unfolding across Europe and bombs dropping on London, there remained political conflict about American aide. Amongst other concerns was America's aspiration to obtain Trade Agreement advantages over the Empire's holdings.

The prospect of having Harriman to head the Lend Lease was a source of comfort. Unlike the former US Ambassador to Britain Joseph Kennedy who was a self-avowed catholic liberal with Appeasement Isolationist advocacy, Harriman was viewed as better suited.

The enemy was gaining. A primary task for the Allies was finding a way for American Aid to reach Europe. Aircraft, heavy tanks, rugged terrain vehicles, Army transport trucks, parts and ammunition were preparing for delivery. Such supply was known to the enemy now bombing targets like ports of entry as well as cities across England.

There was one supply line. Fresh off-the factory-production, aircraft planes had been shipped to the west of Africa in parts. At a secret plant in Ghana they were reassembled, and from Takoradi they were flown to Cairo through Nigeria and the Sudan.

The question was how to provision the Allied Armies with greater American supplies for the war effort in Europe?

* * *

A British victory against the Italians in Somaliland and Eritrea gave them the Somali port of Berbera in the Gulf of Aden for landing. Massaw on the Red Sea was another access point. But even as Addis Abbaba and Amba Alaji fell to the British, Iraq was infiltrated by pro-Axis leadership, and the British garrison at Habbaniyah Airport, just sixty miles west of Baghdad, was under assault.

The battles for North Africa raged on. It was here that some of the greatest assets overseas were positioned.

British troops held fast at Cairo, but the Axis forces had penetrated Syria to such a degree that it was proclaimed an enemy-occupied territory. A second British offensive campaign must succeed. The German siege of Tobruk came under attack with serious losses to both sides. The German Commander Rommel could not advance towards Cairo for the lack of tanks. He waited.

For Churchill, timing was everything. He exchanged General Wavell with Sir Claude Auchinleck. General Wavell proposed that in the interest of India's defense, Iran "should be made secure against German subversion."

Three hundred tanks were successfully delivered to the Allies from America around the Cape of Good Hope and up the Red Sea to Cairo. Supply lines from the United States around Africa and up through the Red Sea showed prospects. British and Russian troops moved to occupy the region with the goal to develop supply routes into the Soviet Union from the Persian Gulf through the port of Basra. Also, they would secure Iranian oil fields, including the main Abadan refinery.

Churchill petitioned Roosevelt to let Harriman accompany him to the Red Sea. Harriman was to provide an independent analysis of the British war effort there and to make a feasibility report on the region's potential as a supply route.

As owner of America's railroad company Union Pacific, Harriman knew the business of delivering government stock.

By the end of May, Harriman was excited about going to the Middle East. "I don't think I've ever seen him so excited about anything. Yesterday he was terribly discouraged, afraid that FDR wouldn't want his Representative to go down there. …Ave feels that he'll be able to help a lot. He's taking 2 experts and Bob along and they'll probably be gone about 6 weeks" said Kathleen.[17]

A cable arrived from Harry Hopkins telling Harriman that he had the President's approval for the Middle East trip. According to his Meiklejohn, Roosevelt's agreement to the request had been already communicated to Churchill June 4, 1941.

Kathleen saw her father off at Pool Station. "His trip was all done in the utmost secrecy. No one was supposed to know, and I've been lying like a rug right and left….All Fleet St. know, but they won't release it until the Embassy gives the word. Thank Goodness."

* * *

As Special Envoy sent by Roosevelt, Harriman had been almost exclusively in Churchill's company since his arrival. Kathleen was viewed as a family dependent who should be accommodated, especially if Harriman were absent.

Kathleen turned age 23. She picked up her pen and wrote of her intention to abandon herself to Bradbury for the weekend in her father's absence. Instead, she went to Chequers where she had been invited. "In case anyone thinks it's poor little Kathleen" alone in England, you can assure them it isn't so."[18]

Two weeks later, Kathleen was back at Chequers "Ave must have asked the P.M. to 'look after' me because I'm being well cared for by about 10 different people" She adds "Last night with the Embassy group I found that I know twice as much about what's going on. That all makes it rather hard. I don't dare open my mouth…" Prone to contrasts, she writes "Life is unbelievably social, God only knows why. ...the only thing people seem scared about here is being lonely, so they date up way ahead…At least that's the way I figure it."[19]

* * *

Kathleen's relationship with the Churchill family was close. She described her weekends at Chequers where she met the Prime Minister. He was "a kindly blue teddy bear … expresses himself wonderfully – continually coming out with delightful statements" (She expected "an overpowering, rather terrifying man") She found him "gracious and …[not] at all hard to talk to…He's got the kind of eyes that look right through you."[20]

… "Mother is a very sweet lady who has given up her whole life to her husband… [often] 'left out' but [having] gracious ways when Averell plays Croquet with her. Mary Churchill, age 18 in whose honor they give a dinner 'since she's running a hospital library'" is described by Kathleen as "full of enthusiasm; childish in the some ways and terribly grown up in others… with a keen interest about public opinion in the U.S."[21]

Pam Churchill, wife of Randolph Churchill serving overseas, made a friend of Kathleen. Writing home on May 30th Kathleen said "She's a wonderful girl; my age, but one of the wisest young girls I've ever met – knows everything about everything political and otherwise." Correspondingly, Lord Beaverbrook – the home in the country was where Pam Churchill kept her child for safety, was described with some dislike as having a big stomach that "tapers down to two very shiny yellow shoes" [22]

Kathleen nonetheless considered herself a reporter on the staff as a Member of the American Press Corps, a role that blossomed in her father's absence and gave her agency. To her sister she wrote assuredly "I started one story with 'It's so easy to forget that there's a war going on in England.'"

Yet Kathleen found it difficult to hold her stride. There were contradictions. How could she contribute to a news worthy story still unfolding? Or, write about a dynamic situation in which her father was engaged? It presented a dilemma.

In England, the familiar and diplomatic world of her privilege put her on the inside. In America, the war was not yet embraced. As a correspondent, she was to inspire Americans to join this war as a worthy cause. But much of what she knew must be gagged for fear of enemy incitement.

Conflicts ensued. Kathleen's activities were overtaken by her father's mission. They visited a munitions factory manned by women workers. She noted their efficiency and work ethic. Next she visited Aldershot to observe the ATS Corps at work, even if she found little charm "The uniforms… make even a pretty girl look like a hatchet-faced battle axe…I've met plenty of the latter too; most are left over from the last war.[23]

And she found safe zones about which she could write. As a member of the American Press Corps, Kathleen was proud of her first spot story at a press conference, Lord Woolton made an appeal to the Woman of America.

Kathleen met the Royal Family and was introduced to Queen Mary. "All us American reporters stood around like a bunch of apes and she was wonderful. She's perfectly beautiful…[she] asked questions…You might have thought she was doing the interviewing." Here, Kathleen defended the Queen's dress code in a challenge to wear uniform. "She's not the type of person who ever ought to be other than well dressed." [24]

The next day Kathleen accompanied her father to see "the first Lend Lease ship with food come in." A photographer's picture captured Kathleen Harriman standing next to the first consignment being unloaded, a woman standing amidst a crowd of men. The image was flashed across newspapers, Harriman and Kathleen representing encouragement and solidarity from the Americans who were not yet officially in the war. Kathleen was both seeking the news, and making news now.

Higher visibility was not lost on the enemy. American Aid to the Allies was a threat, and danger lurked for those who aimed to supply it.

Weekends at Chequers were worthy of commentary to her sister as if she were writing for the American reader, often itemizing the news "Word of the fall of Crete came while we were there. I don't think I'll ever forget the look on the P.M.'s face when he came in and told us. Words can't describe it."[25]

Her pen moved across the page, and Kathleen was unflinching. That night she was to go to Plymouth to stay with Lady Astor; next week to Liverpool for the christening of a submarine and where she would find the docks in ruins – "at least the warehouses back of them are – for blocks and blocks."[26]

London suited Kathleen. It gave her agency and encouraged a sense of independence. "London is…nervously gay – with lots of nice night clubs and places to dine and plenty of people to go out with…"

Kathleen enjoyed her job. She viewed now as a patriotic contribution to the war effort. "I'm only beginning to appreciate what a wonderful picture I'm getting. Thanks to my job I see one side of England; Ave and his friends show me the other." She added "The 'powers that be' want bombers to come over England so that they can get at them and down them. The bombed people have a different idea; they don't want the bombers. Seeing both sides is fascinating." Kathleen closed her observation with "Age over here makes very little difference – that also is something new to me. ..."[27]

Kathleen was not without youthful friends. She went downtown with her colleagues at the Press Corps; American staffers and English hosts. But it was a mix. She referred to one previous weekend at Chequers where "Various members of the RAF were also there. The men who decide what is to be done nightly. Getting their reaction is like entering a new world. The war, the bombing is so completely objective to them; at least they make it so."[28]

* * *

The situation in the Middle East was now essential for Harriman, and not without peril. He travelled across the terrains of North Africa with an eye for transport and supply. He met with Wavell, Auchinleck, Tedder and Cunningham on various Middle East possibilities and strategy. The port of Basra was of particular interest. Farrell, First Secretary of the American Legation and Paul Knabenshue in Baghdad received him and Minister Kirk in Cairo hosted the tour.

For Harriman's stay in Cairo between June 23rd and July 10th, Churchill appointed his son Randolph as his aide. He was serving in the British Eighth Army in the Middle East. A photograph was taken of Harriman and Randolph at the BOAC flying boat station on the Nile. They became friends. Randolph was the husband of Pam Churchill, Kathleen's friend in London.

* * *

Official cables were written and securely delivered in code. Harriman discretely left for England by way of Malta and Gibraltar in a Sunderland flyboat boat. They made notes. Especially observations for delivering military needs. In one passage of his final report "Special Envoy to Churchill and Stalin" Harriman referred to their passage from Lagos, Nigeria to Cairo, "The long journey across the African continent in a Lockheed Lodestar, from Lagos to Cairo, was filled with hazards, short air strips, no navigation aids to speak of, treacherous weather and only the sketchiest of weather information. ..We would fly only in the daylight hours – about five hundred miles a day…These appalling conditions may have accounted for the large number of wrecked fighter planes we saw at each of the airstrips. The ferry pilots – mostly Poles – were too few to handle the traffic, and many of them had come down with malaria. At El Fasher in the Sudan we were put up in a bit tent in a blinding sandstorm" Harriman and his party reached Cairo on June 19, having traced the ferry route from Takoradi by way of Kano and Maiduguri in Nigeria and across Lake Chad to El Fasher. While impressed by the 'quality of the British civil servants at these out-of-the-way posts, but [they had] not efficiency of the air ferry service. Harriman recommended the ferry route be taken over by United States pilots."[29]

* * *

Kathleen was concerned for the safety of her father. On June 6th, she received a call. The Prime Minister's Parliamentary Secretary Brendan Brecken asked her to meet with him for lunch. She assumed he had bad news for her. "I am in a complete stew." Bill Batt at the Embassy phoned to assure her. "Ave's on his way home." [30]

If there was urgency, there was also stealth and silence. London was under siege from nightly bombing; personnel under close scrutiny by the enemy. Every precaution had to be made, every plan devised with secrecy. Kathleen should be shown harmless, even as she was exposed to the knowledge of sudden meetings and clandestine activities. She smiled, and she smoked, ever the young writer with little to say, her nerves of steel and her heart pounding.

Harriman reappeared at home July 15th, barely long enough to show his face. He had to take off at dawn to greet Harry Hopkins just arriving in London from Washington DC. Harriman promised Kathleen that he would stay a few days in London before leaving himself for Washington to report to the President.

Kathleen understood. But she could tell no one.

As head of the Munitions Assignment Boards, Hopkins was on a special mission for the President. He was to proceed to Moscow to meet with Stalin once again. There was much to share with the new ally. Munitions, supplies, troops, passage and combat joint planning. Russia, they estimated, could not last longer than six weeks before collapsing to the Germans. Hopkins was to find out more from Stalin. Harriman, moreover, had much to discuss with Hopkins.

Meantime, arrangements were ongoing for a secret rendezvous between Roosevelt and Churchill. In that regard, a Royal Navy ship quietly slipped her moorings and set out to sea, her movement unnoticed.

Harriman left for Washington. Wrote Meiklejohn "He wished to meet with the American civilian and military authorities [on] information and recommendations he had already presented to the Prime Minister [Churchill] and the British authorities with reference to the prosecution of the war in the Middle East."[31]

For Kathleen, her father had been in London for two weeks.

* * *

It had been just over a month since Germany invaded Russia.

The information that Stalin gave Hopkins was alarming. It alerted the Allies to a new understanding of the German force. Repeatedly, Stalin told Hopkins that the British had underrated the Germans.

By the end of July 1941, Stalin informed Hopkins of the German strength with which they were preparing to invade Russia. Of the 175 German divisions stationed along Russia's western front now were 232 divisions – with another 300 divisions preparing to mobilize. Each division approximated forty thousand fighting men.

As defense, Russia had only 180 divisions available, most of them immobilized by the Germans. Stalin stated that although he could increase his force to 350 divisions under arms, it would take a year. This, while he wanted to engage quickly so his troops "learn that Germans can be killed and are not supermen" [32]

Nothing was lost in translation between the Russians and the Americans. With the aid of an interpreter, Stalin informed Hopkins on the strength and depth of German reserves; their weak spots, their logistical efforts. Russians were now using raiding tactics so that "many thousands" of German troops from the front lines now had to guard and protect the supply lines.

Stalin said Russian mechanized and "insurgent" forces were attacking the axis powers now "many miles" behind the German lines. "Even the German tanks run out of petrol" Stalin had said soberly, they had no "lack of fuel, but rather, had 'transportation' difficulties." [33]

Hopkins reported a Russian comment "moving mechanized forces through Russia was very different than moving them over the boulevards of Belgium and France."[34]

Stalin itemized his arsenal and his lack, noting that steel – used for the manufacture of tanks was in short supply, and that "it would be much better if his tanks could be manufactured in the United States" – especially since Russian tank manufacture occurred during the winter when German production could outpace them.

Long into the nights, Stalin discussed the superiority of the German air force, now outfitted with 20mm cannon in their fighters along with machine guns. He offered Hopkins an inventory of the size and number of Russian bomber types, "but Russia [needs] US trained fighter pilots from the US". He gave Hopkins the general locations of most of his munitions plants, with the clear warning that the Germans could destroy most of Russia's industrial capacity on short order. He thought that the Germans were "tired" but he felt he could defend Moscow, Kiev and Leningrad, less than 100 kilometers away after the 1st October when the rains came. Britain, urged Stalin, should bomb the Romanian oilfields.

Stalin told Hopkins that one of the biggest problems for the war effort were the ports of entry for supplies. Archangel was difficult to keep open because of ice, and Vladivostok "was dangerous because it could be cut off by Japan at any time"

Nor were the railroads and roads in Persia adequate... [35]

It was a sobering report that Hopkins had given to the President. In London, Hopkins would confer with Harriman and Churchill for ten days, then proceed to Moscow for more meetings. [36]

There was one more thing. The threat of a Japanese bombing upon Russia did not go unnoticed by Roosevelt. Russia and Japan had signed a Treaty. To hold against Japan would violate that pact. Manchuria was the focus of Japan now. To incur upon that territory would unleash upon Russian troops the full assault of Japan. For Stalin, it was a matter of readiness.

* * *

The severity of the war was now pressing. For Kathleen and others, the words of Stalin left little else for attention.

Harriman was engaged in constant work and communications: Kathleen attempted to keep life on an even keel by accepting Harriman's many evening engagements in the hope that he might be free to attend them – but instead having to cancel them at the last minute for the lack of his availability.

The crisis was mounting.

Kathleen felt she was losing her value as a correspondent. She discovered that her stories as a journalist could not be published by INS. She complained. Thus, while interviewing Red Cross American nurses who delivered accounts of bombing casualties, she wondered if her words would be published. Frustrated already by censorship of her personal letters, Kathleen realized that the press was likely being gagged. Information might aide the enemy. Or so the British said.

By the end of July, the war was all business. Kathleen's days were attended by men in positions of leadership. She wrote "…tonight my favorite RAF man was here, Pierce, the C in C of bomber command." Even Harry Hopkins, "quite a different Harry, I gather, from the White House" makes a sociable impression on everyone. "He's quite in his element."[37]

Still, the itinerary was full. The next day she inspected five of Britain's biggest bombers on display. She was given much information yet was refrained from reporting it because the Prime Minister "asked me along as Ave's daughter, not as a journalist." Kathleen knew too much to be a news reporter.

With the curtains drawn for nightly blackouts and her typewriter clattering, Kathleen was writing insightful letters. If for the familiar ears of people she could trust, her words did not condescend or lapse into sentimental fillers. She typed quickly, elegantly, briefing the reader with as much precision as she could encase in one line, and once regretting that she had not been trained as a journalist while in college.

By early August, Kathleen noted a sharp increase in levels of anxiety in Britain. With a keen sense for what mattered, she wrote to Mary that Britons "are not fighting for any ideal". The people at the ground level "are now fighting for their country's survival". She claimed the "English people had confidence in their Government so they followed them into battle..."[38]

Occasionally, Kathleen turned elsewhere for friendship including local girls and Wrens. They idolized her for being an American. She wrote "even if my job isn't a success, I'll be glad I came..."[39]

Kathleen's job was giving her fits. Neither did her disappointments offer alternatives, nor was she getting anywhere with her complaints when she took them to her father. He insisted she keep at it.

Rarely was Kathleen caught unprepared. In London, a hostess had introduced her to someone "extremely beautiful" who talked "about her work, women's contributions and the Wrens..." Kathleen had walked off, finding her conversation "rather dreary." Ave was "horrified," she wrote "God damned if it wasn't the Duchess of Kent." [40]

* * *

The Harriman's had a residence at a country cottage outside London near Dorking.

"For the first time since I've gotten here, I'm really away from the war....I'm sitting out on our porch enjoying the birds and the cold summer evenings."[41] The country air, as the English called it, did not dull her pen, but her perspective was allowed to wander somewhat.

Not that she was much alone. Pam Churchill and Kathleen had become close friends, and Pam came over to stay. The Harriman hospitality was generous. Still, the notion of staying at another's house was presumed by Pam to be an entitlement. Kathleen remained gracious.

Unfortunately, Kathleen missed observing a cultural phenomenon at her feet. Pamela, as a houseguest, was a city-life distraction.

The rural demographic was doubling. It would have been of more interest to families in America than any information of Pam.

Whereas most urban women joined the war effort by working in a factory or wearing a uniform for service, those left in the country by their enlisted men faced new challenges thrust upon them.

Large numbers of city children were being sent to the country for safekeeping.

In addition, military camps sprang up in rural communities everywhere for the billeting, training and briefing of Special Forces. Rural infrastructure, already outpaced by city progress, was now engaging in extraordinary effort and sacrifice for Great Britain.

In generous measures of local domestic charity, women in the countryside showed support by collaborative good works like sharing resources; recycling materials and offering commodities. An array of options occupied the rural culture. Mending clothes, "making do" on food rations, heat and fuel. It brought many together in a English countryside bleak, rainy and often isolated. When the siren alarm filled the air in advance of a bomb raid by the enemy, small acts of heroism were demonstrated - where one remained behind in the kitchen to stir the jam-making while the rest went below to safety.

If spun from straw and frugality women in the rural communities uplifted public morale with planned events of light-hearted entertainment like choral recitals and theater.

Had Kathleen reported on how homemakers were contributing to the war effort, her insight would have earned the deep respect of those at home in America reading about Britain. Especially since commended by British Women's Institutes which were underwritten by influential and well-heeled women. Such distinction gave them a grace as the greater heroic village movement. [42]

Whereas Air attrition had been high, British training began to demonstrate a measure of superiority. The RAF was gaining by only losing one plane to six German plans in daytime bombing attacks.

July found Kathleen surrounded by "fighter pilot friends." At the country estate, they felt "beaten up" by friends flying their planes as if they were "practicing dive-bombing." Kathleen was not amused, and on one occasion when she was "working quietly on the lawn" at Chequers a sudden Spitfire passed twenty feet over her. Pam's child "young Winston" was whisked up from his playing and pushed under the main bed for safety.

* * *

Nothing was considered safe. "Am very happy in my flat but am not buying anything unnecessary in the way of fixtures, etc. so I won't have any investment if we get bombed out" said Meiklejohn from London.

For Kathleen, the war was now turning into long days of hard work. The hours for enjoyment came only rarely. She and Pam went to a pub for an evening with friends. After dinner four of them, pilots, got up promptly at 10.30 PM and left for night duty. "Seeing them leave and wondering if they'd all come back gave me a funny feeling…."[43]

One boy told her that when he got depressed… "I guess they all do", she added "he showed me a paper he carried around with him. It was Churchill's bit at the RAF. 'Never in the history of the world has so much been owed by so many to so few…' "

At the same time, Kathleen was attending official soirees with the leadership. Eisenhower and Harriman were frequent guests. The Americans were a favorite in London with a relatively steady pace of achievements, if hard to measure. It was acknowledged that Harriman kept his Mission clean, especially under the long and hardworking management of Meiklejohn. Yet political danger lingered in the minds of many.

Mary Lee Settle, a writer transferred into the Press Corps in London would comment on the group of leadership. She labelled it "a caul of privilege" sustained by access to "wondrous U.S. military post exchanges."

The Churchill Club, located not far from Westminster Abbey was an exclusive place for Americans enjoying both orientation and entertainment. Another center were Headquarters to the Eighth Air Force headed by General Carl "Tooey" Spaatz. At the end of the day, "it was like entering a crowded cocktail lounge."

Kathleen was uniquely in the circle of the media as a member of the American Press Corps, especially working in the London bureau of William Randolph Hearst's International News Service (INS). Some present were actors like Burgess Meredith and Paul Douglas making U.S. government films in London; James Steward, Clark Gable. Others were writers and novelists in London included Irwin Shaw, Ernest Hemingway, Mary Settle. War correspondents included Ed Morrow, Eric Sevareid, Herbert Agar, Bill Walton and General Robert McClure, Allied Supreme Headquarters Chief of Information and Censorship. From London, they wrote in a sort of edgy world of populist warmongering in order to stem US isolationism - Roosevelt's greatest challenge.

It made for a heady stratification of society. For some, like Pam Churchill, "It was a terrible war, but if you were the right age… and in the right place, it was spectacular."

Yet Kathleen remained skeptical about a society unprepared. Whether referring to Heads of State or to local citizens coping with war in Britain, she found an appalling discontinuity between the prosecution of a war and the vacancy of popular engagement. As an American she found this difficult to reconcile.

On a personal level, Kathleen had sympathy with those who tried to speak out. She noted the naivety of Mary Churchill who spoke out openly and was teased. Mary, she said, as the youngest daughter of the Prime Minister managed "okay" when at Chequers surrounded by old generals and politicians, "but she has no idea about conducting herself with young people…"

* * *

On July 30th, it was raining. Harriman was leaving town. A Bentley car showed up, and a party of three climbed into the back seat. Meiklejohn was seated in the front, Kathleen and Pam Churchill in the rear with Harriman. The ladies were seeing him off.

Harriman and Meiklejohn flew to Prestwick Airport and quartered at the RAF base. According to Meiklejohn, planes littered the airfield shipping for repairs and outfitting for ammunition. Spitfires, Hurricanes, Sterlings, Bombers, Fighters, Liberators suggested preparations for a pending invasion.

From Prestwick, Harriman and Meiklejohn got a break in the weather to fly over the Atlantic to Gander Newfoundland where they saw dozens more Hudson aircraft (bi-motor bombers) waiting to be ferried to the Allies.

It was dawn when they landed at Boling Airbase in Washington DC. General Spalding was there to greet them and escort Harriman directly to meet with the President.

Meiklejohn reported for work at the Washington office of the Union Pacific Railroad. He was still an employee serving in the offices of Harriman & Brown Brothers. He lunched with Blanchard, the UP Press representative at Washington and spoke on behalf of Kathleen. Then he left for New York. He would take some time off with his father. Harriman had insisted on it.

In Washington, Harriman was delivering his findings on the Middle East. Also in attendance were civilian and military advisers.

Later, he was introduced to the new official offices of the Lend-Lease Administration in the Federal Reserve Building of Washington DC.

Harriman left for New York for a few days off, then left for Boston to join a secret Advance meeting of the pending Heads of State.

One week later, Prime Minister Churchill and his party steamed into Placentia Bay in Newfoundland. There, they would meet with President Roosevelt and his staff to discuss Anglo-American efforts against the Axis powers in light of Soviet involvement in the war.

The British party had travelled from Scapa Flow on the battleship HMS PRINCE OF WALES, and President Roosevelt was arriving on the cruiser USS AUGUSTA. The meeting occurred August 7th 1941, as the HMS PRINCE OF WALES hovered off the Newfoundland coast. This came to be known as the First Atlantic Conference.

Churchill showed the President every deference, offering Roosevelt an outline of the war status in each theatre. He took from Roosevelt a little territorial teasing, if not early "understandings" between the two nations. The Americans, it became clear, expected to be in a position of superiority. As Harriman would explain, if both of them were sharing a mission on a hypothetical island…they should work side by side said the President. This, Harriman reported almost verbatim.[44]

Immediately a good relationship developed between the two men. Churchill expressed the belief that the United States and the British Empire could and would "establish an order of peace in the world, which – after the war was won – would lead to a golden century with prosperity and security undreamed of for all classes of society and all peoples."[45]

Roosevelt responded with similar sentiments, his hope being that "peace and prosperity would reign during the lifetime of his grandchildren."[46]

However, it was clear Roosevelt had a private opinion about British Imperialism.[47]

In comparing American expansionism with British exploitation, Roosevelt found British Imperialism as combative – even condemning it on moral grounds whereas American history showed expansionism as a force of civilizing and protecting. This opinion he shared with his son who was with him.

Historian K. Burk noted that the United States viewed Britain as an economic rival. Historian Justus Doenecke asserted that "Roosevelt's picture of American history was highly chauvinistic. American action in the world arena reflected sheer altruism."

For now, Churchill was conciliatory, even as Roosevelt determined to use Lend Lease as coercion for trade concessions. Churchill indulged the populist President.

In their presentations to the President at the Conference, British officials offered their chief concerns. The fortitude of shipping in the Atlantic was discussed, especially with regards to US Aid. U-boat aggression was especially worrisome. In the East there was concern for the West Coast of Africa. In the Far East Japanese force might disrupt the "participation of Australia and New Zealand" including their support of the Middle East. The help of the United States was essential for the neutralizing of the Japanese forces – if they entered the war. They posed a threat.

The President asked about British bombing targets. He was told "limited resources of the R.A.F required them to select areas which seemed to be most vital within the economic range of their bombers."[48]

Hopkins then made his report directly. He told them everything Stalin had said. He itemized the needs of the Soviet Union for provisions. Churchill recommended a further conference in Moscow for a "more long term policy, since there is still a long hard path to be traversed before there can be won that complete victory without which our efforts and sacrifices would be wasted….We realize how vitally important to the defeat of Hitlerism is the brave and steadfast resistance of the Soviet Union and …we must not fail to act quickly"

The President left on August 10th, 1941. After the meeting, Churchill and Harriman got in a dinghy" reported Meiklejohn, with half a dozen sailors to row them ashore."[49]

The dinghy beached and Churchill climbed ashore playfully. It allowed for some unofficial talk, a time set-apart that was to bond them in their mission for the rest of the war. Then all of a sudden, Harriman recorded, Churchill tumbled down the steep embankment. "I thought he would break his leg..."

For the United States the Atlantic Conference offered new awareness of the gravity of the situation. The President returned home knowing that America would enter the war, and in the following weeks, he took several steps to prepare. He requested from his Secretaries of War and Navy their recommendations for production allocations and supply needs through June 30th 1942. He instructed the Office of Production Management to submit their requirements of raw and intermediate materials for the manufacture of equipment that could be made available to Russia by July 1942. He asked his Secretaries for their conclusions about serious ramp-up of US production – a program that would come to be known as the Victory Program. Finally, he proposed a conference in London to be held mid-September.[50]

Work aboard-ship at the First Atlantic Conferenced produced consequences. Less than a week later, the "Atlantic Meeting" issued an official communique delivering the statement that the United States Congress had passed the "Lend Lease Act." No longer a program used by Roosevelt, this was law.

Further, the Conference showed Russia as agreeing to attend the conference of October 1st 1941. With their new ally, this would produce binding Agreements and policies for signing. [51]

In addition, Averell Harriman would be Chairman of the special supply mission to the USSR with the rank of Ambassador to Moscow.

* * *

2.

In London, with her father absent, Kathleen was attempting to find her balance as a professional journalist. Constricted by censure, secrecy, Kathleen was in a dilemma. She was being drawn into a role that defined her less as a working journalist and more as Harriman's daughter – a member of the entourage of Roosevelt's Representative.

As her father described in a quick letter to Kathleen and Pam, who was staying with her at the cottage in Dorking, "This is a bit of a scrawl. I am trying to write in bed – not too successfully…I am too comatose to make much sense. We think and talk of you both on all occasions. You have many friends in this group. The President said that you Kath were one of only two (Mrs. Winant the other) American women allowed to go and live in England. I haven't asked all your questions about our job yet, but you don't have to worry anyway. Your articles according to Steve's office are well received. Your New York boss says you are a "find"…"

Alone with her thoughts at the end of her day, Kathleen had reservations. In those hours Kathleen would write home. There was much she had to reconcile.

Her relationship with her father for one; she and her sister Mary were children from Harriman's first marriage – a marriage that ended in divorce.

Another, the relationship between Harriman and his present wife Marie, a New York City girl contemporary with Kathleen. Correspondence with Marie was congenial. Still, in one letter to Mary,

Kathleen makes mention of a sense of loss with regards to their mother.

Further, there were issues, and Kathleen was concerned. Harriman was operating under extreme pressure, having stepped onto a stage unrehearsed for conditions that might corner him in suggestive ways. Especially if planned at the hands of political rivals in the press. The war posed threats from many fronts.

On the 15th of August she wrote another letter to Mary and reflected on one man who owned a newspaper business and belonged to the Labor Party leadership. "I hope you meet Lord Beaverbrook while he's in the States. He's a fascinating old gentleman who at first I found exceedingly terrifying...

...On Tuesday I went to the Minister of Information's Press conference with the American press. All around it was pretty disappointing, I thought. The really good people didn't talk at all and Brendan didn't put himself over at all satisfyingly.

...On Wednesday I had my first non-restaurant meal since I've arrived. The Stratt Allens still keep their house going – at least a small part of it and I dined there. It was very pleasant. He works in the Ministry of supply and at the moment on supplies to Russia. He says their efficiency is unbelievable. They get ships docked, unloaded and refueled in a minimum amount of time, much less than what the English Dockers take..."

* * *

By August 14th, Harriman was back in Washington and staying at the Mayflower Hotel for a week of work. He did commute to his family home in New York on the weekends before returning to London where Kathleen was waiting.

On August 25th, in Washington, Harriman and Meiklejohn were invited to Darryl Zanuck's private showing of his Film "Sun Valley Serenade" with ski scenes taken at Sun Valley, Idaho.

Roosevelt had another mission in mind for Harriman. His mind was clear about the state of American readiness for war. Harriman was to go to Moscow to obtain for the President from the Soviet government full information on Soviet productive capacity and their requirements. It was imperative to keep the Soviet forces in the field fighting the Axis powers. For his Moscow visit, Harriman had his orders from the President on August 29th, 1941 while he was in Washington. In the commission of this directive only, Harriman was handed temporary pocket authority of Ambassador.

"Reposing special faith and confidence in you, I am asking that you proceed at your early convenience to the Union of Soviet Socialist Republic, there to act as my Special representative and as Chairman of the Special Mission …with the rank of Ambassador…

The joint Anglo-American trip to Moscow was announced on September 3rd, 1941.

"…You will, of course, communicate to this Government any matters which may come to your attention in the performance of your mission which you may feel will serve best the interests of the United States"

In the next ten days, Harriman managed to shuttle to New York for the weekends; dine with the Soviets in Washington DC and meet with the President at the White House before boarding a US Navy four-motor flying boat to Scotland September 13th. He landed two days later.

At Stranraer, he was met Lord Beaverbrook, Anthony Eden, US Ambassador Winant and Kathleen. Making the most of their time, they travelled together to London where they spent the afternoon with Beaverbrook before meeting with the Prime Minister for dinner that evening.

The London meetings were fruitful. However, it was becoming increasingly clear that there existed some political conflict underlying issues amongst the British, including those concerns of the opposition party expressed by their political leadership.

Harriman would have to find a way to appease any conflict.

The "Eight Point Declaration" speech was approved by Beverbrook "unqualifiedly." Harriman informed him of the decision to bring US supplies up through the Mid-East.

Beaverbrook expressed his concern about Japan entering the war, such that "if the cruisers of the Japanese navy should be loosed in the Indian Ocean to prey on British Empire shipping that would create havoc [and make it] impossible" for the continued participating of Australia and New Zealand in their support of the Middle East.[52]

There were issues stemming from adverse publicity and propaganda matters. America was clearly divided about entering this "European" war. Separatists culled from it wrong ideas. Roosevelt was casting about trying to answer to an anti-Empire sentiment needing American bail-out.

From Beaverbrook, now exerting his influence as a powerful newspaper man, this was a political warning. Churchill, he suggested, was under pressure from Roosevelt to reform the notion of a "British Empire."

Beaverbrook, only slightly less the wordsmith than Churchill, was wary of the cost of American help.

Roosevelt's position that Britain pay America for its Lend-Lease by breaking down the British imperial preference system of trade was considered unacceptable. It held to an economic network of trade that penalized importing good from non-empire countries. A rivalry for global trade was at play. America coveted British bases in the Pacific and oil concessions in the Middle East.

Fueling his impulse to rely on Russia for England's survival, tension arose when "the Beaver" as he was called, wanted to leave immediately that week for Moscow. Harriman wanted to stay in London.

Kathleen records the evening dinner, a meal steeped in military jargon and supply to Russia. "..I got so 's I thought I'd scream if I heard the words "tanks" or "Russia" mentioned again...I enjoyed watching Ave and Max fight. Lord Beaverbrook doesn't like being contradicted and he's inclined to be set in his ways and view about people". The following day, with Churchill present, she writes "dinner tonight was a sharp contrast with last night - with the P.M - one's a gentleman the other is a ruffian. Ave luckily can talk both languages"[53]

Kathleen was writing home from the center of whirlwind where they were clearly overtaken by events on a daily basis.

Pam Churchill, the daughter-in-law of Winston Churchill who had befriended the Harrimans was now ensconced as "one of the family." Her child, like all children at the time, was kept for safekeeping in the home of Lord Beaverbrook, a ways distant but also in the countryside. She was considered a trusted party while her husband, Churchill's son Randolph served in Cairo, Egypt in the British Army.

Harriman was frequently at Chequers, Churchill's country residence which Kathleen described as "a strategic policy center." There they gathered as leaders and strategists formulating interim, medium and long range tactical strategy for the prosecution of the war.

At the same time in London, Harriman's office never let up. The work of Harriman's Mission continued with urgency.

The joint party to Moscow left on September 21st They embarked on the Cruiser HMS LONDON. It would take them two thousand miles around the North Cape.

In spite of a British Embassy in Moscow, Beaverbrook observed Harriman's quick response to Russian needs. Harriman had alerted Roosevelt to send Hopkins to meet with Stalin already. Where there was an ally, there was opportunity.

* * *

If Kathleen felt that she was an "annoyance" to the British, she was essential to the Americans. That night she was a guest speaker on a B.B.C broadcast.

"'London to the Continent'…I'm doing it again on Friday for the Ministry of Food." She thought she might be nervous. "It couldn't be easier" she said.

Without the guidance of her father, Kathleen was occasionally caught off balance.

She had written a brief note home two weeks earlier complaining about Elliott Roosevelt who "got drunk with Piccadilly tarts every night and got his picture on the front page of the papers for one escapade."

The President's son, Elliott Roosevelt had received a captain's commission in the US Army Air Corps as an Aviator during his father's election 1940 campaign - a post disputed as favoritism.

General Arnold asserted that there had been no favoritism involved.

It was generally unknown at that time that President Roosevelt was an invalid. He had contracted polio in his mid-thirties and was confined to a wheelchair. With the aid of a brace he could stand, and the media rarely photographed him confined to a wheelchair. Thus his political image remained that of a stalwart man, his face affable and his demeanor bright and astute as a world leader.

Roosevelt needed the use of an aide at his side. Transportation, trust and intelligence-gathering would be his primary needs as President. Elliott's qualifications to serve the President were ample.

After his brief military duty at Wright Field Ohio, Elliott Roosevelt passed an Intelligence Training Course and served with the 21st Reconnaissance Squadron at the new US facility in Gander, Newfoundland.

Elliott was with his father at the Atlantic Conference on board the USS Augusta, having been that summer in London while searching for suitable air-base sites in Labrador, Baffin Island; Greenland and Iceland for the landing of factory produced US aircraft. For this critical mission, he had the consent of General Arnold and Winston Churchill.

Elliott had the confidence of Roosevelt's most harbored aspirations, especially when told before the war by his father that England should disabuse herself of her Empire if she wanted American help. "We've got to make clear to the British from the very outset that we don't intend to be simply a good-time Charlie..."

Kathleen was not entirely informed of his mission when she complained of his exposure as a *bon vivant* "he should have behaved better, being in uniform..."

Nor were things going well for her on her job. Fleet Street, the news district, complained of Americans being paid to write "propaganda." The Ambassador [Winant] called her in and "told me in exact words what to say if I was questioned again..."[54]

Perhaps unknown to Kathleen, Winant did have a concern.

The British had been warned not to compete with American Lend-Lease goods for economic gain. Designed to allow for American penetration into global markets theretofore held by the British, this matter was negotiated as a trade concession for American aid. It took Gil Winant, the US Ambassador, much effort to get the British to agree to sign this Restrictions Agreement.

Clearly, it had been a difficult political issue. Not all were in agreement with Churchill's concessions as head of the government. Lord Beaverbrook, Minister of Supply - whose personal financial wealth was rooted in the newspaper industry, opposed matters that might hurt British labor interests.

* * *

In September, Kathleen found censorship to be a handicap to her freedom of speech. In addition, her father's position required particular discretion, and she was looking at a blank page on a typewriter for a Press that cried for explanations. Still, for the family at home, she attempted to keep them abreast of her activities with shreds of palliative news.

"I haven't heard from nobody for the last few weeks…" she wrote to Mary from London at the end of the month. "I hope Marie was able to make heads and tails out of my wire, but at that point no one was supposed to know that the mission was already on its way…[Moscow] Harry Hopkins always knows his whereabouts, if you ever want to know"[55]

Kathleen was aware of Roosevelt's position at home. The US had not yet entered the war. "Averell took Quent [Quentin Reynolds, Commentator and Press Officer for the Harriman Mission] along with him to do some work for him – propaganda on religion, religious freedom in Russia. I gather the U.S. has to be sold on that score."

The strain of the war was showing. "Today I wrote two not too good stories, trying to see [what] the U.S. [is doing] on helping British prisoners of war in Germany – at least I hope they will – even though I didn't say anything about that. I feel now that if I see one more letter …rather depressing"[56]

Kathleen felt lonely. "Talked to Mr. Allen, the head of the American Red Cross, today and he seems to think that I …do some work for them…"

* * *

Harriman's Moscow meeting was under observation. Dinner at the Kremlin was for "over a hundred people including all the US Mission staff and our B-24 aviators; the British mission and some of the Embassy staffs with Russian delegates and officials"[57]

Meiklejohn made notes and Harriman would describe the environment of their meeting in his reports to the President. For the Americans, this would be a precursor for what lay ahead.

"Catherine the Great's room…With her initials inscribed upon gilt carved and painted shields atop columns" was a room of "plaster walls and hardwood flooring furnished with red velvet curtains and a …red runner[carpet] down the center connecting …one end with the old ballroom which had been rebuilt into an enormous meeting room for the Congress… the other end with the ante-room in which we had [gathered]."

Seated at the head of a long table that stretched two rooms, Stalin was flanked by Lord Beaverbrook and Harriman. "The dinner was the usual affair of endless hors d'oeuvres, beginning with caviar and various forms of fish, cold suckling pig, hot soup, chicken and a game bird, with ice cream and cakes for dessert."

Stalin was opening up. He ate and drank plentifully but very selectively according to Beaverbrook. Harriman added "It is true the red wine bottle was brought in special, as was the Champaign bottle."

When the conversation later turned to the war, Stalin said that it should be won by the Allies of the three countries meeting. Of the news he received, he said that there were difficulties in the south. The Crimea was strong "as it was reinforced by troops that had been taken from Odessa. Leningrad's news was better."[58]

Over thirty toasts were raised. Harriman raised his glass. "To the Soviet solder. As the American tank or gun came into the hands of the Russian armies they would, I know, feel the comradeship of the American people who sent it to them."

After dinner, over coffee in an adjacent sitting room, a British presenter informed Stalin of the military situation. Stalin listened attentively. Finally he recommended a strategic growth of Army troops for Britain, and perhaps less reliance on its naval supremacy.

Two movies followed in a smaller theater room. One, an older war picture; the second a comedy about theatrical entertainers "which included some rather good singing…" noted Harriman[59].

The Russian ballet for the visiting Mission was stunning, if altered. "The performance was in four sets and the ballet was changed from the original version where the swan dies to a happy ending with the "evil Genius" dying" noted Harriman. "The whole performance…was exceptionally fine… "Several of the subordinate dancers were extremely good, including Khomyskov, the clown." He notes one exception. "Moscow's top ballerina, Lepeshinskaya, sat in the box"[60]

Suddenly, on September 30th, 1941 the Germans resumed their attack on Smolensk, planning to reach Vyasma in a week. That placed them ninety miles from Moscow. In his order of the day, Hitler delivered to the German Press Chief Otto Dietrich on October 9th "for all military purposes Soviet Russia is done with."

The Agreements were accelerated. Stalin suggested that Beaverbrook and Harriman meet with Molotov the next afternoon, October 1st, 1941 to prepare such a "protocol". The agreements would be officially ratified and signed.

The Soviet draft of the Protocol of the Conference was submitted to Harriman and Lord Beaverbrook early. The final formal meeting of the British, American and Soviet delegations took place that afternoon at Spiridonavka House (British diplomatic offices in Moscow.) The formal signature of the Protocol took place at the Kremlin the next day, Thursday, October 2nd, 1941.

The Agreements included monthly deliveries of Medium Bombers (100 from the USA); Fighter planes (200 from the UK, 100 from the US).

On October 4th 1941, the ink not yet dry on the documents, Harriman was cabling for delivery of the shipments and war materials. In Secretary of State Cable No.1757 Harriman said to Hopkins "It is considered urgently desirable that the greatest possible amount of critically needed materials may be shipped at the earliest possible date in order that the spirit of our conference might be translated into actuality....100 medium tanks, and 66 light tanks…As many as possible A-20 and P-40 aircraft…"[61]

Three days later, Hopkins replied "In addition to the foregoing the following military items are being made available for delivery during October. '4 Guns, 90 mm…94 Tanks, light…6 tanks…30 Mortars…8,000 shell, 3,000 shell, 30 planes, 65 planes...100 bombs, 139 bombs…300 bombs, spares…' "[62]

Within 72 hours, October 10th 1941, Moscow began evacuating. The German Army was advancing.

The Agreements, hastily concluded, did not address how the supplies were to be financed, the details were left for subsequent negotiation. At the time, Harriman considered the Moscow mission a success. He confided to Meiklejohn that in just four days, the heads of Mission "have succeeded in making an agreement with Stalin that is mutually satisfactory."[63]

Ultimately, Meiklejohn noted in his later log, "the supplies were financed under Lend Lease and delivery to the Soviet Union was provided primarily by the British and Americans at the cost of tremendous losses in shipping, particularly on the North Atlantic on the route to Murmansk."

Like Napoleon's advance, Berlin issued on October 22nd that snow storms and freezing nights were impeding operations on their Moscow front. It was the coldest winter in forty years. This would allow the Soviets to repel the Germans, and victory was announced mid-December, 1941.

Meantime for the Harriman team exiting Moscow, transportation home was little less than a scramble. They had boarded four transport planes at Moscow airport, Harriman intending to work the minute they lifted off the tarmac, but within a half hour they encountered bad weather of such turbulence that it was all they could do to hold on. Four hours later, at Archangel, they landed for lunch, then transferred to the yacht of a local Soviet Admiral "Pearl of the North" to sail down the river past the large town of the harbor where their baggage was transferred onto the British minesweeper HMS HARRIER. They sailed out to the open White Sea in gale force winds so strong that the minesweeper had to make several attempts at rafting to the heavy Cruiser HMS LONDON, waiting offshore.

Harriman worked his staff with paperwork while at sea. On the 9th of October, they arrived at Scapa Flow and anchored. A British destroyer carried took them to Thurso where a launch brought them into town. Harriman sent out a number of cables before embarking a train south. At Inverness, Bill Batt met them with paperwork from the office during their absence.

On October 10, their train pulled into London. So essential was their mission to Moscow, that they were met by no less than a contingent of British dignitaries and a fleet of cars from the American delegation office.

Their Mission to Moscow had alerted the enemy. They were thrust into a propaganda war. At a press conference given that afternoon, it was said that a copy of Harriman's letter to Stalin had already reached the Germans. Meiklejohn recorded "the text of the letter WAH [Harriman] brought to Stalin from Roosevelt…was cabled to us at Moscow in code and I have the only copy supposed to exist on this side of the world. They didn't get it from me."[64]

* * *

Harriman and Kathleen checked into their Hotel. As an American Industrialist accustomed to execute the responsibilities of his office, Harriman had to struggle to keep his equilibrium in a London culture of wartime exigencies.

At Beaverbrook's behest, Pam Churchill was there to greet them personally.

She had been placed well within his sphere of influence, her role that of a social functionary to the Americans.

Harriman knew she was a member of the Churchill family, not a member of the Prime Minister's government cabinet. However, before free to leave his hotel, and armed with sensitive material of strategic importance to the Allies, Harriman was obligated to meet first for lunch with Mrs. Randolph Churchill.

That afternoon he and his party went directly to Chequers to meet with Winston Churchill for dinner and long days of discussions.

Harriman arranged to leave immediately for the United States. His next report was to the President.

By 15th October 1941, Harriman was on his way to New York where he would meet with Roosevelt at Hyde Park, the President's family home. With him were Lord Beaverbrook and Harold H. Balfour.

* * *

In her father's absence, Kathleen was advised to circulate amongst military personnel. "I picked up some miscellaneous bits about fighting the air battles over the weekend…since [they've] lost some men that they've at least realized that flying over enemy territory means business and not just excitement…"[65]

In her next letter home, Kathleen referred to an outing that occurred while Harriman was in Moscow, a small matter of some distaste to Kathleen now.

She had been invited to the Churchill's for a family party. The occasion was Sarah Churchill's birthday, eldest daughter of the Prime Minister. Kathleen referred to Vic Oliver, Sarah's husband, who "felt himself compelled to explain" his side of something called the "Newhaven fiasco." There was a sense that Kathleen neither thought this appropriate for a birthday party, nor pleasant to know. He said "Half way through apparently, negotiations changed hands at the Berlin end and that's when the attempt to double-cross was started." Clearly, this incident informed Kathleen's value less as Harriman's party and more as a news writer.[66]

Her professional job had become a matter of concern. Kathleen felt that her role as a writer has been diverted. "Miss Knowles, head of the prisoners of war parcels, phone me last night in tears. Had I written anything to America? She's been in touch with the families on this side and now it looks as though there'll be no exchange for some time to come."[67]

She ended her letter with "Excited about Averell's return – can't wait to hear all…"

Clearly, Kathleen is not only justifying her role as a professional, but her necessity on post as a family guardian.

* * *

Harriman was essential to Roosevelt. Ever the pragmatic executive of successful ventures, Harriman now saw that the American public was still unsold on the vision expressed by Churchill at the first Atlantic Conference. "To establish an order of peace in the world, which – after the war was won – would lead to a golden century with prosperity and security undreamed of for all classes of society and all peoples…"

For Roosevelt, this public sentiment presented a growing problem. Aiding allies to fight an enemy overseas was a far cry from defending your shores from a global menace.

Unlike the liberal altruism of Ed Murrow or Ambassador Gil Winant, or the rivalry over Imperialist garner, Harriman wanted to capture the vision of victory for Americans by cultivating a spirit of free agency. Like everything else he knew, it would be done by populist branding and youthful enthusiasm!

Harriman, the businessman, was familiar with publicity. He understood the need to focus the message of this war in such terms that made Americans feel good about themselves, offering moral liberation while encouraging new markets; new innovation, new fashions. It became the hallmark of the American GI in WWII.

Harriman turned now his attention to a media campaign.

Kathleen wrote home saying that he would be on CBS, and had given a press conference with Lord Beaverbrook in London. It was a joint statement of support for the cause which she dubbed "a mutual-admiration society." With some pride, she added that Harriman consulted her for his material, and the two of them discussed his content over lunch…

Kathleen had been in London six months, and she might well have wanted to go home. But in her second letter to her sister, she reported an exchange with her father, revealing a touch of resistance at home from the Roosevelt family "they…dislike me more in Washington than they do here and …there'd be no conceivable chance of my getting over here again."

Harriman assured Kathleen that she was making a huge contribution in her capacity as a member of the American Press Corps. Her message might propel America to aid this war with greater resolve. Harriman encouraged his daughter to feel that she was adding to the greater good. Kathleen wrote "If I came home now, I think probably after a month or so I'd regret it, because I'm just about beginning to get the swing of my job."[68]

Still, Kathleen was somewhat reticent about her standing as a member of the American Press Corps. "Averell and I had a long discussion at lunch today about my work. He was full of accusations of my lack of initiative, etc. I tried to hold my own and explain reasons for my position in INS and reasons why I couldn't force the office to spend more time educating me."

By the end of October, most of Europe had succumbed to the enemy. England was engaged, Russia

48

ramping up, and still the United States was holding back. "Besides, I think I'd go mad arguing with all my various friends – from their letters I gather they tend to isolationism or towards non-interest, which is even worse…."[69]

There were options. The Red Cross was very active in London, and because of its exposure to Ministers-in-exile residing in London, it was a milieu rich with European source information for journalism. Kathleen had been invited to join them. Harriman considered the Red Cross invitation a bad idea. Kathleen's work would pick up, he assured her. It did. In addition to featured articles which came "in bunches", she landed a serious interview that day as a news assignment from INS.

Later that evening, a soiree was given for her father. They saw a Noel Coward show hosted by Mr. and Mrs. Eden followed by a dinner hosted by Beaverbrook. The party was also attended by Ambassador Winant, his demeanor piqued because he had not accompanied Harriman to Moscow. "[He was] more silent and Lincolnesque than ever. I think he did say "Yes" once during dinner!" Notwithstanding Kathleen's dislike, she recognized his position of influence amongst the British.

The level of effort and its many conflicts were adding up. Fatigue was creeping in. "Averell was unbelievably rude at dinner tonight. He went to sleep after the last course and practically snored once we moved from the table."

The dinner, if pleasant, showed some resentment building about American reticence. A few light-hearted sarcastic references were made by Sir Hastings Ismay who had attended the mission in Moscow as the British military man. His charm, which only Kathleen appreciated, was lost on Harriman. Her father, whom Kathleen called "His Lordship" apparently hated his guts and called him [Ismay] Puggie. [70]

In America, as Roosevelt's biographer James Burns wrote, the people of America were not responding to Roosevelt's call to arms. "the United

States seemed deadlocked – its President handcuffed, its Congress irresolute, its people divided and confused."

* * *

Pressure for America to enter the war was everywhere prevalent. Lend-Lease was Harriman's sole responsibility. Roosevelt's prevarication, – as it appeared, was a problem for Kathleen who was at the center of media, its outcry in popular communication persuasive. She had to walk on her toes on more than one occasion to avoid conflict of interests.

Pam Churchill, now Kathleen's roommate at the cottage in Dorking was turning into "a loose cannon." Her attitude was grating on Kathleen. Information about American materiel being ferried to the allies overstimulated her enthusiasm, and she announced at the end of October that she wanted to join the ATA, the women ferry pilots. Whether for personal or for professional reasons, it took all of Kathleen's persuasion to curb her impulse. "Today, thank god, the whole thing collapsed. Much as I like Pam, she's not the right type."

Anthony Biddle, US Ambassador for Exiled governments was overwhelmed by leaders of fallen governments. "Poles, Dutch, Belgians, Norwegians and what have you" noted Kathleen. Mrs. Biddle implied she could use Kathleen's help… "but I flatly refuse."

Kathleen was given the assignment to write about the opening of an Orphanage home supported by Mrs. Roosevelt. Mrs. Winant was absent, and Kathleen accompanied Mrs. Biddle for the event.

They were introduced to the Bishop of Chelmsford. His wife thought Kathleen was a sort of "Lady in Waiting" to the Ambassador's wife. As conversation turned to the war, the Bishop remarked that the Germans would be totally intimidated "if the Americans get in."

Increasingly, Kathleen's role as Harriman's consort was drawing public attention. As the visit to the orphanage was led by Biddle who "wore her Red Cross uniform with trimmings," the newspaper photographs focused on Kathleen playing with the children. It became a BBC Newsreel. "Quite aside from the fact that I hate public participation when I'm reporting, it was rather embarrassing as it was her show. (At least it gives you an idea of what they think of Ave over here! Each day there are squibs about what he's saying in Washington…)"[71]

Harriman was in Washington when Kathleen noticed a sharp wind in the political climate. Social tension and political frustration in London about the progress of the war was palpable. Kathleen recognized it immediately and reported home. "There's a terrific wave of frustration over here now. People feel that because there's no bombing; no invasion (2nd front) – [that means] the government isn't doing enough. They're all uneasy, itching to do something other than listen to radio reports of how Russia's faring."[72]

Kathleen had tea with resident Belgians who had escaped from Europe. They told her of refugees arriving in England through any means available, including a boat which they rowed across the channel. Amongst other items, they listed an appalling lack of food supply in Europe. Belgian cities were empty and "foodless." She wrote "France is better. Spain is unbelievable – no food anywhere."

Kathleen recognized a growing criticism of America. She presumed a quasi-diplomatic role in her reporting. There were rumors circulating amongst the "little guys" that "Anglo-American relations" was going from bad to worse. "Result, our boys go home mad at the English. The fault lies on both sides. Neither knows how to handle the other…"

The following week, Kathleen attended a party at the home of the Belgians. This time they informed her of intelligence about high-ranking officials who had remained behind. In her letter home, she wrote carefully and with cheerful resolve to avert attention by censors. And she added her touch "Two toasts were drunk, one before lunch to the King; another before coffee to Liberty."[73]

It was November, and Kathleen hosted a small party for "all the people who we owe meals and things…"

Relaxing at her cottage, Kathleen received a private visitor. She explained that he "had fought with the British Ministry of Supply about having his business included in the war procurement lines." His business was the manufacture of anti-tank guns. As head of the Ministry, Beaverbrook apparently declined, citing the Restrictions Agreement. "he [Beaverbrook] declined to offer the hospitality of his home" said Kathleen.[74]

* * *

During Harriman's absence, Kathleen found her stride. Far from being a tourist, she knew she had a responsibility, and she used her pen effectively. She wrote that she was "taking life fairly easy and at the moment, concentrating most energy on writing the Sunday night postscript, - which as you may not know is the most listened to program of the week"[75].

Kathleen was aware of social clashes in America, especially American unions in riot. During a visit to Birmingham at a light tank factory, she noted that it was "one of the 1063 factories in Birmingham manned mainly by girls". Her observations drew upon contrasts for evocative attention. "I met them, talked to them…In some of the quiet rooms music is played, and the girls sing while they work. I liked that. When I walked through, they sang American songs…" She proceed to itemize their work conditions and hours "The factory runs its own buses; frankly I saw little reason for the union to beef. All the night shift workers their hours…The funny thing is that no matter what a girl is doing, whether it's boring a hole, sorting tiny parts, she thinks her job is interesting." [76]

In the same letter home she reported that "five Republican isolationist Congressmen arrived yesterday. They are all tough, unadulterated Americans. It was nice seeing such unsophistication."

Harriman arrived in London during the third week of November.

Thanksgiving party plans were overdone by overzealous friends seeking familiarity with the Americans. A Thanksgiving Day Dinner Dance for the American Press and a large crowd of other guests gave Harriman concern that British hospitality might leave the wrong impression about Americans. Kathleen wrote "Unfortunately, too, they met all the worthless West End women. However, the damage is done..." She complained of two official lunches – one the Thanksgiving Day luncheon that her father made her attend, and the other for Eagle Squadron. "Winant spoke equally badly at both. Anthony Eden spoke of him yesterday as being 'one of the men who can influence the tide of world affairs.' God help the world affairs! Poor guy, he misses his family terribly..."

It is unclear when Kathleen penned her next letter home since she tended to carry on with notes for days before the Courier pouch was sealed for a night flight. On December 4th she referred to a speech delivered by her father. "It was a terrific success over here. He told the British just what they wanted to hear...He's been taking things quite easy and is looking better and seems more relaxed. He's been a great help with my work. We argue most of the time...Its fun."[77]

It is conceivable that Kathleen was finding guidance from her father about news she should write for the American media. This, combined with her assignments to satisfy a lackluster news reporting service, might have been the cause of some consternation. She was after all, a woman in London working as a reporter.

News to her sister was showing gravity. She cited the reaction to a second front offensive, then recited her interview with Beaverbrook after the opening of 'Commons debating.' Not all was without dispute within the halls of power in Parliament.

She added news from Dick Scott - a "Sun Valeyite" just returned from the Continent. "DeGaule is politically hated because he's the *Front Populaire* which is more feared than Hitler." Kathleen reported on the conditions of food, false information, public apathy, small victories, and civilian populations complaining. So you see, you can never tell who is right." [78]

By December 1941, Kathleen was showing concern about the visiting Congressmen. While acknowledging America's political divisions on the issue of war, Kathleen sensed the danger in the lack of consensus. As American political Isolationists disinclined to enter this war she wrote "They are a pleasant… not too brainy lot...amazed to find a will to fight to the end among the British. They seemed to think that if Hitler offered a good enough peace, the British would accept it..."

If war-time profiteering was the indictment, apathy distressed her more. Kathleen wondered at American resolve. She wrote "they see things like the determination of the British to see this thing out, their unity and cooperative spirit, I of course always did take for granted. It's interesting to find some people at home don't…."[79]

More fundamentally however, a greater problem was revealing itself. The lack of truthful information circulating amongst the voting public was seriously compromising America's responsiveness.

* * *

At the Harriman Mission in London, it was known amongst personnel that Meiklejohn's father was ill.

On November 18th 1941, Meiklejohn noted "Mr. Harriman thoughtfully agreed that I take a four week vacation so that I could take my mother and father to Florida and spend some time with them…"

He added "our staff in London, now experienced in his ways, would be able to take care of Mr. Harriman's needs there until my return to London."

For this vacation, Meiklejohn travelled to Florida on a pass on the Seaboard "Silver Meteor" streamline train specially arranged for him by Union Pacific. A family picture was taken on the beach at Ft Lauderdale. "A very welcome and restful interlude sadly terminated with my departure on December 14 to return to New York and Washington." On that date of his record he said "Heard the radio news of the Japanese attack on Pearl Harbor December 7th on our return from a sightseeing boat trip…"[80]

* * *

In Washington DC, the developments that followed the Japanese bombing of Pearl Harbor followed swiftly. One week after the attack of December 7th 1941, America officially declared war. Troops were mobilizing with the full concurrence of the United States Congress.

Almost simultaneously, Great Britain declared war on Japan. Within days, Hitler declared war on the United States.

Off Malaysia, Japanese aircraft flying from Saigon bombed the HMS REPULSE and the battleship HMS PRINCE OF WALES – the ship on which the British Prime Minister Churchill had travelled for the Atlantic Conference and met with President Roosevelt. Both ships sank.

In Washington, all military branches were activated; all prevarication swept aside. The American population and the President were determined to fight this war. Playwright Robert Sherwood said "they cast off isolationism readily, rapidly, even gratefully…"

* * *

In New York City, Meiklejohn reported in for duty.

The Harriman offices of Brown Brothers Harriman and Company Bank knew that Harriman's mission overseas would keep him exclusively engaged with the war. But as the crisis unfolded, the whereabouts of Averell Harriman was officially unknown.

Security protocol had taken hold, clearly. Orders for the defensive protection of all key leadership were immediately executed, including those working in conclaves overseas; representatives and executive heads of state of government. Suddenly sequestered, essential personnel were immediately "sheltered in place," or moved away under tight secrecy.

While in New York, Meiklejohn met briefly with Secretary of State Mr. Stettinius who instructed him to reserve a room at the Mayflower Hotel in Washington DC.

On December 22nd 1941 a newly commissioned British ship HMS DUKE OF YORK arrived at Hampton Roads, Virginia. Churchill, Beaverbrook and Harriman stepped off together and went directly to meet with the President in Washington DC.

Kathleen remained in London.

It's unclear when Averell officially vacated London, perhaps leaving a note in lieu of a family farewell. Kathleen wrote a letter home on December 16th, its tone defensive. "Please thank Averell for his note and tell him I won't do nothing rash…" Having found her father gone, and having been called in by Ambassador Winant to be so informed, she wrote "please tell Averell he's a hellova lousy guardian angel!" [81]

If the event provoked insecurity or any conflict within the family, it was quickly redeemed. In a trait that remained the hallmark of

Kathleen's ability to make light of a crisis as a means of reassurance, she choose to deliver an account of "my lovely social errors last night."

While out for an evening of entertainment after work, she described how she and Pam had been introduced to a gentleman who was an obvious foreigner. "They were both being very funny and I thought perhaps drunk. I was introduced…I never listen to names…Pam curtseyed and made a hellova fuss. It turned out to be the King of Greece!" She added "we had a drink with them so I was able to mend my ways!"

Kathleen was on her own. She immediately started reporting with keener perspicuity.

On the topic of the Middle East she wrote "our geography is being rapidly improved." On the European fronts "Petin resigned and I had to get a statement from the Free French quarters." She wrote about the amassing troops on the Iberian Peninsula, the locations of key leaders like her father and Churchill, adding that she was informed that they were "to have his Christmas dinner in the White House."

Kathleen revealed her instinct for deeper foresight, reporting that on a night out with the Polish Ambassador and friends, (amongst them Mrs. Eden whose proclivity to socialize long into the night was well known) Kathleen found a source of information worth cultivating. He described for her an account of enemy Russian infringements upon his house and gardens.[82]

* * *

With Churchill in Washington DC, the Second ARCADIA Meeting of the US President and the British Prime Minister took place.

Mandates, subsequently ratified by US Emergency Powers' Executive Orders, directed resources from both countries to be dedicated to the defeat first of Germany, then Japan.

Four main strategic decisions were to be deployed immediately.

A unified command of the armed forces – Army, Navy and Air would be consolidated for British and American action in all theaters. The creation of a "Combined Chiefs of Staff" was established and charged with "coordinating and directing military strategy under the general direction of the President and Prime Minister on all fronts where British or American forces were engaged."

A "Munitions Assignment Board" was created with combined British and American committees in both Washington and London, for "advice on all allocations of munitions from British and American production– including 'others in the United Nations.'"

A "Combined Shipping Adjustment Board" (for merchant shipping) and a "Combined Raw Materials Board" (for production) was created.[83]

Harriman and Beaverbrook were not involved in military deliberations that took place at the White House. But Churchill and Roosevelt had such a close relationship at the White House that they shared notes, maps, plans and dinner parties.

While in Washington, Harriman remained focused on a revised "Victory" production program which greatly raised the production thresholds of the United States.

Harriman's Mission in London was to be now added the updated priority for joint Anglo-American supply to Russia under the First Protocol Agreement.

Winston Churchill, before leaving the United States as visiting British Prime Minister, addressed the U.S. Congress in mid-January.

Harriman stayed on to recruit additional staff for the new Harriman Mission overseas. He commenced his return journey to London at the end of January, 1942.

* * *

Kathleen wrote Mary on New Year's Day, 1942. Only one issue was addressed.

She received a phone call from a gentleman who informed her that he had a flat for them to move into at No. 3 Grosvenor Square. Two bedrooms, two baths, and a living room and dining room. Kathleen noted that the latter (dining room) "can be converted into a bedroom for when Pam comes to visit for her work."

Housing was a premium concern for the task of managing war-time affairs in London's proximity. All possible accommodations had to be considered.

Kathleen viewed their new housing accommodations with some reserve, explaining that while "it is very difficult to get housing not far from the Embassy in a "strong building to suit his majesty [Harriman's] conscience when he leaves his poor little daughter alone in England near improbable German bombers…" she must assert herself. "SERVICE on the house is my one requirement. It is a full time job getting food, hassling with rations and servants. I didn't come to England to become an efficient housewife…"[84]

* * *

By mid-January, without news since America had declared war, Kathleen reported to her sister that she was circulating amongst the "free-governments" and seeing for herself the futility of old regimes… Norway fell to Germany, and the inter-allied conference was held. Heads of state decried the collaboration of "quislings" with the occupying enemy and warned of retribution after the war. Kathleen observed, "it seems rather fairy-tale like…in St. James Palace…so damned unimportant and remote from the war."[85]

On the topic of Stalin joining the allies, Kathleen was uncertain. She described it as a feeling "(Different from Averell)... [as they] distrust him and fear him and figure he's doing a good job of out-smarting the Americans and Britain"[86] The matter was put to rest by Brendan Bracken, she declared. As the official spokesman, he was "speaking against the future motive of our

'our brave allies'." Kathleen asked "Is there any like feeling at home? [in America}"

At 23, stranded in London at the outbreak of the war, she felt alone. "There is no word of Averell," she reported. "Nor anyone."

* * *

The attack on Pearl Harbor had a profound effect on the two Allies.

It was February 1942 by the time Averell Harriman returned to London. Coming from New York with messages from the family, and with the nation officially at war, Harriman had much to tell his daughter. She should understand the urgency of those conditions and the priorities before them, including personal and family matters on the home front that needed resolving.

More importantly was the added responsibility vested in him by the US President. There might be changes in the future, he warned her.

Clearly, for the Harrimans, this separation caused by the attack on Pearl Harbor had been frightening. Averell Harriman would never again leave his daughter alone and unattended.

She did understand.

With her father back in London, Kathleen was encouraged to turn to her reporting like a professional. She found much to report on. There was news copy of events; war developments; personalities to report about. The ups and downs of allied leadership; the bravery of men; the social conditions, the fear of war. She wrote in London as a serious member of the American Press Corps.

However, she was unprepared for the rapid events that occurred next. A change within the British government took them all by surprise.

Kathleen telephoned Sir Stafford Cripps and had a few words with him following his new appointment as the Head of the War Cabinet. The interview she received from him as a journalist was published in the US Press and she was acknowledged as author in a byline. Kathleen was proud of this accomplishment. America wanted news about the leadership of their ally.

On the other hand, with the United States at war and her father head of the Lend Lease Mission in London, Kathleen now recognized a dilemma. She was someone exposed to inter-allied affairs. She must remain impartial, and informative as a reporter without compromising security. It was not an unfounded concern. The British media accused the Americans of writing propaganda.

Young as she was in a community of working Americans, Kathleen had to be discrete, and held her own as she took her place beside her father. It was a challenge in a city at the center of a war.

Professionally, Kathleen wrote articles of general interest topics related to public affairs. But there were private concerns amongst the leadership that flooded her thoughts.

To her sister she wondered what would happen to the war production output of England under the new Labor administration. She had her answer "…but as Averell says, the war won't be won or lost by ten less planes a month." [87]

With the British government in disarray and military matters preoccupying every aspect of the day, the US Consulate and the Harriman Mission became Kathleen's primary focus.

"Tonight" she said "Averell speaks to occupied Europe on the Colonial Britton V program and then the speech is translated into every conceivable language."[88]

Increasingly, the US Mission Offices in London were overtaken by logistical crisis. Military cargo from America crossing the Atlantic to Europe in supply ships were being sunk.

On February 10th, Harriman's appointment was confirmed as US Representative on the Combined Shipping Adjustment Board. His counterpart on the British side was Lord Leathers with whom he consulted.

Neither did his duties as Roosevelt's Special Envoy mitigate. Colonel Victor Taylor, US Army General Staff, appeared in Harriman's office with a copy of the General Orders for General Wavell, new Commander in Chief for the Far East theatre. It described the full Pacific fleet strategy; the areas to be held, and the ultimate goals of all Allied operations. Nor did Harriman have any guidance or warning of the ways of the British Government making abrupt political adjustments.

The Americans now felt like an autonomous satellite operation in Europe.

* * *

The affairs of Parliament were in disarray. A maelstrom of criticism surrounded the British Prime Minister's Government following a series of military disasters in all theaters of the war.

In North Africa, the British Army lost almost half the territory gained - almost three hundred miles to Gazala. Field Marshal Rommell had received a massive delivery of tank reinforcements without resistance, and used them to drive the British Army back into the open desert, south of Tobruk.

At sea, a British battleship and battle cruiser were both sunk. Further, a fleet of German battleships and cruisers slipped their blockade off Breste and returned for action via the English Channel.

In Asia, Japan had advanced so rapidly after Pearl Harbor that Singapore fell by mid-February.

Britain's War Cabinet was changed. Lord Beaverbrook, Minister of Supply was shifted to Minister of War Production. Sir Andrew Duncan took his place and Lt Col Moore Brabason continued as Minister of Aircraft Production. Col. Llewellyn was named President of the Board of Trade.

Five days later, Beaverbrook resigned from the War Cabinet. Churchill's Government resigned, and a new government was formed. Lyttleton returned from Cairo and replaced Beaverbrook as Minister of War Production. Sir Stafford Cripps was now head of the War Cabinet as the Lord Privy Seal.

In the new War Cabinet, Churchill was to proceed as Prime Minister, First Lord of the Treasury and Minister of Defense; Clement Atlee was to serve as Dominion Secretary; Sir John Anderson as President of the Council; Anthony Eden as Foreign Secretary; Lyttleton for Production, Ernest Bevin as Minister of Labor and National Service. In such a manner, Britain was preparing for the Allied commands of the war.

Almost all those included in the formation of the new government like Leathers, Sinclair, Alexander, Gregg, Wolmar, Morrison, Dalton and Portal were known to Kathleen. Secretary of the Colonies and Leader of the House of Lords, Lord Cranborne she would meet.

Yet there was greater political malaise. With Americans finally brought into the war, the British were dwarfed, if not threatened, by a sense of rivalry. While Churchill and Roosevelt entertained a close and binding relationship at this stage of the war, there were doubts in England about Roosevelt's aspirations for their Empire. Especially since Roosevelt had openly talked of giving India her independence.

While embracing the concept of anti-communism together throughout the wars, the British and Americans were not without dissimilarities. Not only had the socialist movement of World War I swept through Europe and left its mark on American society, but the world was now mapped on a global scale of commerce.

* * *

The Harriman Mission was fully focused, if with American-style reservations about what was happening around them.

Bets were on that Churchill's new government would collapse. It was a dynamic situation fraught with watchful urgency.

Harriman, who by day was delivering speeches that began with "Your Excellencies, My Lords, and Ladies Gentlemen" was by dark delivering cables to Churchill's No.10 Downing Street as they arrived from the US President.

He brought his portable radio to the office where he and Kathleen; Forester and Meiklejohn listened to President Roosevelt's "Fireside Chat" broadcasts at one o'clock in the morning, London time.

London was cold, the city difficult to navigate, and the streets often deserted.

The war news was not good. When invited to meet the wives of the new London leadership, Kathleen found them distracted and lackluster.

Meiklejohn, suffering with a bad cold, took the time to check into the bookkeeping accounts of the Harriman Mission. "We are broke! We have used up our original $75,000 allocation so I composed a cable and supporting letter asking for another $100,000." [89]

Later in the day a cable arrived from Harry Hopkins showing Washington to be equally stretched for key personnel. Mr. Lewis Douglas, who was scheduled to arrive as Harriman's Deputy, had been re-tasked to a senior position in the newly created War Shipping Administration under Admiral Land and "will not be coming to London" [90]

Still, there prevailed a feeling at the Harriman mission that they were in full readiness.

* * *

Kathleen wrote "Dined with Beaverbrook last night. I interviewed him…This morning I made some amplification of my own interpretations…Hope to hell he won't take it off on Averell…"[91]

Kathleen, now understanding the intensity of British politics, lamented that American interest in the affairs of the world remained tepid. "<u>Please</u> write and tell me who in the US knows in the British government. What are they interested in?" Adding "Incidentally, Averell spoke on the

Colonel Britton program to Europe on Friday night – a propaganda speech on American production which I thought was excellent".

Two days later, Kathleen made a remark about Pam's husband, Randolph Churchill. "Averell was a terrific success at a huge lunch today. I'm really extremely proud of him…" Adding "Randolph, who is always under the impression that the world has no great speaker other than the two Churchill's, was quite bewildered that Averell hasn't spoken before…"

Ruminating, she said "I imagine it's rather hard at home to realize the strength of Averell's position over here and what a wonderful job he is doing towards consolidating Britain's and U.S.'s production"[92]

Kathleen Harriman was now a fully opinionated American staffer at the center of activity.

* * *

The hours were long, two clocks showing two continents attempting to work in tandem. Meiklejohn reported "Worked till ten at night without supper getting up copies of the speech for the BBC ... Had a Marine driver and car take me to the two offices with the text of the speech… [afterward] to get a sandwich at a place near the Leicester Square Theatre that turned out to be run by a Mormon missionary from Salt Lake City who got out of Germany after the war started and couldn't get home. A nice place and got real Coca Cola." [93]

By the end of February, American Ambassador Winant left and Harriman's office was now delivering cables from the President to the Prime Minister at 10 Downing Street on all topics. The Embassy was by default taking up hours of daytime effort at the Harriman Mission and gradually, within the American leadership the Harriman Mission was overtaking the Embassy mission and logistics. Its staff was being augmented; office space expanding, furniture procured and tasking growing in scope as they monitored overseas information. Few others in the war effort at this time, were as fully reliable as the Harriman Mission for the management of American interests abroad.

Still, Harriman has his unique challenges. He had to pacify both allies and assuage their fears. "The boss says today he is getting another carbuncle. Some day he will learn to stop working under such pressure." Neither did the politics of the two allies coincide, nor did their leadership make easy concessions. Roosevelt was again pressuring Churchill to offer India her independence, and staffers primly observing "the Prime Minister does not yet understand what happened at Singapore except that it wasn't supposed to happen" [94]

Harriman the pragmatist managed to keep them all focused on priorities. He viewed Harry Hopkins from the White House as preoccupied with political matters; military men with military matters, but what of food supplies…?

Neither was the traversing or sharing of information or intelligence facile, especially when arriving by courier pouch through the tortuous routes travelled by seaplane Cutters via Lisbon etc. Yet for Averell Harriman, his imperative remained focused on distribution; logistics and strategic needs above all else. His correspondence saw no detail too minute in the execution of range and scope in his responsibility. Yet Harriman knew his boundaries.

It fell upon Harriman to answer the neediest of questions for the President. How was the United States to be paid for its stream of supplies going to Europe? Was it all by Congressional mandate a gift, or was much of that mandate confined to just men and material…? What was the limit exactly, of the Lend Lease Program with Britain, Russia, others…? When and how was payment to be made to the US delivering aid to the Europeans? Harriman was the accountant.

Already some sizeable deposits had been made for American aid. But things were progressing slowly. In March 1942 William Schubert, Vice President of the Bank of Manhattan, arrived by train after a week of travel via Clipper to South America, West Africa and Lisbon before landing in Bristol for a train to London. He was an assistant to Paul Appleby of the Department of Agriculture who arrived next day via Ireland. Problem solving was not easy, let alone payment arrangements.

Spies were everywhere present. Those in key positions feared intelligence leaks, infiltrations, conflicting war sentiments in all quarters --from Washington to London.

Until recently Harriman had been staying at the Dorchester Hotel. Now, London was increasingly under attack and war conditions closing in. Londoners living on rations in blackouts and gas shortages sustained nightly bombing raids, sirens, falling rubble and burning fires.

The British leadership reeled with ambivalence and frustration. It was a documented commentary that the British seemed to be embracing Stalin over Churchill, even encouraged by Cripps, "a pious damn Socialist" wrote Meiklejohn in utter frustration.

For the Harriman Mission, the work was relentless. Harriman moved into his flat. The prospect was met by his staff as "more hovering by a boss" who worked all hours; awoke late and often worked from bed; showed up at the office late, and didn't get to open his mail until 7.00 PM before responding to classified cable traffic well into the night.

The staff was exhausted. Harriman got the message and offered some respite for everybody. He suggested that his staff take alternate days off; or leave at three in the afternoon. Regardless, everyone was harried, picking up after Harriman or bolting out for a quick dinner with classified documents tossed into the vault while trying to build a social life around "him."

Still, London life had its moments of relief. Lunch with a companion might have been at the American Club, or at the Berkeley "Buttery."

There were some local entertainment, movie theaters; dinner and dancing at Landsdown House. Shopping for clothes came from Regent Street such as for "a wool suit".

Rations were mandatory, if favors came from unexpected quarters they were fragmented. The Embassy chauffeur, Smith, was handing out two eggs apiece - gift from his wife in the country. But the eggs were locked in the Safe and forgotten overnight because letters were being typed up all night to Harry Hopkins at the White House. Colonel Taylor was leaving at dawn by Clipper and would deliver the mail, so the eggs were left.

Not that Harriman was mindless about compliance. "Last week his nibs had us check the gas consumption in our cars and found it comes to almost two hundred gallons a month. He was very conscience stricken for a few hours but it hasn't changed his habits.[95]

That included weekends. Cited was at least one motor ride to Chartwell, Churchill's home for a Sunday afternoon tour of the gardens and ponds which he built himself. Kathleen observed "The war's tiring and aging him [Churchill] terribly…"[96]

In addition to the assumptions of the duties of American Ambassador by default, Harriman was still without a Deputy. If stress and fatigue were mounting as Harriman pushed his staff -including Kathleen, it was because the war now gathering force.

By March 6th, 1942 with American troops arriving on British soil, the Allies suffered military setbacks.

Kathleen interviewed the first arrivals of American troops at their "barracks hotel" where she went from room to room interviewing groups at a time. She stayed for hours until she reached the "top floors" with stories for her news articles. The next day she wrote to her sister "N.Y. kept coming back for more and more [articles]. I wonder if you saw it, under my byline"[97]

But as Kathleen knew, the reality of this war was elusive. "…America certainly isn't what you might call in the war spirit, is it?"

Harriman mounted a media campaign of public information. Designed less for Europeans than for Americans at home, Harriman was offering deals on the promise of Lend Lease money. He invited to London Darryl Zanuck, a 20th Century Fox movie producer and acquaintance from his days at Sun Valley, Idaho. As history has shown, Hollywood did much to idealize the American hero of WWII.

Kathleen engaged with local broadcasters, telling them of their poor performance on *BBC North American* broadcasts. This, while noticing growing disaffection amongst leaders of the British government. To her, this was most disheartening.

Things were not going well. She wrote '"Batavia, Bandeong, Javas as a whole is going, Rangoon too. They'll probably all be gone by the time this reaches you. India and its seas too, for that matter. Then soon we'll no longer be able to look forward to the Russian communiqués and say "well, at least the war's going well on one front"'[98]

Nor was there any abatement of domestic sentiment. "The one real point we agreed on was that England is very socialistic, getting more and more so…"[99]

By mid-March, so disparate were the public opinion that Harriman addressed a joint session of the Parliamentary House of Commons and House of Lords secretly to discuss production and Anglo-American relations. He spoke about "what should be done to forward them."

Kathleen was allowed to attend.

There would have been little that Harriman could say to Parliament that they did not know: Certainly, news of the American commitment to their cause would have been expected – if not welcomed in their darkest hour. But they regarded progress with suspicion. This was Harriman's greatest barrier.

The dilemma that Britain faced was the sea of cultural change that had arrived upon her shores from the previous war – the Great War, which had introduced "modernism."

Whereas modernism was already in the American lexicon, it had arrived less timidly for the British.

As historians assert, the " fact that the Great War's artillery shells burst amidst the artistic and intellectual questioning of the shibboleths of the nineteenth century's social and intellectual norms has generally *not* been viewed as a coincidence."[100]

Europe had been 'cast into an unpredictable future' – redolent with what Robert Wohl termed a general infusion of mistrust for progress. WWI had "'dealt a serious blow to the official bourgeois culture that was already coming under heavy attack during the years before 1914'. The war [WWI] changed the very circumstances in which *avant garde* intellectuals acted and in which their ideas could flourish: 'progress' was thoroughly discredited, history was no longer viewed in terms of certain laws, discontinuity came to the fore…"

Further, "a new perception [had] permeated its culture to include all of society. As Allyson Booth has put it, 'the Great War was experienced by soldiers as strangely modernist and … modernism itself [was] strangely haunted by the Great War'."[101]

From Harriman's perspective, if his address to Parliament was somewhat audacious, it was timely as American soldiers were about to step into the foray. Also, it was at this time perhaps, that Harriman knew his time in England was ending: He was informed by Roosevelt that US Admiral Standley was appointed Ambassador to Russia as an Interim only, pending a new appointment…

Some improvement did follow, suggesting that this had been Harriman's greatest challenge. By the end of March Kathleen observed that "Averell seems to be more rested than he was. He works English hours. Works in bed in the morning, goes to the office at about 11, and seldom gets home before 8.30. His secretaries get a great deal of sympathy from me but they don't seem to mind their extraordinary hours…"[102]

* * *

Kathleen managed to divide her time between her obligations as her father's consort and her job as information officer. Following the announcement of a British Commando raid on St. Navaire by the German's broadcast she said "Being general stooge and water boy, I got to stick around until we're sure no further details are forthcoming..."

She found ways to write copy. On one occasion she interviewed an escapee from the Gestapo, a Norwegian, and she was able to report on the lack of food availability at the front lines. On another occasion, she sat through two long luncheons; one "intimate" for the King of Norway, another "boring" for DeGaule. And dinners, one "amusing" with Alexander Korda hosting, the Maiskys and H.G. Wells, plus Leslie Howards."

Still, having moved into their flat, Kathleen observed her father's responses to the conditions around them. "Averell is adamant; we're to eat our own food. He figures that if other people can live on their rations, so can we" [103]

Kathleen then added "Averell always has somebody business-minded to lunch and then there's usually three or four of us for dinner. As a full time job, I'm not too keen on housekeeping and that's what it is over here…"

Kathleen was kept busy. "My job is to find out what the troops want in the way of entertainment, particularly officers. That involves all sorts of problems …[104]

Kathleen met with Mr. Amery, Minister of State of India who gave her time as a friend and informer. He talked about India, Gandhi's support, the dominion-status parties and the power of the Rajah states. Kathleen's world was unending amongst key leaders.

3.

Harriman was chasing the gold.

Harriman focused on the First Protocol of Moscow wherein the Soviet Union was to pay in gold. His primary task was to receive payments for supplies and troops offered through Lend Lease exchange. But there were complications.

Communiqués showed wider concerns. While Roosevelt viewed the Pacific theatre his immediate priority, he had intonated at the Arcadia Conference in Washington that a cross-channel invasion might be feasible in 1942 to relieve the European Eastern Front.

The Joint Chiefs in Europe thought that such a crossing was premature if not lacking in logistical support. They were being stretched. Further, neither was the war going well for Britain with continued ship loss at sea, especially with setbacks for General Auchinleck, nor was the public confident in their political leadership.

Roosevelt sent Harry Hopkins and General Marshall to London. For the visit, Harriman invited Hopkins to the weekly staff meeting of the Harriman Mission where Hopkins made a few observations to his staff.

Hopkins spoke softly and told them that for the moment the White House had no victories in sight; that Bataan was hopeless, and that food rationing back home was implemented by curtailing retailers' supply so that grocers did the rationing-out. He told them that US manufacturing plants were waiting on raw materials for airplane production, and that the "good neighbor policy" of supplying certain countries with critical provisions had been curtailed for the lack of shipping. He offered the awful numbers of submarine attacks, even of one sub entering San Lucia for multiple sinking's without submerging. He explained that now, collecting insurance on sunken cargo was too onerous for private insurance companies. Ship carriers were now running without precautions in dangerous waters. The staff found his words sobering, and Meiklejohn would record them in his logbook.

Harriman, Hopkins and Marshall stopped in Ireland for a few days, ostensibly to inspect the first American Army units. But secret arrangements had been made to ship gold owed by Russia. It was to cross the Atlantic to America under British escort. Much of the gold was already lodged in British vaults, and with England's cooperation, loaded onto ships for America. Unfortunately, the gold never survived the Atlantic crossing. Two key supply ships in the convoy was sunk by U Boat torpedoes.

Russia was pressing for a cross-channel mission. Code named "ROUNDUP," an assault was to occur in about a year with a smaller invasion codenamed "Sledgehammer" to occur earlier if the situation became desperate. Stalin was to be appeased and not drop out of the war. Simultaneously, a major Anglo-American invasion of North Africa should be planned. It would be Codenamed 'GYMAST' and 'TORCH.'

Harriman returned to his post in London on April 19th, 1942 and within the week, he fell ill. A call was made to his doctor in the United States. Finally Kathleen found an American doctor residing in England, Dr. Gordon from Harvard. Harriman was diagnosed "with some kind of typhoid."

* * *

If Pearl Harbor enabled Roosevelt's hand for a Declaration of War, what began on that day in the White House as a "fog of war" was now a full throttle conflagration in the Pacific Theatre.

At the same time, with American troops now in Europe, the Harriman Mission at the American Embassy in London changed complexion. No longer limited to Lend Lease operations for aid, the mission was now fielding multiple front-line issues.

Kathleen was caught up in the fray. She could not report from select information, nor could she reveal any political positioning held by her father. Especially as her status at the diplomatic colony increased. She turned to information from other sources.

It is not known from the public records whether the Harriman Mission was exposed to matters of intelligence or espionage outside their mandate. King George VI set the general tone for public resistance, his words serving as a beacon for all who could aid or sympathize.

If she drew attention for her proximity to privileged information, she could not betray trust. If resented for being the only woman on station, she could not flinch. There was a vacuum, perhaps filled with words to her sister in letters, especially when her father travelled. Kathleen felt a measure of isolation.

If her father was too distracted to entertain her, she remained steady and calm. For one so young, she walked a tenuous line. Meantime, there was the matter of Harriman's health.

Harriman's recovery was slow. Kathleen arranged for a nurse to oversee his progress, even as she arranged for fun and outings for all. Meiklejohn was recruited to offer his arm as an escort. Harriman was popular, his health a matter of concern to many and an outpouring of sympathy followed.

Meiklejohn reported that a crate of oranges was made available for his wellbeing - a rarity procured by a ship carrying food supplies to various US installations and missions. The ship, he recounted as a matter of interest, had cited explosions in the boiler room and been forced to return to Newfoundland, yet it made its way to England with oranges.

By May Kathleen wrote to her sister about the "highlights of my career" involving General Anders, Polish Commander in Chief residing now in London. Two interviews were exclusively arranged for Kathleen. The first was conducted by an interpreter for Sikorsky, head of the Polish government in exile who was hosting a cocktail party for 500 people for Anders, the second in French "while hundreds of important admirers and associates sat in the next door bedroom."

Kathleen described his "release" -told to her in the first interview which she got published; and the second where "we had a nice general chat about his home his family and the war." She added "We, the press must never let on or remind the forgetful what happened to the 2,000,000 Poles transported to Russia. This guy is their head" [105]

While noting the futility of sensationalism, Kathleen came to fully understand the gravity of her father's agenda. "Yesterday and today I ...around to the nine free governments and collected...figures in the occupied countries."

Kathleen was opening up deeper seams. "Met a Greek escapee yesterday. 40,000 died of starvation in the Athene-Piraeus area alone during the Oct-Nov-Dec! The Germans and Italians hate each other as rabidly as the Greeks hate them! Italian officers, anticipating their end, have purchased mufti, to facilitate...get away. That's all in a story, which you'll never see!"[106]

To her sister she spoke in controversial tones about issues, perhaps nuanced for censure.

"You asked about India" she said, implying that any aspirations for its independence pressed by Roosevelt must wait. Churchill, she knew, was adamantly against it. Paul Manning and she had discussed the matter at lunch together. He explained to Kathleen the chaos of Indian commands.

Unfamiliar with conventional assault combat orders, organized warfare was beyond them. "They've never heard of congress and nothing its leaders could do would change them overnight. Paul's comments rather contradict Avery's statements."[107]

* * *

Kathleen's role was at times doing double service. She said "When [Ambassador] Winant and Stark arrived, I was there – reporter and reception committees. Being on both sides of the fence helped…"

On May 11th, Kathleen took her father out to the country to convalesce. From there he used a scrambler phone to do business with the office. Meiklejohn said he used it relentlessly.

* * *

Life in London was a strange mixture of celebrity hubris and revolutionary fervor. Whereas a driver was taken ill, a replacement was found quickly on the recommendation of an American friend. The driver turned out to be a woman of some European wealth.

Americans in London were gathering in numbers. While officially introduced to English culture and orientation, their presence and prestige abounded. Kathleen, riding all classes of English society found herself by day in the company of titled nobility, exiled sovereigns, heads of state and leaders of military, and by night mixing with the Avant-guard set of the literary media and press.

For the American staff there was a range of activities from the Royal Mid-Surrey Golf Club to theatre-restaurants like the "The Players Theatre" near Berkley Square. Kathleen went easily with trusted friends to their favorite haunts.

In this time of war, like so many London places in the cellars of historic buildings, it was fashionable to enjoy low-priced entertainment in quasi club-membership milieus to comply with liquor laws. One place, at Albemarle Street Piccadilly, was reputedly the haunt in the 1840s of Dickens Thackeray and Landseer who ate steak and chops at the Grill alongside the "very best men about town." Meiklejohn observed "there's as much chance of sitting down to steak and chops now as of sitting down with Dickens and Thackeray."[108]

* * *

By the end of the month, the fruits of the earlier London visit by Marshall and Hopkins became apparent. A contingent of American military leadership including General Arnold, Admiral Towers and General Somervell were to conference in London for the coordinated supply and buildup of United States forces in the United Kingdom - code named BOLERO. The full scope of this war was only now taking shape.

Present at the conference were Brigadier General A. J. Lyon, Army Air Corps; Brigadier General Grosse for Transportation, (for Supply); the former Vice President of US Lines Colonel Franklin (for Shipping); Major General Lee, and Colonel MacKeachie.

Meanwhile, Oliver Lyttelton, British Minister of Production was to go to America to meet with his counterpart and with Mr. Donald Nelson, War Production Board Chief.

On June 2nd 1942 Harriman accompanied General Arnold; Admiral Towers and Lord Louis Mountbatten to the United States.

Kathleen saw her father off at Northold Airport. If she left London for the States, she would not have been able to return. No Americans, particularly women, were allowed overseas in this time of the war. Kathleen's contribution to the war, by staying, made her unique and vital.

For Kathleen, it turned out to be a very busy month.

* * *

Harriman spent days in June with President Roosevelt and Mr. Hopkins at Hyde Park. Just over a week later, he was in Washington at the White House participating in additional meetings with Churchill and the President. A cross-channel invasion launched from England was being discussed, perhaps commencing as early as 1942. This, to keep Russia viable as an ally.

However, the meetings were overtaken by other news unfolding out of North Africa. German Field Marshall Rommel was on the move. Not only had he advanced three hundred miles from El Agheila to Gaza in May, but he captured Tobruk and moved the British back to the Egyptian border.

The Washington meetings turned exclusively to focus on halting Rommel from reaching Cairo where lay some of Europe's vital interests.

Singapore had fallen in the Pacific. Added to the defeat of Tobruk in the Middle East, the events were considered strategic disasters. Churchill said of Tobruk "Defeat is one thing; disgrace is another."

Roosevelt agreed to immediately dispatch three hundred American tanks to the Middle East to help the British defense. England was in trouble, its people in turmoil.

Harriman returned to England with Churchill June 25 1942. They travelled on a British owned Pan American Clipper from Baltimore by way of Newfoundland before crossing the Atlantic. Churchill had achieved the support of the US President and the commitment of military aide. Above all, the gesture achieved moral encouragement and reinstatement of confidence in the British Prime Minister.

Kathleen reported that there was "quite a gathering at the station to [greet] the P.M. in – all sorts of cabinet ministers and uniforms and hundreds of press…"

"The P.M. looked very well and all set to squelch anyone who is still stupid enough to think that he's about to fail…" observed Kathleen.

Harriman's role at Churchill's side was largely symbolic of US friendship. "Averell…apparently took a good bit of money off the P.M. at backgammon on the way over. I guess Winston didn't realize he was tacking one of U.S's pros…"[109]

Concomitantly, Kathleen's stature rose both in diplomatic circles and in her career. As family, Harriman showered her with gifts from home and recognized her support in London, particularly for having nursed him back to health during very difficult months in 1942.

Kathleen had been in London a year. She explained that now one aspect of her divided role – her professional position of the last year was ending. "Now that Averell's back I'm suddenly realizing what a completely different life I lead when he's here. It's sort of like waking up from a dream or moving out into another world."[110]

The reason behind this decision may well have been predetermined in Washington when Harriman resolved to augment public relations of this war. One can assume he received the full concurrence of the President. "Averell's full of me resigning from INS…."

Perhaps more related to the politics of Washington than to her journalistic performance – including her safety, Kathleen's assets as a staff writer were vaunted, even as the war was heating up and Americans vulnerable.

Neither did Kathleen complain, nor did she relinquish her aspirations to be a writer at this time. Perhaps she knew why. "Added to my new list of friends is the recently arrived managing editor of Newsweek, now Major Joe Phillip. He's terribly nice, a believer in the possibility of opening a second front almost tomorrow…the British lack the offensive spirit (always have and always will sort of idea), an optimist about Russia – all of which I couldn't disagree with him less." [111]

Clearly, Harriman had future changes in mind. He would deploy Newsweek to inform the public about this war.

* * *

By July 1942 it was clear that the Allied Commands would be centered in London. They had a strategic objective to accomplish. It was kept secret.

But the war was still a political liability. Richard Myers wrote "The apathy of the people seems to be still prevailing, but I think it is more apparent in New York City than elsewhere. And it is more noticeable among the upper class than in the masses. There are certain people who simply cannot forego their luxuries..."[112]

So uninformed were the British about Americans in general that US Ambassador Winant, a former history teacher, went about the country speaking to the English about Americans and their history.

Harriman's drive never slackened. The Harriman Mission, having now been established as an operational unit in London, was at the center of the American mandate overseas. Fred Winant, the Ambassador's brother arrived on his way to Egypt to be the Lend-Lease representative. "Gave him an office and took care of him in our space" said an office said Meiklejohn. "Warned the Army we would bounce them out of five of our rooms and ordered six each desks….hiring new help….We are getting quite popular."

Kathleen reported insider observations in a letter to Mary at the end of the month. There had been several transitions and upheavals. Ed Stettinius, head of Lend Lease in Washington had been scheduled to arrive midmonth. "Ed. Stettinius I like a lot, particularly as he crashed through with a Virginia ham and some lemons" [113]

Lewis Douglas of the Combined Shipping Adjustment Board arrived. "Averell gave him a big build up which has fallen rather flat" said

Kathleen. "Our generals are a success...unfortunately, they aren't very social-minded."

By mid-month William Bullitt, former Ambassador to the Soviet Union and to France arrived as the new Assistant Secretary of Navy. For Kathleen, he was a "disappointment." The next day Harry Hopkins and General Marshall arrived.

Ostensibly, Hopkins and Marshall had travelled to London to develop with the British joint plans for a cross Channel invasion scheduled for April, 1943 - code name ROUNDUP. Also, there was a contingency plan in place to relieve pressure from the Russians fighting on the Eastern front.

Meanwhile, General Auchinleck had stabilized the Egyptian front at El Alamein, but his strength to hold was dubious, such that the President delivered a report written by Harriman on July 16th that American soldiers should engage the German Army somewhere in 1942. "I do not believe we can wait until 1943 to strike at Germany" said the President. "The theaters to be considered are North Africa and the Middle East" [114]

A full house of Americans arriving demanded immediate and quick plans for accommodations and entertainment. Harriman wanted to hitch a ride up to Scotland and back to London in an Army flight with Marshall and Hopkins to meet with them in advance, but he was foiled by weather. He would find another way to arrive in with the leadership.

The girls got out for a break in advance of the arrival party; Kathleen and Pam Churchill grabbed Meiklejohn to escort them to view a movie "Son of Fury." The following morning was no less hectic. "Up at six thirty and Captain Buttles of the Army (he will be General Marshall's aide, was formerly General Chaney aide) took me to Euston Station to meet the big shots at 8 AM..."

"The train came in ahead of time but the celebrities were all on the platform. Hopkins, General Marshall, Admiral King, Steve Early, and the president's Press Secretary. For the British,

Cmdr. Thompson (Churchill's Aide) and Lord Louis Mountbatten waited ….Churchill was receiving a hero's welcome.

Said Meiklejohn "Kathleen and Mrs. Churchill had sneaked into the Bentley [intending to greet them] but didn't dare get out of their car because it was a stag party"[115]

The Harriman Mission was busy with their mandate to deliver critical supplies. The staff kept up the work pace. By the end of the month, their quarters occupied twenty rooms at their premises at N. 3 Grosvenor. Meiklejohn said cheerfully "Quite an organization, and so far as I can see I run the show with my left hand."

It had its moments of fun. Harry Hopkins was in love. "His one subject of talk was Louise. We went through every step of the engagement campaign time and time again, evening every evening. It's so nice that he's getting married" said Kathleen.

Meantime, the Harriman mission responsible for the delivery of supplies could not belie a growing threat. By the end of the month, Harriman and Douglas were drafting a cable to the President informing him that due to enemy sinking's, there was a serious shipping shortage. Most were carrying essential supplies and deliveries to Russia promised under the Agreements of the First Protocol in Moscow, - an Agreement authored by Harriman.

Neither was the pressure felt any less by the British. Lord Beaverbrook endorsed strongly a second front of attack sooner rather than later. Said Kathleen "people are taking bets like mad." She described a rapacious dinner hosted by Lord Beaverbrook who gave them "a long harangue on the second front, the whole works, with much crashing of Champaign bottles and thumping on the table…His line is that if we stop the Russian convoys (which are getting sunk anyway, he says) and use the ships that would be diverted for that route, along with the supplies of tanks, aircraft and munitions for the opening of a second front, we'd be doing more to help Russia. He's against maintaining the Middle East and seems to honestly believe that by landing a few divisions in France, we'll be able to get Hitler to divert a goodly portion of his troops off the Russian front" [116]

Kathleen reported home on accommodations at their building for Americans. A flat for the Randolph Churchill's was to be procured – the younger sister also. She mentioned that the Prime Minister intended for his son to take a bigger part in British Parliamentary affairs.

The American Red Cross was causing a stir. In something viewed as a rebuff of British hospitality, the ARC wanted sole responsibility for the American troops arriving, including their entertainment. They insisted that the British personnel wear American uniforms. "That's a lovely little idea, conceived I gather in Washington, between some G.I. General and that doddering idiot Davis."[117]

As a parting shot, she noted that the Navy was everywhere present and behaving admirably. Either she held some contempt for the Washington administration set, or there was more. The Red Cross was the banner of Washington's leading women, including the First Lady at the White House who might be using the system for inappropriate political gain.

The Roosevelt family had been long time acquaintances of the Harriman's. While her father had contributed largely to that family's political aspirations, there was something about their patrician attitudes that made Kathleen, now coming into her own in a London environment, overly sensitive.

In a world of Democratic Party partisanship, socialism and uneven economic growth, concentrated wealth for any mechanism was anathema. The Harriman fortune amassed by Kathleen's grandfather had been publically disparaged. The Roosevelt's, as far as Kathleen was concerned, had climbed on their political platforms to appeal to the average Joe mainly for his vote, not for his brain. As far as Kathleen was concerned, no one worked harder than her father. And no one was seeing the brunt of the war as they were in London. She thought dimly of the Red Cross capitalizing on their agenda. "London's been getting every-other-night raids. Unfortunately, I can't get much interested in them - never having had reason to be frightened by bombing, the recent ones hardly do more than partially wake me up. The so called ack-ack makes lovely looking fireworks…"

Kathleen spent the next two weeks writing editorial content from the offices of the exiled governments.

* * *

By August 1942, the unequally yoked burden of an allied coalition was seeing disparities amongst leaders.

Britain's sea losses were intolerable. Shipping convoys to Russia had to stop. Churchill would take it upon himself to inform Stalin that they could neither advance a cross-channel invasion as promised, nor continue deliveries to Russia by sea. He felt he should explain these reasons to Stalin personally, and left for Moscow late July by way of Cairo and Tehran.

This left Harriman sitting in London with an American commitment to Russia that could neither be performed nor excused. Harriman realized that it compromised the President's promise, and worse, might jeopardize the credibility of American troops coming into the field.

If there was long term vision following this war it was foreseeing a future of commercial opportunity. For Harriman, it informed his mission overseas and filled his reports, even if such vision might exceed the boundaries of a President under siege by domestic issues. In subtle ways, such notions were neither lost on the President, nor discouraged as a primary impulse for agency.

Harriman may well have discussed this dilemma with Winant, the American Ambassador to England. Kathleen says "The other week Averell and

I went out and spent the night with the Winant's. They've got a house outside London, swimming pool, tennis court, etc. but we were too late and the weather was too cold to make use of either of them…. The evening was, oddly enough, rather fun."[118]

By August the 4th, Harriman was talking to Anthony Eden, British Foreign Secretary about joining the meeting in Moscow with Churchill.

Roosevelt, who had a proclivity for competitive statesmanship, feared that Harriman might somehow dilute his impending appearance with Stalin. If he went as an "Observer" only, Roosevelt said it might create a precedent. The next day however, Churchill sent a cable to Roosevelt asking for Harriman to accompany him.

That night, at a dinner party at his apartment, Harriman received a cable. The President was ordering Harriman to join the Prime Minister for the Moscow meeting. Seated at his table was Mr. Harold Balfour, Parliamentary Undersecretary of State for Air; Air Marshall Sir Christopher Courtney; Brigadier General A. J. Lyon, Air Member of the Harriman Mission, and Mr. Philip D. Reed, the newly arrived Deputy Chief at the Harriman Mission.

Mr. Balfour got up from the table and issued instructions to hold up a British B-24 bomber scheduled to leave at midnight for Cairo from Cornwall Airport.

Earlier, Harriman had met with Air Chief Marshal Sir Charles Portal, British Chief of Air Staff. Now he called Eisenhower and said he was leaving in a few hours, could they get together before he left?

The time for departure passed and the flight was delayed as Harriman consulted with General Eisenhower well after midnight. Eden and Winant were calling him. Fred Winant, the Ambassador's brother was already in Cairo as head of the Lend Lease and would receive him there. Meanwhile, Kathleen was packing his bags. Harriman finally left London by car at three thirty AM.

Harriman took off at eight thirty in the morning of August 6th, stopping in Gibraltar and arriving in Cairo early August 7th, 1942. Other leaders from the Allied commands were also using the secure flight to shuttle across Europe. On board the same flight were General Charles de Gaulle, head of the French government in exile; his aide, and three high ranking Russians.

Of that evening Kathleen wrote "There was great excitement the night Averell left. He had a stag dinner. I came in at about mid-night. Most of the guests had left. Then finally at about dawn, he got off, in great spirits. He's certainly been lucky getting in on all the big shows!"

Kathleen spent the weekend at Lord Beaverbrook's country estate with Randolph and Pam Churchill. "I got lots and lots of sleep that came as a much needed pleasure"

She returned to town, and, missing the luxury of car travel said "I tackled the underground and found it just about as easy as the N.Y subway once you set your mind to it...that means walking at night…"

Kathleen now had a place to publish her work. Thrilled with herself for getting her story published in N.Y. she explained that the interview on Mihailovitch was more about a second front in the Balkans rather than in France, something which justified her "good twelve hours in one of the Yugoslav offices."

She was "making the rounds" of military advisors; garnered assessments about riots in India which contradicted AP sources "God know who their source of information is…"

At the same time, Kathleen was mindful of the need for discretion. She was exposed to secret sources of information and caught up in the political world that surrounded her father's mission. She lunched with Mrs. Churchill, the Winant's, Ministers, Lord Leathers and his wife, Col Llewellyn, Minister of Aircraft Production, and others.

Thus, at age of 24, Kathleen Harriman remained careful, declaring to her sister that she was less interested in her own professional career needing story-leads as a reporter – but not because she was without "my own rather violent present views on the subject of Anglo-American relations served up every morning, noon and night… " – but because she believed in the care needed and cause of the Allied war. [119]

* * *

Moscow was not easy. In addition to Harriman and Churchill, the delegation included Brooke, Chief of the Imperial General Staff; Wavell, Commander in Chief of India; Air Chief Marshall Tedder and Carogan, Under Secretary of State for Foreign Affairs.

Stalin was furious. He handed them a Russian summary statement of the previous days' discussions asserting that the organization of a second front in Europe – decided upon and agreed during Molotov's visit to London in June – now "complicated the situation of the Red Army at the front and prejudices the plan of the Soviet Command."

Churchill pointed out that conversations with Molotov in June did not constitute a binding commitment. However, from the previous day's statement submitted to Russia, plans offered by Britain represented the best that could be offered in the way of assistance to Russia, and should be considered Britain's final statement of intention.

Stalin turned to Harriman. Harriman confirmed that the position taken by Mr. Churchill was also that of the United States Government.

Aside, Harriman had coached Churchill into an overnight lawyer. When Stalin charged that the Allies had not fulfilled their commitments under the Protocol of October 1941, Churchill reminded him that the Protocol did not require the Allies to deliver the supplies but that, nevertheless, every effort had been made at "great cost in loss of men and shipping"

In the tense moments that followed, Stalin said that higher sacrifices were called for, and that in his view, it should be possible for the British and Americans to land on the Continent. He accused the British Army of being afraid of the Germans. The room went silent.

Churchill said he pardoned Stalin's remark only on account of the bravery of the Russian Army. Churchill explained that the Allies planned a landing in North Africa and that this was the thrust "to the belly of the Crocodile".

Stalin backed off, but Churchill felt challenged. He promised a raid on Europe "to make the Germans anxious about an attack across the Channel. It would take place in August. Some eight thousand men with fifty tanks would be landed..." [120]

By dinnertime, Stalin accepted his Allies as friends, sharing complete confidences about Russian front details. For Harriman, the meeting would mark the beginning of a long relationship between him and Stalin.

On August 16th, the party returned to Tehran from where Churchill went on to Cairo.

Harriman remained behind to inspect the Persian Railroad. He was interested in its facilities and he especially wanted to visit the Persian Gulf Ports. Three days later, he joined Churchill and cabled the President recommending that the American Army take every precaution for the Persian Railroad. It would be an action that under the Persian Gulf Service Command headed by Don Connolly, would make deliveries to the Soviet Union by road and rail of needed supplies.

On their return, Churchill authorized the diversionary invasion on Europe at Dieppe. For Harriman, it was a fruitful trip.

In her second letter home of August, Kathleen was preoccupied with the Dieppe raid. In it she asserted, perhaps with words overhead from her father, that any continental landing in Europe "will be no picnic". In the citations circulating amongst the Air Force, it was well known that the Canadians had participated on the Dieppe raid. Her quote was that of an officer who said "My God, but those Canadians are fighters."[121]

Kathleen wrote home on September 9th 1942. At an after-dinner party Mr. Brenden, Chief of Information offered movie clips on "some wonderful bombing newsreels about the Russian version of the Moscow mission. All very good. Bill Paley's comment: 'Someone ought to tell Averell never to arrive again in Moscow unshaven'" [122]

Kathleen recounted the greetings of her father's return. His celebrated reception was clearly an indication of satisfaction with the Americans.

* * *

Harriman got his own B-24 Bomber. It was the Liberator COMMANDO which had flown him and the Prime Minister to Moscow. Modified, it had two rear compartments behind the bomb bay opened into an area of upholstered benches facing each other and a Forward cabin rigged with airplane reclining armchairs. In the general radioman's quarters, hammocks were rigged and a complete staff of ten were able to travel and work comfortably. They were thrilled with the new arrangements. Harriman could now fly to the United States from London in his bomber.

Armed with new and critical information about the Russian front from Stalin, Harriman proceeded within a few days of arriving in London to report to the President. If pressed by urgency, they were up to the task at no cost. The trip took 25 hours of flying via Newfoundland, and Meiklejohn reported that Harriman *was* in need of a shave – but there was no water on the plane, only coffee in the thermos bottles. They made light of it. Harriman "would have shaved in black coffee but he was darned if he'd do it in coffee with sugar and cream."

The Press had a way of waiting for dignitaries disembarking. As it was, they landing at the far end of Washington Municipal Airport with nobody around and started in a taxi. But as they passed the front entrance of the Airport, they found a Secretary waiting with a White House car to take them directly to the President, unshaven.
123

* * *

On the Eastern Front, the ground war was digging in.

In a staged maneuver, the Russians were luring the enemy into a territorial combat zone. It was a trap. Stalin explained to Harriman the outline of the Soviet plan.

The Germans had concentrated a large force in the Ukraine. They had broken through the front and were coming down in two streams; one South toward the Caucasus and one East toward Stalingrad and Voronezh. The Germans had intended to break through Stalingrad, but failed to reach the Volga.

Stalin was waiting for them. At the point when they realized their error and could not return on the Moscow front at Voronezh, the Soviets would take Rzhev and move south to cut off Smolensk. Using large reserves North of Stalingrad they would sweep to Rostov, which, together with the Southerly direction, would isolate the enemy forces in the Caucasus.

Harriman briefed the President at Camp David of the top secret information. This allowed for optimism amongst American military circles. News that the Soviets might halt the ongoing German offense on the Eastern Front was hopeful.

Further, Harriman suggested to the President that they utilize the Iranian Railroad to deliver supplies to Russian under the Protocol delivery commitment.

This was a revelation to the President. Harriman pressed. As corporate owner of the Union Pacific, Harriman knew how to use rail.

Furthermore, he had gone to the Middle East and inspected the facilities; the track and its capacity to deliver cargo…

They agreed. The railroad should be used to supply their Russian Allies. And it would be defended with personnel.

Throughout the war it remained the principle supply line by which American aid reached Russia.

* * *

In London the mood was dark. Kathleen was getting frustrated. In her letter of September, she said the prospect for victory was not good. Amongst other things, the Duke of Kent had died in an airplane crash in Scotland. She was pleased to know that in Washington, Harriman attended a memorial service for him at the National Cathedral.

Kathleen went to Parliament. She heard dissent and witnessed a leadership in disarray. Things were going from bad to worse. Supply ships were being torpedoed. North Africa was showing little success. The Germans were marching on Russia. The Pacific was falling like dominoes. The Americans were slow arriving, and the Soviet Army seemed to be in retreat. "Went to the Commons yesterday. Disgraceful performance on the part of the MPs." Churchill spoke. "I enjoyed the P.M.s speech, but then I always do. It was received with a certain amount of apathy by the House." She said "Today Andrew Bevan shot his mouth of, called the P.M. a paranoiac. Andrew, unfortunately, is a very good speaker." [124]

Moreover, on the streets of London morale was low, panic beginning to surface. Nightly bombing was taking its toll on the city.

Shocked by the appalling deterioration of their world, Kathleen was becoming opinionated. "Stafford Cripps made a complete ass of himself and proved once more what a lousy leader of the House he is. As you can gather, I'm not much of a Stafford Cripps admirer."

At the American Red Cross, Kathleen talked to a "couple of mid-western young boys who had just returned from the Dieppe raid." She found their American fight spirit encouraging, and she spent time with them, taking notes for an article. "I got a great story today."

She had been working behind the information desk at the ARC when they came up and asked where they could contact Quent Reynolds. "Ages 19 and 25, from hick Minnesota towns. One an ex-butcher boy, the other fresh out of high school. They were terrific. We chatted for ages…Praised the Canadians, the RAF, and the R.N. sky high, but sort of forgot to say much about their own guts…"

Kathleen kept her bearings.

* * *

A major military landing scheduled for North Africa brought Harriman back to a busy schedule in London. Large convoys set sail from Iceland in early September with an escort of seventy-five British; Canadian and American warships.

Twelve ships were sunk. Another convoy was deployed.

Harriman had planned for more media coverage and had been making arrangements. There was a serious need for larger broadcast of public information. In this dissemination of information, Kathleen would be of help and hit her stride.

In her letter of September to Mary, Kathleen reported "I did the inevitable, resigned from INS" Her boss Leo Dolan was much upset "but I think I convinced him that the resignation was not due to any hard feeling, just that I was considering a better job, namely Newsweek. Now that they have a London office, it really makes more sense that I work for them. I can get the kind of information they want and the type of query work they require… [to accomplish] far larger in scope than what INS does."[125]

At the American Press Corps, Kathleen had been writing for the *International News Service*. Founded by William Randolph Hearst at the turn of the century, the INS had been banned from using Allied telegraph lines to report news during WWI because of unfavorable reporting about British losses.

To continue its reporting service, it used the sources and news of a competitor, *Associated Press*. The AP brought legal action seeking to enjoin INS from copying news. The case was tried in 1918, and the Court found in favor of AP. The ruling only aggravated the debate on copyright and the public right-to-know. Especially with regards to profitability for news mediums. By WWII, the Doctrine of Misappropriation failed to provide for the needs of public information. Moreover, it left the staff at the Press Corps scrambling for "hot news" contrived from public news, somehow compromising the nature of verifications and source identification for reliable information.

Clearly, with Congressmen showing up in London wondering if the British might accept an offer from Hitler just weeks prior to the bombing of Pearl Harbor, the failure of the media was embarrassing if not an impediment to Allied progress: It had insufficiently informed the American public about the state of the war let alone alert its leadership to the dangers, effectively compromising national security.

Harriman had worked tirelessly. He had given speeches; encouraged news articles and offered as much information as he could share in his reports home. Neither the Department of State nor the President were able to inform the public.

Harriman turned to his own media publication *News-Week* - a magazine which had merged in 1937 with a journal he founded five years earlier called *Today*. Both he and Vincent Astor were principle investors.

Malcolm Muir was now president and editor in chief of *News-Week*. They used interpretive stories; issued international editions, utilized breaking news stories; provided analysis, reviews and commentary.

To this Kathleen could now write, appreciating the tireless efforts made by her father, and showing care for his endurance. Kathleen closed her letter with Harriman's health. Fully recovered from his illness, he was now described as being "in fine shape."

* * *

In London, Anglo-American plans for a cross-Channel invasion of the Continent were beginning.

Following an earlier visit to America by Mr. Oliver Lyttelton, British Minister of Production to meet with Donald Nelson of the American War Production Board, it was agreed that a second consultation was needed in October. The tasks of allocating war production; mobilizing the war effort and dividing resources between the two nations was enormous, especially since Mr. Nelson had been unable to detach to London since Lyttelton's visit.

Harry Hopkins offered to come in his stead - such was the critical need, but in the end he felt that the two parties should work out their logistics and a meeting was scheduled.

With Lyttelton making his second trip to the US, Harriman decided to join him, and the total party going back to the US took several Liberator bombers. They would leave London for Scotland on a train with twelve cars able to accommodate them as a working platform while waiting for safe flight conditions, such was the routine of staff returning to the United States: Safe passage opportunities across the "Northern Route" of the Atlantic took time, patience, and readiness for the right moment at Prestwich Airport in Scotland.

Meantime, the London Harriman Mission office was now under increasing pressure. Space allocations required constant upgrading and expanding at No 3 Grosvenor Square Headquarters.

It was an American depot for those serving at all levels of authority, and from various capacities.

Henry Morgenthau, US Secretary of the Treasury was quartered at the office. Others, like Grover Leoning shuttled to the US; Colonel Green, presently waylaid at Prestwick waiting for transport and a panoply of key people were populating the Embassy and premises including those commissioned to the Signal Corps like Douglas Fairbanks, Jr.; Edwin G. Robinson. The traffic never stopped. When the Northern route was shut down by the Army, personnel were shuttling on the Clipper Plane only on a top priority basis, or boarding the QUEEN ELIZABETH ocean liner as it crossed the ocean for a five day passage. It made for enormous administration, nor was it getting easier to manage.

Nighttime electric-lighting blackouts across Great Britain were mandatory, November weather was closing in. Dark nights were described as windy landscapes bathed by a moon close to the horizon casting long shadows on an "eerie" world.

In London the war in 1942 took on an otherworldly effect, everyone lifting their collars, working tirelessly around the clock amid the unremitting destruction of Europe.

Kathleen watched it all. Then under stealth of security, an event occurred that altered her routine.

The President's wife, Eleanor Roosevelt was in London on an unofficial state visit. In a public campaign of support, Eleanor was conducted on a tour of various Depots; Women's Associations and Service Auxiliaries, and she became the focus of the media. As a reporter now for *Newsweek,* Kathleen was to cover the activities of the President's wife in London.

In her letter to Mary of October 22nd it was clear these two families knew each other. But this was London, and it was Kathleen's London. Playfully she remarked "I'll be God damned if I'll let a grandma like Missus R get me down, so I'm taking a moment, while she's off to too-secret-for-the-press-to-go- places, to repair a part of the physical and mental damage I've acquired while trailing her the past 4 days."[126]

An unexpected surprise came her way. "Tonight I was writing my story down at the U.P office and trying to locate my dinner date (it's much easier to do more than one thing at a time in a newspaper office, helps distract from general noise) when I discovered Ave and I were dinning at No. 10, quite an (un)expected pleasure for me. Dinner was just the three of us…He's such a wonderful man. I do wish you could know him…"[127]

Kathleen was behaving like a media member – if not an *avant-garde* young professional, but there is no doubt that she remained cognizant of the importance of Eleanor's visit to England. "She's reformed me, indirectly I must admit. I rise at seven, or a very little later…" She pouted "and as yet haven't had sufficient energy to go out for pleasure in the evenings…"

Further to her sister, she wrote "Last evening, Winant threw an all U.S. bigwigs' gathering. I was the only non-bigwig but had a very nice time flirting without starred uniforms and bald-headed ministers and embassies."

Eleanor Roosevelt was regarded with mixed feelings amongst many at the Harriman staff – an understandable disaffection with politics while in the grips of war. "We have that old war horse, Mrs. Roosevelt on our necks."

Eleanor Roosevelt did pen articles. "She [Eleanor] is selling that drivel column of hers exclusive to the 'Express'" wrote Meiklejohn. "I have just cancelled my subscription."[128]

The President's wife did have her duties to perform in England. Kathleen said "Today starting at 8.30 we set out to tour USAAF 'dromes and stations. We caught a fleeting glimpse of Eleanor at 12.30, then lost her again until 4 pm (due to the P.R. O's usual inefficiencies). Must admit I didn't mind at all. We, the press, got dumped at a bomber airfield where there was a very nice little bar with excellent rye. The afternoon continued with more waiting, gin rummy, and a flying trip that ended us at Elliott's station the same moment Mrs. R. turned up (she by car.) She talked to us, told us what she'd been doing, apologized for having lost us, etc."

If less than thrilled, Kathleen performed her duty as a working reporter. Her role did serve the interests of the bigger picture, and she was careful to be in full attendance. "The whole of the daylight hours had been spent in the pouring rain following Eleanor from ATA to ATS station and depot after depot. The party started at 8 and ended for me at 5 minutes to 8, which meant less than 5 minutes to dry my head and stop my chattering teeth. The latter I did by [sic] downing a half tumbler of scotch. The net result, I arrived at the party half stewed, anyway, feeling wonderful."[129]

Yet in a subtle shift, (and perhaps by Eleanor's nod) it would appear that Kathleen was just too visible to hide. She became a member of the viewing party. "Today "we" inspected the national Fire Service, listened to a brass band, watched tuniced gals [girls wearing tunics] and men do amazing acrobatics; ride motorcycles in drill and go through flares – all very exciting I can assure you. After that we dashed to the other end of town and watched some civil defense squad go through a very gruesome and lifelike rescue scene."[130]

Kathleen remained assured enough of her own position, having already completed the viewing circuit in her own right as the ranking American woman on Mission in London. "Thursday. I've now caught my second wind. Yesterday we had the afternoon off while *Mrs.* saw the various heads and kings of the guerilla governments. (!) A much needed holiday, [for me], I can assure you,"[131]

Lend Lease first delivery,
Kathleen, Center.

... Tomorrow I go with Ave (Harriman) to see the first lease lend ship with food come in and after that we got to the Churchill's for the Weekend.

Kathleen, (R) May 30, 1941.
First US Lend-Lease Supplies to UK, 1941

HMS PRINCE OF WALES, First Atlantic Conference, 1941
Newfoundland.

Courtesy Library of Congress

First Atlantic Conference, 1941.
President Roosevelt and Prime Minister Churchill (Foreground);
Harriman (Back-left),

Courtesy Library of Congress

American Press Corps London 1941.
Kathleen Harriman, Member. (Third from left)

Courtesy Library of Congress

Harriman's Bomber, "Becky" 1943.

Courtesy Library of Congress

4.

The British party that arrived from London was ample. From the British Ministry of Production came Sir Walter Layton; Mr. Morris; Mr. Poynton; Mr. Griffith. Air Ministry was represented by Air Vice Marshall; Slessor; Hindley and Vice Marshall Sorely. From the Ministry of Aircraft Production was Professor Jewkes and Mr. Curson. The Office of the War Cabinet sent Mr. W. J. Haslor; the Admiralty sent Commander Currie and Graham-Smith; the War Office Lt. Gen Weeks and Major A.C. Geddes; the Ministry of Supply were represented by Sir William Rootes and Mr. Morris.

The U.S party comprised of three, Harriman; Brig-Gen A. J. Lyon and Meiklejohn.

In Washington the logistics, living and office accommodations were arranged by the British Supply Council and Joint Staff Mission. They worked tirelessly, unfolding the war between them.

In Harriman's book "Special Envoy to Churchill and Stalin" it was recorded "The month that Harriman and Lyttelton spent in Washington together resulted in a set of far-reaching decisions, the most important of which carefully apportioned the resources of Great Britain and the United States for the last, long pull to victory. They met with the Combined Food Board, the Combined Raw Materials Board, the Combined Production and Resources Board, and the combined hipping and Adjustment Board. Roosevelt accepted the scaled-down British import program of 27 million tons for 1943, including 10.5 million tons of food (less than half the 23 million ton level of prewar allocations) and 16 million tons of raw and industrial materials. [Note. Figures for dry cargo, exclusive of petroleum products]. Arrangements were concluded to have the United States replace British merchant shipping sunk by German U-boats, the Americans at this stage of the war having more new ships than they were capable of manning, while the British had more idle crews than ships." 132

In his office log, Meiklejohn reported Harriman as saying "'We finally carried out many of the decisions I had been fighting for over nearly two years on both sides of the Atlantic,' He added 'The Washington decisions in November of 1942 laid the foundation for the enormous buildup that made possible the Normandy landings in 1944."

After the meetings, the Americans took a few weeks off - Harriman shuttling between New York and Washington to catch up with his private bookkeeping before returning to England.

Finally, with the year drawing to a close, Harriman, Oliver Lyttelton, Sir Walter Layton, Air Vice Marshal Slessor, Lt Gen Weeks and others of the original party left for London on a US Army DC-4. They took the Northern route home.

Harriman had authorized Meiklejohn to take off from work and have as much time as he could in the U.S. His father had just died from a protracted illness. Meiklejohn and his brother David - now a commissioned officer in the Navy, had to relocate their mother to Washington DC. Meiklejohn was to join Harriman in London on a later schedule.

In writing his account of his return voyage to London following Harriman's departure, Meiklejohn described the tenuous nature of their war-time transportation. He spoke of one "false start" by a Pan American Clipper; one YANKEE CLIPPER that failed to lift off; delays that passed Christmas day in New York and finally a second Pan American flight that took onboard a full party of associates now joining the Harriman Mission.

One of that party was Arthur Kudner, a prominent Advertising Executive; another was Otto Jabelman, an elderly railroad engineer from the staff of the Union Pacific Railroad. The cross Atlantic trip took them all from New York to Bermuda, Azores, Lisbon, Foynes and on to Bristol before London. It was strenuous.

Sadly, Meiklejohn's first task of the New Year was to organize appropriate arrangements for the sudden death of Mr. Otto Jabelman who suffered a heart attack shortly after arriving in London.

* * *

In London Kathleen was entertained by those familiar to the Harriman Mission. Some invitations came from office friends, others were social and diplomatic obligations. But the winter days had been long.

Kathleen leaned over her typewriter to see the words typed. It was dim, the curtains drawn at night without lights lest they enlighten enemy planes. The city was to remain dark. Regulations. Neither was there any sound of the city about, also regulations. Doubtless the moon danced intermittently between the clouds passing above them. But the tiny candle by the typewriter flickered. Kathleen lit a cigarette, a small luxury in a world of food rations and restrictions. Embassy stocks were good though, and dinner had been satisfactory. Cigarettes and liquor "were always in abundance."

But the war was not going away.

"Dear Mary" she wrote, flicking some ash in a tray…

She paused. How to cram your heart inside a few cryptic expressions? Thank God at least for the Embassy pouch and secure exchange of correspondence by courier between Britain and the United States. Yet here she sat, wondering how to phrase her sentiments, stranded overseas on a mission that only her father provided -or she would be back home, like every other aspiring American. Travel was strictly enforced by the US Department of State. So alone she sat, a reporter ostensibly. But also a young woman needing to talk to someone in the family about her personal experiences here in London.

Christmas in London had presented a measure of celebration and cheer. Plus her father had made it back from Washington DC in time to be there for some festivities. And there had been no end to hospitality for the Americans by the British leadership. She did feel upbeat. It was January.

"…Tomorrow I'm giving a cocktail party, the British Ambass to Moscow wants to meet the American press…." [133]

She was typing when a screeching siren pierced the night air outside. Kathleen jumped, cursed. With all the lights doused, perhaps she could continue. She tried. Just to finish off…a bit longer?

But the phone rang.

The baby! she muttered

"Al" she called out. "Come on! Let's go!"

The letter remained undated. It had to wait for a later installment, and she would describe the events of that night. She explained that if such a raid siren required them to remove themselves to a shelter she had made arrangements to pick up the baby, 'Young Winston' son of Pam and Randolph Churchill. Their apartment was in the same building and Pam, the mother of Baby Winston, was out of town during the Sunday raid.

"As a phone call from the proper authorities advised that he be taken down into the shelter, Al [a domestic staff member] and I marched over to Pam's flat. We found Butch [the child] already dressed and ready, wide awake, trotting around saying "Guns going boom, guns going boom" which alternated with "No more booms, no more booms." He was quite unfrightened, or pleased at the idea of going out than anything else. So, armed with his favorite toys, a black velvet "demon" and can of blackberry preserved stuffed in the other arm, he was very excited. Nanny, however, I gather hated the shelter, and somehow I don't blame her. Shelters aren't design for luxury…."[134]

Yet Kathleen articulated an archness for the compulsion to seek shelter. "…Anyway, all went well and Al and I came back to the apartment just in time to run into a couple of pajama clad (hanging below uniform trousers) senior U.S. officers, tearing towards our shelter well-armed with gas masks and tine hats. I'm neither brave nor blasé over the combined dangers of bombs dropping and ack ack shrapnel, but I thought that performance was mortifying."[135]

Still, she was sanguine. "The idea now is to keep the [German] planes up high, with ack ack, and chase them out of the London area where the [London] night fighters are waiting to catch them. A bomb-loaded bomber causes quite a mess if it's shot down! As I daresay you can imagine…"

In fact, the Germans unleashed a rain of fire upon London. Bombing raids over the city in the cold January of 1943 were relentless. Ack Ack, falling bombs and search lights filled the city; sirens called for endless scrambles to bomb shelters. Many were terrorized and fled. The American Embassy held fast and Harriman's staff worked tirelessly through the nights, days and weekends. Cable traffic was endless, all encoded communications filtering out to US Departments, agents, executives and private industry support infrastructure. The White House was in constant communication, including the President. It made for little regard of the clock, and it clearly made the enemy nervous.

However, what preoccupied Kathleen in her letter to Mary the following week were her events during January. She conducted Press interviews and talked with Exiled leaders from European governments, most of them still uncertain about Russia as ally.

London was a hybrid of émigrés fleeing Europe, making it a center of Head-of-State officials now living in exile who said London was their "Last Hope Island." They were allies with Britain and America against Nazi oppression.

London, holding in its palm sovereign legitimate governments overthrown by the Axis powers, became home to foreign Royals staying in mansions overlooking St. James's Park; Chester Square, the Rubens Hotel, Stratton House, Belgravia, Kensington, Mayfair, Knightsbridge and St. James. Over 100,000 European pilots, soldiers and sailors had collected in England – Soho their center as they integrated with the English on all levels, offering social vibrancy and fervor if not their services for duty.

"I had a very enlightening talk with the ex-Russian ambass to Poland (he's also accredited to all the other exiled governments.) He's a talkative individual (in French) so I got a lot out of him…" And whereas Tony Biddle, the American Embassy Press Secretary receives official lines from Bogolomov when he joins them, Kathleen stays on to observe the sense of intimidation exerted by a "huge Russian map of Europe. The countries were all colored in light pastel shades, with the exception of Russia which was dark bright red." Kathleen notes with remarkable perspicuity that while talking the map became the focus of attention "That had rather a catching effect – soon both Tony and I were looking at the map too. Russia certainly looked very big and ominous... The Ambass's line was forceful "our breaking off Nations, not Goebbels. We have cleansed the ranks of the United Nations of fifth column elements, just as we cleansed the army of fifth columnists in the purge…"

Kathleen closed her letter with an observation "And at the end, when I left, I felt more depressed than ever, not only for Poland, but for all the countries that border Russia. You can't blame them for having the jitters…"

* * *

It was in the dead of night, the moon low and the stars out that the wind blew with a howling call. English soil was in total blackness, and something was happening.

A "cover plan" was in place according to Harriman's account in his book "*Special Envoy to Churchill and Stalin.*"

At the airport, the Prime Minister's Liberator bomber COMMANDO was preparing to lift off, key personnel preparing for a special mission of the utmost intelligence and secrecy. It would land in the morning of the same day, and take off again at approximately the same time. *That* was the cover plan.

Clearly, the enemy was watching.

Harriman assembled his papers, and in so doing, it became obvious that he was off to one of the most important meetings of the war. He said to Meiklejohn that he would have invited him, but for reasons of secrecy it was best he go alone. Win Brown, another member in the office was told to prepare himself for a trip to North Africa. Meiklejohn came anyway.

The car came to pick them up. Together, they went to the airport, put on parachutes, flying suits, and boarded the plane. Destination was cited as Dakar. But in a sudden sequence, they all secretly were taken off the plane and returned to London in a different car. Others, evidently, were to take their seats on the plane!

The next day, Win Brown was told he was going to the Lend Lease venue in India. Harriman, Brown and Meiklejohn drove to an airport in the town of Stanton-Harcourt where a number of planes were aloft, dozens more dispersed on the field. They ate supper at the officer's Mess then retreated to a back room to go over papers. Meiklejohn noticed that the airfield was not too far distant from the Prime Minister's country residence.

Once again they all boarded the Liberator COMMANDO, now outfitted for Ministerial comforts, and Harriman turned to his Assistant to disclose that they would be joined by the Prime Minister. The destination was to remain secret. They understood.

As a security precaution Brown and Meiklejohn then disembarked and returned to London, their seats taken up by the Prime Minister of Britain and Commander Thomson his Aide; Sir Charles Wilson his physician and body guards.

The next morning, in the Harriman Mission a cable arrived from the Russians for "Harriman Eyes Only." The cable was taken to a senior British Admiral who said "He won't be seeing any Russians where he's going!"

5.

Casablanca. The President of the United States, Prime Minister Churchill and Harriman were conferencing to discuss the next phases of the war. Stalin was supposed to join them.

On the agenda were targets for special assault missions against Germany. Bombing sites included submarine construction yards; aircraft industries, transportation oil refineries and critical enemy war-industry targets.

In addition, troop-lists were now drawn for crossing the Atlantic from America to Europe, along with the intensified prosecution of anti U-Boat campaign, complete with the provision for air cover of Atlantic convoys.

Little did Kathleen know that it was her father's activities in Casablanca, coupled with Roosevelt's unprepared Press remarks, that incited the enemy to shower fury upon London.

Two months previously, on November 4th, just before Anglo-American forces started landing at Casablanca, the British Eighth Army had captured El Alamein from Rommel in North Africa; then Oran and Algiers on November 8th 1942.

Within days, as the Germans occupied Vichy France, Admiral Darlan came over to side with the Allies in Morocco and Algeria, allowing for their planned occupation of Bone on the Western side of Tunisia. A full attack on Tunis was scheduled for the 25th of November. At the same time, the French fleet at the naval base of Toulon France was scuttled.

Rommel had beefed up his force in Tunis. Torrential winter rains forced the Allies to abandon Tunis on Christmas Eve. On Christmas day the French Admiral Darlan was assassinated.

This, only weeks after news from the Eastern front on November 22, 1942 that both prongs of a Russian assault at Stalingrad had surrounded the German Army under the command of Field Marshal Von Paulus.

There had been a plan for the meeting. On January 4, 1943 Harriman had been called to 10 Downing Street. The scheduled conference was arranged and shrouded in absolute secrecy. Casablanca was the site chosen for Churchill to meet with President Roosevelt.

Once there, the leaders stayed at private Villas outside Casablanca, their staffs holding at the Anfa Hotel. The meeting opened on January 14th and lasted ten days.

A number of key decisions were made at the Casablanca Conference. Amongst them, a basis of cooperation between General Charles de Gaulle and General Henri Honore´ Giraud, head of the French African Allied command was established.

More plans were laid for the next move of the Allies in North Africa.

In Europe, an intermediate step to occupy Sicily (Operation HUSKY) was scheduled for July, 1943.

Operation BOLERO was to resume for the cross-channel invasion as a buildup to operation OVERLORD. Here it was decided to schedule the massive invasion for the following year.

Amongst other strategic decisions like bombing targets; anti-U-Boat campaigns and Atlantic convoy's protection, supplies to China were also decided with arrangements made for the traversing of the Himalayas, an ambitious plan.

It was not lost on Harriman however, that the presence of the Chinese at this conference made for Soviet shyness to attend, if only on the grounds of a prior Soviet Agreement made with the Japanese regarding the Manchuria. For the Americans, any reticence by the Russians to join them against Japan was worrisome.

Following the Casablanca Conference, a final agreed Joint-Communique was drafted and released. Roosevelt provoked unexpected response with an unscheduled statement calling for the absolute "unconditional surrender" of Germany, Italy and Japan.

The conference concluded, Roosevelt took a tour of Marrakech at the Foothill regions of the Atlas Mountains. Then the American party returned to the United States; Harriman to England.

Harriman travelled with the British party in one of two planes landing at Lyneham Airport Wiltshire, 29th January 1943. He disembarked, and was walking away from his plane when the second plane, carrying all others from Casablanca, crashed. Brigadier Dykes, Joint Secretary of the Combined Chiefs of Staff; and Brigadier Stewart were killed.

* * *

"Hear! Hear!"

Kathleen was all dressed up, she leaned over the rail from the gallery. Winston Churchill, the Prime Minister of England looked up and, with a smile, emitted a knowing salutation of acknowledgement. Up there in gallery was a member of the American leadership come to join forces to defeat the enemy of Europe. She was there, as promised, to listen to the words of the British leader addressing his Parliament. Kathleen was there by invitation.

The war was going badly.

Churchill, encouraged by what he heard at Casablanca, inspired his nation to keep going.

"He was in great form" wrote Kathleen to her sister on February 16th, 1943. "However, I must admit that his announcement of Ike's appointment went ungreeted by even one "hear hear" from his fellow honorable gentlemen. Actually, Alexander's back in his original job. As C in C of the First British Army, he was "given" to Eisenhower."

Kathleen was referring to Montgomery whom she had met at the Prime Minister's residence at Chequers. "I met him once, actually, and was not too impressed. ...He's dapper, untalkative..."[136]

Harriman called a staff meeting. He had just survived a situation that crashed a companion bomber carrying key members of the Casablanca conference, and he had buried one of his senior expert engineers at Union Pacific come to London. The meeting was conducted by Colonel Forgan and Colonel Green. The news was grim, precautions necessary. They announced that the British had given up on finding Colonel MacKeachie whose plane was lost flying back to the United States thirteen days ago. "Search flights have been abandoned."

Lt. Griggs took over the meeting. Formerly employed by Harriman at Brown-Harriman & Company in New York, his task was to brief the Harriman Mission staff in London on security. Cable traffic regarding financial affairs was to be now encoded. Private industry had been using coded cables related to finance and treasure for decades.

Meiklejohn appreciated the talk. He said it was for "our most secret Navy cables, and we worked out a satisfactory procedure for handling them."

The Harriman Mission in London had reason to be busy by February 1943. Its complete compliment of staff included 25 secretaries and a new office Manager Bartlett. Meiklejohn, now in the US Navy even as he continued his duties for Harriman knew that this was no time to be delinquent on details.

Meiklejohn was swamped. Housekeeping for the office required supplies ordered from Washington for a total of about $3,000. He noted "We have gotten too care-free in our ordering in view of the increased size of the office..." For the semi-annual financial report to the State Department Meiklejohn said "We have spent close to $50,000 at London in the past six months."

By the end of February, Harriman and Kathleen were able to drove to the country for some much needed rest and recreation. Harriman, while recuperating from his illness, was never far focused from his mission.

He toured Cardiff, a major seaport, with the Mayor of the City. There he gave a speech, and augured the people well with the help of American aid. A few days later, March 17th 1943, he attended a garden party given by King George.

Meiklejohn was officially sworn in to serve the United States Navy. He held the rank of Lieutenant serving on the staff of the Harriman Mission. He received a phone call of Congratulation from Major Geddes, Aide to General Weeks and Vice Chief of the British Imperial General Staff, and was invited to dinner with Geddes and his wife along with another couple. For a young American working on the staff of Harriman, he found himself having a wonderful evening in his own right, saying "I think they all have Dukedoms or palaces in peace time. Never the less, he had leather patches on the elbows of his uniform and he rides a bicycle to work"[137]

* * *

At one o'clock in the morning on March 7th 1943, a silver combat plane flew low over the city. "It shone like a moth" in the night as it hovered over the American Embassy and the Harriman Mission. The air raid sirens went off and gunfire followed, but no bomb exploded.

Some said it was a retaliatory flight following a raid on Berlin on March 1st by the Allies. Clearly, Hitler knew about the Americans.

Moreover, tension was mounting within the Harriman Mission. Harriman's high profile required him to push his staff hard. Many found it difficult to work under him, complaining that he was remiss in "thoughtfulness or consideration for the people working with him" - a trait "that characterizes WAH's every act."

A four-hour train ride to Cardiff, Wales was arranged. As a railway man, this was Harriman's preferred way to interchange with people, especially with privileges to work at a desk if necessary in a rail car. A private railroad car was assigned to Colonel Ryan, Transportation Officer for the U.S. Army in England. Harriman was to open a new Seamen's Hostel for the War Shipping Administration. On board the train with Harriman were USN staff; War Shipping Administration staff, Embassy staff and a Vice President of the Railroad. It is entirely possible that the train was used to transport heavy cargo.

Stress was everywhere evident. To a nation wearying from war in London, the United States appeared to be dragging its feet. Harriman stepped up the pressure as the days of 1943 unfolded. By mid-March, the US Coast Guard arrived to look into safety measures relevant to the berthing of U.S. Ships in the United Kingdom.

A subtle turning of the war occurred at all fronts.

Since the Casablanca Conference, Field Marshal Rommel's Afrika Korps, which had been in retreat before the British Eighth Army, joined forces with the Dietloff von Arnim's German Army in Tunisia behind the Mareth Line. Previously, they had succeeded in breaking the American eld Kasserine Pass, forcing the Americans to withdraw by the end of February. But on March 20th, 1943 the British Eighth Army attacked the Mareth Line and, following a three day battle, succeeded in joining forces in April with the American Army under General Patton at Gafsa. A final drive on Tunis and Bizerta was successfully achieved by early May. Thus, with the surrender of those retreated to the Cape Bon Peninsula, Egypt and North Africa was cleared of enemy action by May.

On the Eastern front, the Soviet Government announced further success following the campaign in the battle of Stalingrad. An offensive continued with the advance of Russian forces westward to the Donets River, forcing the enemy to retreat from the Caucasus, from the Caspian Sea to Rostov.

In Europe the US Army Air Force announced the first Eight Air Force daylight attacks on Wilhelmshaven using Fortress four-engine bombers. Liberator bombers also bombed targets in northwest Germany, only three losses reported.

In the Pacific by mid-February, the US announced that all resistance in the Solomon Island and Guadalcanal had ended, followed in early March by the Battle of the Bismarck Sea in which a twenty-two ship Japanese convoy carrying reinforcement to Lae in New Guinea were destroyed.

Still, the build-up preparations progressed in Britain. By the end of March, Churchill expressed his concern that it might provoke the enemy. Churchill asked the Americans to arrange for another Conference in Washington DC.

There was more to discuss.

* * *

The war was taking its toll. Fear and danger lurked at every corner. During the Spring months of 1943, the record shows that Kathleen was without letters. But much was going on around her. Heightened security for one, spying another…

In one cable between Harriman and *Newsweek*, Kathleen's name came up as journalist discounted either because of her professional insufficiency or her exposure to danger. She was after all, a woman. While it is clear that Harriman was lobbying for her job as a professional, it was also clear that she was too vulnerable to write with a byline. She could write anonymously.

From Kathleen's perspective, it is entirely possible that Harriman was taking home letters for her. Kathleen remained discrete and secretive.

In the months that followed, Harriman did travel. But it was dangerous. During his next trip to America, by sea, Harriman left a note for his office regarding the disposition of his war papers in the event of his demise. This, as troops come pouring across the Atlantic from America in oceans filled with enemy U boats inflicting extraordinary losses.

The Conference called by Churchill to confer with Roosevelt in Washington DC was confirmed. Harriman, Churchill and his party were to cross the Atlantic by ocean liner.

The boarding of the QUEEN MARY was done when the ship was in Clyde, Scotland scheduled to rotate her crossing back to America.

For the parties going to America from Britain, it offered commodious facilities; communications and plenty of room for staff and operations. Upper decks were reserved for top officials able to rest and catch up on discussions, the luxuries of ocean travel a pleasant respite. Still, they were surrounded with working apparatus, including a fully operational and clerk-staffed "map room" command center with naval-tracking table. Harriman could receive – but not "transmit" cables.

However, security precautions were ample. The ocean liner, carrying some three thousand passengers was also seen taking onboard over a hundred Afrika-Korps German prisoners kept in the hold.

Further, the QUEEN MARY was under escort with circling Spitfires and a small anti-aircraft cruiser, HMS SCYLLA. She was to rendezvous with a full convoy of American destroyers while at sea. Her course, set for New York, took a southerly route so as not to pass her sister ship the QUEEN ELIZABETH carrying 15,000 US troops to Europe.

The Harriman itinerary included docking in New York from where they would take a train ride to Washington DC to meet the President for the TRIDENT CONFERENCE scheduled for May 12-25th, 1943.

The conference was a success. Cited by General Marshall later as one of the most important military conclaves of the war "for here the specific strategy to which movements of the land, sea, and air forces of the British and American allies conformed were translated into firm commitments."

Most importantly, plans for the cross-Channel invasion were affirmed at this conference. Code named now as Project OVERLORD, (instead of a previously named ROUNDUP) a forceful battle plan were taking shape to occur in the spring of 1944. It would later be known as the D-Day invasion.

Also, the Combined Chiefs of Staff decided that Italy should be forced to withdraw from the war, pending further decisions beyond TRIDENT.

Above all else, it was decided that an unremitting offensive against the Japanese was requisite. General MacArthur and Admiral Nimitz were to take the Aleutian Islands; the Marshall Islands; the Carolinas the remainder of the Solomon Islands; the Bismarck Archipelago and the remainder of New Guinea.

Further decided was that the flow of material "over the Hump" of the Himalaya Mountains to China should accelerate, with aggressive land and air operations made in order to establish surface communications with China.

Before leaving, Churchill again addressed the U.S. Congress. On May 19th, 1943 Churchill left Washington with General Marshall and Field Marshall Alan Brooke for General Eisenhower's headquarters at Algiers.

Harriman, Lord Leathers and Lord Beaverbrook remained in Washington to complete discussions on the Anglo-American effort of shipping and production. Harriman met repeatedly with the President and Mr. Harry Hopkins, dinning often at the White House. The President asked Harriman to coordinate with Churchill for a special personal meeting of Roosevelt with Stalin.

It was perhaps at this time that the President took Harriman aside and asked him to consider the post of Ambassador to the USSR to succeed Ambassador Standley.

The results of this Conference were immediate. Within weeks, the British Government announced the appointment of Field Marshall Archibald Wavell as Viceroy of India; General Claude Auchinleck to succeed him as Commander-in-Chief in India with the intent of an East Asia Military Command, a posture for the offensive against Japan.

Harriman, Meiklejohn and Assistant Secretary of War McCloy inspected the amphibious force training facility in Norfolk, Va.

The US was in full war time production. New technologies and capital investment were behind every endeavor. For Harriman and Meiklejohn - so long insulated in cramped offices and dark nights, it was an eye opener. Here were forces preparing for project OVERLORD.

They were escorted to view tank landing craft as well as low-lying planes. They boarded the YAG, an old wooden hull used to practice boarding and disembarking by landing nets; observed fully armed troops in training. They inspected Landing Ship Tanks to deliver tanks ashore with an opening of the ship's bow. Prototypes of amphibious vehicles with wheels and propellers; new technological simulation shops making topographical models of landing areas were for them to inspect in earnest.

While in Norfolk, Meiklejohn hoped to see his brother David, now serving in the Navy on station. But the reunion did not occur.

Harriman took Hopkins and other company to New York for the weekend before returning to Washington Sunday night. There was much to attend to, and much to consider for himself. Finally, he took ten days in New York to regroup.

During this visit to the United States, Harriman felt entirely that his work in London was not only redeemed but that his own career path was about to change direction.

Kathleen, undoubtedly, should go to Moscow with him.

* * *

The naval officer walked deliberatively for the elder lady at his side. They strolled through quiet groves and plantings at the Child's Farm at Falls Village in Connecticut. It was a beautiful early June morning for Lt. Meiklejohn and his mother. They had come up to choose an appropriate monument for the gravesite of his father.

The trip was arranged in haste. They had come up from Washington, spent the night at the Roosevelt Hotel in New York City and travelled up by the New Haven Railroad. The headstone ordered from the local Limerock Cemetery, they retraced their steps, satisfied that their task was complete.

At New York City Grand Central Terminal, Meiklejohn looked down at his uniform and realized that the calendar had advanced. The official US Navy season dress-change deadline had passed! He dashed into the men's room for a quick change into his summer whites uniform and dashed back out to find his mother laughing at him.

That evening, they enjoyed themselves at the invitation of family friends who owned a French Casino in New York. They had dinner out and watched "*Follies Bergere*". The outing, his mother knew, was less about the loss of her husband than about the precious time allowed for her son's stay in the United States before taking off again. Later that night, they boarded the Pacific Railroad "Congressional" to Washington DC where Meiklejohn would doubtless join his boss waiting to return to London.

By the third week in June, Harriman had collected quite a party returning to England. Amongst them was the gregarious Lord Beaverbrook, all of them travelling on a British Boeing Clipper BANGOR via Botwood Newfoundland, Foynes Ireland to

Poole England. In Newfoundland, however, Harriman rushed out briefly then handed Meiklejohn nine lobsters to take to London. For Kathleen, he said.

On the same evening of their arrival in London June 23rd 1943, Harriman, Beaverbrook and Kathleen dined with Prime Minister and Mrs. Churchill at No. 10 Downing Street. The Lobster was good; the night long since Harriman stayed on to deliver several messages from the President.

Harriman petitioned for the President's need to meet with Stalin in a Soviet-American meeting, a courtesy on account of the Prime Minister's meeting with Stalin the previous summer, absent Roosevelt.

Churchill argued for a three-way meeting, complete with the Chiefs of Staff in participation for close military liaisons. He wanted a meeting of the "Big Three" allies.

Further, Churchill recommended an Advance party meeting of the three Foreign Ministers' to lay the groundwork for Agreements to be accomplished by the three Heads of State.

Harriman stayed with the Prime Minister for the weekend at Chequers. Other matters were discussed, including his potential new mission to Moscow. More importantly, Churchill's devotion to the idealism of free market capitalism imbued Harriman with a confidence that would sustain him through difficult times, and divided American policy.

The British had long kept an Embassy in Moscow. After all, the Czar's family had been related to the King of England. Now they were Allies. Still, Russia was a revolutionary communist regime. The two doctrines were not necessarily compatible after the war, unless other possibilities existed. They explored the ideas of a post war Europe.

Harriman suggested he return to Washington to discuss Churchill's concerns about Roosevelt's meeting with Stalin. That, and his appointment to Moscow as Ambassador.

The trip was scheduled.

* * *

So far, the Americans were represented in Moscow by an Ambassador with a full complement of Military and Naval Attaches. If Harriman went, he planned to head the American Embassy with another Mission of his own. It would be the US Supply Mission, affecting matters on the Russian Lend-Lease supply program.

Much later, in writing the history of the Mission to Moscow for foreign policy, Harriman would outline the interests of the United States that sent him there in 1943.[138]

Roosevelt and Harriman understood the Soviet foreign policy as aiming to dominate her neighboring countries by military oversight (secret police); and political and economic influence, especially for "political penetration to a greater or les extent in all other countries through Soviet inspired communist parties."

In America, this was perceived as being motivated by an urge to obtain defense in depth, and a political atmosphere in other countries that would enable "further acceptance of Soviet foreign policies by the governments of these countries and also as an offset to the political influence of anti-Communist organizations"[139]

However, there was a sense of need by the Soviets for American friendship. Not only were the Russian people cited as friendly and sympathetic to Americans, with special regard for the relationship between the two countries, but the leadership sought to fulfill the promise of better days. The Russians had made little progress since the Czarist-overthrow. As an insulated nation, public information about affairs outside their boundaries was scarce. Only war-returning soldiers could speak of overseas improvements and capital investments.

Further, it was observed that the Russian people, who had undergone great suffering and sacrifice prior to the war, were told that they had won the war. As a result, they expected to receive rewards that might improve their living conditions. Thus, failing to "Provide this reward will present grave problems to the Soviet Government and aid from the United States will be almost essential."[140]

Harriman recommended "a continued firm but friendly attitude on the part of the United States [that] will best serve this end."

* * *

Winston Churchill had a lot on his mind. He was pacing. Rather, pacing and talking up and down his "quarterdeck" as he called it, the space between the entrance to the room and big window at Chequers.

"Tommy!" he called. "Do put on a good marching band will you?"

Tommy played the gramophone, and knew the Prime Minister's favorite marches.

Churchill stopped suddenly. "We are going to win this war!"

There was much to be pleased about.

In Italy on July 10th 1943 a massive American, British and Canadian amphibious force landed on Sicily as planned at the Casablanca meeting of January. Thirty eight days later, all organized resistance in Sicily ended. Then, following the agreements of May at a military conference of the Prime Minister and Generals Marshall and Eisenhower at Algiers, 521 planes of the U.S. Ninth Air Force were procured over the rail supply yards at Rome. Before the end of July, King Victor announced Mussolini's resignation. His replacement, Badoglio, placed the country under Martial Law.

On the Eastern Front, the Russians won a series of battles that regained Belgorod and Orel, forcing a 300 mile front retreat for the Axis forces.

In the Pacific the U.S. Navy landings at Rendova Island; New Georgia and Solomon's Islands annihilated the Japanese garrison and the action was followed by landings north of Guadalcanal. General Marshall began an amphibious campaign with the Australian/U.S. forces and succeeded in taking Mubo.

More importantly for Churchill, he was meeting with the President for the Sixth QUADRANT meeting at Quebec. Planning was already underway.

* * *

Meiklejohn noted that the Harriman Mission in London had grown. Its operating budget reflected $200,000 for thirty six executives and a support staff of thirty eight. In space, it occupied twenty six of the twenty seven rooms at No. 3 Grosvenor Square.

Barely settled back into his London accommodations, Meiklejohn received a cable from the President for Harriman. "Hope you can come with the Colonel." They both knew what it meant. "Colonel Warden" was a code name ascribed to the honorary position of Warden of the Cinque Ports once held by Churchill, a term for Churchill used only for the highest security measure. Harriman was to join Churchill on his trip to meet with the President.

This time, Kathleen would go.

The Prime Minister invited Mr. Harriman to travel with him to Quebec and on August 4th the official party left London by train for Greenock Scotland where the QUEEN MARY would take them to Halifax, Nova Scotia.

The ship ostensibly, was to take Queen Wilhemina of the Netherlands and her Dutch government to the United States: It was a cover plan as security precaution to take the Prime Minister and some 230 British personnel across the Atlantic, even as everything from the bathrooms to the hallways were festooned with placards written in Dutch.

The invitation to join them in travel had come as a surprise to Kathleen. In London a meeting of high level ministers was shrouded in such secrecy that only four days' notice was given. Meiklejohn said that such a surprise might once have set him "on all a twitter" but since he had been through it so often "I know all the ropes, and the office for once is in apple-pie order to wag along without me…" Nonetheless, no one knew *where* they were going, or *who* was going.

Kathleen was the only woman on station in London, and her post was considered a job with the American Press Corps. With the exception of Mrs. Biddle, wife to the US International Ambassador to displaced Sovereigns, there were no women allowed on mission. Thus, by the summer of 1943, whereas her father had been back to the States multiple times and travelled to several other locations for high-level meetings, and with the ground war in Europe raging and bombs dropping upon London, Kathleen Harriman had been in Britain for over two years without a break.

Harriman knew more. If he was about to be re-appointed on a new mission, his daughter was family.

Since Kathleen's passport had been issued with exception, it was unlikely she would be allowed to return to Europe once returned. Thus, on August 2nd 1943, Harriman called on Commander Thompson (Aide to Churchill) to make special arrangements for Kathleen to travel with the party going to America.

Said Meiklejohn, she was not to inform her Media office since "she will probably be fired for it." Neither was the staff at the Harriman Mission informed as to the nature of the covert trip. Only the following day would Harriman tell his Deputy, Colonel Green and Win Brown that he was leaving for a meeting. "We need no passports so the Embassy need not know our plans…" he said.

Harriman must have known that Churchill was bringing his wife and daughter Mary on the trip.

Thus, if "Mrs. Warden" and "Miss Warden," the Prime Minister's wife and daughter Mary were in the party, then of course Kathleen should be arranged to go home for a spell.

* * *

For Kathleen, the trip was the beginning of a new adventure. She had her role to play, her hands were full of baggage.

On 4th August, Harriman did not leave for the Addison Road Station at nine with his daughter and staff. Instead, he dined with Lord Beverbrook and left from Kings Cross Station at midnight.

Nor was the Prime Minister to look as if he were travelling. His baggage was sent on ahead with Kathleen and staff while he pretended to be going to the country for a few days of leisure.

For security precautions against any spying enemy watchman, the sequence of events was carefully orchestrated and secretive.

Harriman left his office at six in the evening. Smith, the driver showed up in the Bentley with Kathleen inside. Meiklejohn got in the car and together they were driven to the station and met with General Ismay (Sir Harold of the War Cabinet Offices) who gave Kathleen a warm greeting. A crowd assembled.

Kathleen was introduced to Lord Louis Mountbatten; a number of ranking generals and admirals including Sir Dudley Pound, Admiral of the Fleet.

The party grew to include 58 Royal Marines; 19 WREN ratings personnel and WREN officers; WAAF officers and a number of female secretaries from the British Ministries.

A large camouflaged train gradually pulled in and they all climbed onboard.

Meiklejohn and two Lieutenant Commanders of the Combined US/UK Operations held accommodations within reach of Harrimans, if in separate quarters of double-decker sleeping couches.

The train did not leave immediately as it should. The minutes passed in delay. There was some concern.

Lord Moran, Churchill's Physician, was tardy. He had been mistaken in his instructions for the time of departure.

Finally, the train pulled out of the station 17 minutes later than had been precision-planned. All through the dark night, it weaved them north through England.

By early 5th August the train was traversing the verdant countryside of Scotland where it stopped briefly for a washing procedure, allowing them a glimpse of Edinburgh Castle as they pulled out of the station. For Kathleen, this was most exciting.

Lord Mountbatten joined the Harriman party to introduced himself to the rest of the American team.

After breakfast, they travelled onward in passenger compartments. Kathleen sat facing Meiklejohn, entirely content with the arrangements. Her father "had told her practically nothing about what to expect or where we were going" said Meiklejohn.

But the day became long as it turned cloudy and started to rain. The train wound down to the Clyde - with purposeful detouring until they arrived at a destination later recognized as Faslane on Garelock. Or was it Roth-Neith up the Firth of Clyde - they could not discern.

Finally a sea harbor came into sight and they recognized three converted aircraft carriers and one fleet carrier at bay. Off Greenock was moored the ship QUEEN MARY.

They disembarked on facilities originally built by Americans for troops arriving by train for garrison, to deploy to the North African campaigns. Now under British management, the facilities were again preparing for American troops.

They unloaded baggage and embarked on a cross-Channel steamer MAID OF ORELANS. It pulled alongside the QUEEN MARY, the wind and rain picking up and the Ocean-liner hull looming like a mountain from the water. It was noon.

Once the passengers disembarked, a patrol boat came up to the steamer and instructed it to follow it to Gare Lock only. The steamer was not to return to port: For security reasons, it would remain anchored and sequestered in the middle of the harbor for four days - the patrol boat circling, until the ship QUEEN MARY was safe and away with her passengers.

On board ship the QUEEN MARY, Kathleen and the Harriman staff were immediately posted to cabins on the top side on the Main Deck. Harriman had his cabin on the Main Deck. Kathleen was assigned cabin no 25 on the Sun Deck.

Staffers noticed differences in the layout of accommodations from previous voyages on the QUEEN MARY. Whatever vestige of peace-time luxury remained – such as a private bar positioned forward on the Main Deck, it had been purposefully requisitioned for the occasion from the Cunard's stocks in Scotland since the QUEEN MARY's furnishings had already been completely ripped out and stored in the United States to make room for troops.

However, due to a complaint lodged by Lady Bevelridge about bed bugs from troops, it was said that new metal bunks had been installed - to swing up for space, and sanitation facilities improved.

Once underway at approximately 4 P.M., all other standard passengers aboard ship were shooed out of the way and the decks cleared along one side of the ship, portholes covered, to allow privacy and security for the travelling leadership party.

Below, on the Main Deck Lobby Harriman appeared with the Prime Minister, his wife, Kathleen and Mary. They came through with a grin on their faces, the feat of secrecy well accomplished!

After taking on her passengers, the ship sailed out swiftly ninety minutes later and within half an hour had cleared the anti-submarine nets at the harbor entrance.

Kathleen was excited. This trip was a well-earned respite. She and Mary were free to enjoy, and they took to the upper decks.

Below, the leadership conjugated for drinks at the Cocktail bar just as the BBC announced the capture of Catania in Sicily, and the Russian liberation of Orel.

Moving to the "Map Room" they observed strategic placements rearranged to comply with the news reports. Here, for now, the strategic Command and Control center of the European Allies was moving across the Atlantic.

Sailing to Halifax through seas containing German submarines presented challenges. As escort, the aircraft carriers HMS ILLUSTRIOUS stood off their quarter, as did the cruiser HMS GLASCOW followed by a number of destroyers. Once at sea, the HMS GLASCOW was replaced by the HMS KENT, and the aircraft carrier HMS ILLUSTRIOUS turned off for others. Tracking were Liberator bombers from Newfoundland.

Kathleen was in safe company. With a calm sea and comfortable trip they adjusted their clocks steadily. Kathleen was an icon and could shine like a celebrity. For the staff it became clear that work would be without prospect, "particularly now that Kathleen is aboard."

Along with Mrs. Churchill and their daughter Mary, others too had been invited as reward.

One of Churchill's guests was Brigadier O.C. Wingate who had led a British column into Burma and returned to India after destroying Japanese communications for an entire air supply mission. Another, was Wing Commander Gibson, a highly decorated twenty-five year old aviator who led a remarkable feat of precision bombing over Germany, destroying a critical Dam before taking out the Moehne, Eder and Sorpe dams of the Ruhr River that caused massive flooding of the entire military-production and industrial regions. However, when invited to deliver his short speech aboard ship to the party in transit, Churchill apparently took him aside and said "Now Dam-buster, don't say over here that we bomb the centers of the cities, let them think we bomb military objectives."[141]

On the evenings of August 5th and 6th, Kathleen was at the dinner table with her father. At these dinners Churchill was discussing critical matters to Harriman for the President's information.

Harriman would enter a Memorandum to the President about the evenings' conversations with the Prime Minister en route the United States on board SS QUEEN MARY. "Thursday evening, August 5, Kathleen and I dined with the Prime Minister, Mrs. Churchill and Mary, Commander Thompson, Lord Leathers (Minister of War Transport) and General Sir Alan Brooke (British War Office, SIGS)."[142]

Continuing his conversations after dinner with the Prime Minister while playing Bezique, Harriman had much to report. He revealed the Prime Minister's concern about the exploitation of the Mediterranean. Churchill said that the lines of (attack) were as "good a place as any" to fight the Germans to relieve pressure off the Russians. Churchill's opinion was that pressing the Italians would defeat other German allies "and the Balkans may collapse as well."[143]

Harriman in turn, asked Leathers for ways to augment the troopship situation from the U.S. for Bolero in order not to take away divisions from the Mediterranean. Leathers agreed that shipping should not be an obstacle.

Personal information was added for the benefit of the President. Churchill, noting gaps in American infrastructure said that he could call his Cabinet members or Chiefs of Staff to Downing Street for quick resolutions and decisions. The Americans, he observed, were not always in such agreement with each other.

Churchill discussed the Pacific battles, including Brigadier Wingate's concept of fighting the Japanese in Burma. That, and the feat of Gibson, his "dam buster"

At the dinner of August 7th, 1943, Harriman reported that the Prime Minister was extremely pleased to be meeting with Roosevelt in the next week so that they could make decisions, political as well as military.

Churchill discussed Beaverbrook at dinner. When Lord Mountbatten asked why he had been left out the present government, Churchill explained that just prior to his retirement, Beaverbrook had some health issues with asthma, a "bit too much whisky."

The Prime Minister, beset by military disappointments and poor British leadership, regretted the absence of Beaverbrook. He said that had Beaverbrook not left his government, he would have him back. However, Beaverbrook was also a source of concern to Churchill, perhaps for reasons of his indiscretion related to some sensitive matters. Regardless, Churchill cited the Opposition party as being Beaverbrook's main detractors.

Regarding Stalin, Churchill was concerned about not hearing from the Russians in weeks, and that he wanted to cable his Congratulations to Stalin for the victory of Orel, but Sicily was pending. Then Churchill looked up and said "would the President care to send a cable of congratulations ending up with the words "It may not have come to your attention that considerable military operations are going on in the Mediterranean which have resulted in Mussolini's retirement'" [144]

Harriman noted in his Memo that, based on his own private dinner at Beaverbrook's before leaving London, Beaverbrook had his own agenda, especially with regards Stalin. Harriman reported that Beaverbrook found Bevin's new Labor proposals untenable in Britain. It might lead to the collapse of Churchill's government in Parliament. This would catapult him [Beaverbrook] into a political position of leadership.

India was discussed. Churchill regretted that the Indian Army had grown too big and said that he never should have allowed it to expand. He was distracted elsewhere, and he would back it up nonetheless. Jacob's remark was insightful. He said he doubted that troop recruits from India would total more than 25,000. While military tradition called for enlistment, most fighting men were not inured to combat, and might not even speak the dialect of their officers.

A number of topics were examined. The Atlantic Charter of two years previously was discussed; the Cairo meetings of the previous year; Jacob's message for Auchinleck; his talk with Gott before his death; the decision to bring on Montgomery. Later, for Roosevelt's eyes only, Churchill gave Harriman a handwritten reproduction of his Orders to Alexander.

Even the great speeches given for public dissemination were discussed. All this in the company of Kathleen, included in their confidences.

* * *

6.

Quebec. At Charny junction, the Canadian Prime Minister MacKenzie King came onboard and joined the procession to gather at Chateau Frontenac, a large and formal place of old world charm.

Harriman took a quick flight down to New York in advance of the meetings, possibly with Kathleen, and within a few days, had achieved his objectives. Returning to Quebec by train, he attended dinner with the President, Mr. and Mrs. Churchill and Mary at Hyde Park, NY.

On August 23rd 1943, the President joined the Conference with Harry Hopkins, Secretary of State Cordell Hull, Secretary of War Stimson and Secretary of the Navy Knox.

In attendance were British Foreign Secretary Anthony Eden and Brenden Brackon, British Minister of Information.

During the course of the Quebec Conference, Harriman took several Ministers on a fishing trip to Grand Lac de L'Epaule in Laurentide Park. He discussed with Harry Hopkins the Russian situation. Back at the Conference, Harriman attended to matters of shipping and supply.

Key to the QUADRANT conference however, were the military decisions made between the President, the Prime Minister and the Combined Chiefs of Staff.

General Eisenhower was to accept the unconditional surrender of Italy; to seize Sardinia and Corsica and establish bases in Rome for project OVERLORD, the cross-channel invasion.

Operation ANVIL was to supplement OVERLORD by an offensive in Southern France along with Air-nourished operations in the Southern Alps.

In the Pacific, General MacArthur was to continue up the New Guinea Coast for the Philippines. Operations in the Gilberts; Marshalls and Marianna's Islands should be under Allied dominion by 1945, and the Ryukyus Islands would be secured as a threshold to the main islands of Japan. Operation GALVANIC was to be the seizure of the Gilbert Islands beginning with a landing in November on Tarawa and Makin.

General Arnold was to establish air bases in China; the Mariannas and other Pacific islands from which the new B-29 Super fortresses could operate.

In the Allied Southeast Asia Command, Vice Admiral Louis Mountbatten and Lt General Stilwell were to include the command of Generalissimo Chiang Kai-Shek. British and US Air forces including the Tenth Air Force were to form under Major General Stratemeyer, and all efforts were to be made to establish communications with China as they proceeded with an offensive in North Burma for the winter months; the Ledo Road from Assam for connecting with the old Burma Road at Mongya, and a pipeline to be built from Calcutta to Assam.

The Quebec Conference was concluded with the promise of a further meeting, plus the understanding that they make full disclosure of the decisions to the Soviet Union, their ally.

With all business finished, Harriman and his staff left Quebec by train on August 25th for Washington with Mr. Knox, Secretary of the Navy.

Following the Conference, President Roosevelt went to Toronto to address the Canadian Parliament. The Prime Minister and many of his senior advisers stayed in Quebec until the President completed his obligations in Canada.

The QUEEN MARY, now outfitting as a troopship, was scheduled to sail back to England from Canada with the Administrative staff used at the Quebec Conference, many of them dropped off in New York for excursion. Kathleen was to join them.

For the leadership, including Harriman, there was much to accomplish yet in Washington DC. Winston Churchill lodged at the British Embassy in Washington during his stay before returning to England.

* * *

The Harriman's country estate was not too far distant from the Roosevelt residence of Hyde Park. Harriman also had premises just outside New York City. There is no doubt that Kathleen was in New York enjoying a warm and long overdue break from the Harriman Mission in London. For someone of her age, it was a welcomed treat.

Thus, it could not have been easy for Kathleen, when the time came, to face the moment of departure from American soil for another endless stay in London – or anywhere else for that matter. However, the duty of attending to her father was her topmost priority. For this, the trust she had cultivated amongst Mission staff would serve her well. Especially when a crisis developed in New York for Kathleen Harriman.

* * *

On the night of August 23rd 1943, Kathleen called Meiklejohn from New York. Having played until the very last minute, she now had a predicament. She said she missed the train, that is, the 11.15 PM train from New York to Quebec. Kathleen begged Meiklejohn *not* to inform her father. She knew she was in trouble.

Meiklejohn was mortified. She was to be in Quebec by 9.00P.M. Wednesday in company with the British delegation returning by train to Halifax to board the QUEEN MARY for her return voyage to England. Missing this connection was serious.

A plane out of New York might get her to Montreal, even if she could get a seat. It was too late to call upon "special favors" flights, he said. He fretted. "Kathleen said she would show up at the airport and see what she could do in the morning. She didn't seem overly disturbed."

Overseas, neither had Kathleen ever been out of sight of her father, nor was Meiklejohn remiss in accounting for the safety of his boss and his family.[145]

He now worried. Meiklejohn consulted the Canadian Pacific traffic Officer at the Chateau Frontenac. He was the general passenger agent at Montreal where he could arrange for Kathleen to meet with an agent at the airport and get priority standing for a seat to Quebec. It was a long shot.

The agent met her. Meiklejohn found Kathleen standing at Lorette Airport Quebec about 2.00 PM. If flustered, late and the weather foul, she stood there wearing a fashionable suit with a hat *de-rigeur* - her bags following on the next flight to London. If Meiklejohn found the Harriman family frustrating to account for, here she was, a grinning Kathleen.

Meiklejohn later reported that had she *not* shown up, Harriman would have blamed him for incompetence. Harriman, after all, could have conjured up a special Army flight for Kathleen.

Kathleen, scheduled to return to England on the QUEEN MARY now serving as a troop carrier, was neither accompanied by her father nor the senior leadership that had travelled westward. Of the "Special Party", only administrative personnel and those supporting military matters were to return on the ship eastbound.

Kathleen's return voyage on the QUEEN MARY was a circumstance of her travelling without a passport and continuance of her overseas stay as her father's dependent on post. Such arrangements must have been considered suitable and cleared by both her and her father in advance. On board the QUEEN MARY Kathleen was to be a member of the "Special Party." And while some officers were on hand for dinner events, Kathleen's days at sea were sparsely populated by Americans.

In her letter to Mary from onboard the ship, Kathleen began by alluding to her last minute connection-crisis with "after my call to you, and Ave's call to me…" Then, Kathleen's personal comforts are recounted. It was not an easy return trip.

The urgency of delivering troops across the Atlantic had packed the ship to capacity. If Kathleen started out with a cabin of her own, she was told to double up. And if she counted herself as amongst the privileged, she was less than charmed. "We, the privileged, have 3 meals a day - Breakfast at 10, lunch at 1, and dinner at 8. Punctually."[146]

Kathleen was stepping over sleeping recruits everywhere - in the hallways, on the decks "Roughing it." She added "But I share a cabin with a hellova nice War Office secretary and share a bath (which adjoins our cabin) with a girl next door."

Kathleen was not amused when she described planned activities aboard ship. Naval officers organized P.T. exercise routines for the "Special Party" - of which she was one. It was a drill made for the leadership to inspire example.

"Can you image U.S. generals dressing up in slacks or shorts and sweaters and making figurative fools of themselves in front of their junior officers, staffs, and little secretaries? I can't - but that's what the British do. We get up there on deck, freezing cold and go through a routine of jumping and skipping and swinging arms and legs, then run relay races, much to the amusement of the troops on board and the crews on the ack ack guns. It must be a nice feeling, not to mind making a fool of yourself in front of others!"[147]

Perhaps missing the presence of her father on board, she popped into the cabin which he had used on the way out. It would have been a familiar place, at least. "I glanced into Averell's suite - bedroom and a sitting room one morning and now it accommodates 24 officers! Plus more on the floor! And of course this is luxury travel, so I'm told. Thank God it hasn't been rough!"

If unprepared for the drills of physical fitness, Kathleen recognized that the war was everywhere prescient. If Kathleen was return to England without her father, then she was preparing for longer endurance.

* * *

Harriman was in Washington DC and commuted to his home in New York for the weekends, often aboard military flights including Forrestal's plane. He was making all necessary arrangements for himself and his family as he prepared for a change of career. If Harriman harbored any misgivings or personal distress, there was nothing to show prevarication about serving President Roosevelt.

When his Deputy Director from the London Mission, Don Reed was boarding the Clipper to return to London, Harriman took him aside and told him that he might soon be carrying on at the Harriman Mission in London alone.

The concept of going to Moscow for a diplomatic mission would mark a turning point in Harriman's career. No longer the railroad executive from an industrial-banking world appointed by the President as his Special Envoy, more now was added to that ministerial responsibility, Averell Harriman would also now serve his country in an official capacity as U.S. Ambassador to Russia. His nomination would be put before the Legislature Senate where he would be confirmed by a vote of Congress for the post. For this process to occur, he was to wait in Washington DC.

As history would show, the political decisions made by the leadership at this time would play a pivotal role in the outcome of the war.

Further, he would earn the respect of the Russian leadership in ways that no other American had done, or continue to do, long after his posting in Moscow.

Especially meaningful was his guidance in Washington as Advisor to several administrations following the war. This would include moments of extreme crisis between powerful entities vying for Europe in the Cold War years.

* * *

Washington DC served as a hub of activity for the nation during the war.

Since the attack on Pearl Harbor by the Japanese, defense production and development was a top priority. On Constitution Avenue, large Navy Buildings served as management offices to an expanding fleet deployed around the world, including the commission of an advanced submarine fleet headed by Rickover.

Across the Potomac River in Arlington, the Pentagon expanded to manage full production; strategic deployment and global planning assault capabilities for the Army. The Air force was budgeted with appropriations for developments that would eventually train airmen for spaceflight.

In Congress, the nation rallied under President Roosevelt. Both Republican and Democratic parties expedited the mission of winning a war, advocates and isolations alike. Of greater concern was the loss of American lives.

Also at this time, it became clear that the country was in the grips of an economic recession. It was hoped that with development of war production, there would come relief in the way of technology, opportunities and jobs. This was a time to rally to the cause, and all embraced the notions of heroism. Military service, for the troops, was nothing less than a patriotic duty.

It was still hot at this time of the year. In the nation's capital a sense of urgency prevailed. Harriman would be immersed in the city's culture for September 1943 before returning to London to join Kathleen, even as he commuted to New York for the weekends.

* * *

Meiklejohn worked at the Department of State for his boss Harriman while in Washington DC. When Harriman confided in him he said "I can't ask you to go...[to Moscow], but I'm hoping you will want to..." He wasn't sure how long they would be gone, "but periodic visits home would occur... now and then..."

Robert Meiklejohn had been in the employ of Harriman since before the war and had seen history unfolding.

Harriman could be a demanding master. Having led administrative operations for Harriman, Meiklejohn was not without options.

While Meiklejohn's first considerations went to his family; secondly to his personal life (if he had one, he said) and finally his future, it was clear that his abilities impressed Harriman, chief among them, perhaps, was his writing. In the years that followed, the language of Agreements at Conferences; cables; communiques; reports and correspondence produced by this team was largely ascribed to Meiklejohn's quickness to put to words Harriman's concepts and perspectives.

Moreover, that Harriman had the complete loyalty, efficiency and intelligence of his Aide was indisputable. Considering the success of the Lend Lease Mission in London, Meiklejohn's contribution had brought Harriman the safety and success he aspired for. Most importantly, he had shown every respect to Kathleen and had earned their trust.

Robert Meiklejohn had by now received his commission in the US Navy and was in uniform. His brother David had also received a commission in the Navy and was about to be deployed aboard a US Navy ship in Boston, Massachusetts. Both brothers, and one adult sister, had just relocated their mother to the Washington DC area following the death of their father. When it was realized that housing accommodations were almost impossible to find, Harriman had stepped in to help. Thus for Meiklejohn, with his mother secured within the community, the determination to serve Harriman overseas was made.

* * *

During the following week, Harriman stayed at the Mayflower Hotel, a venerated establishment in Washington DC patronized by many in positions of leadership and privilege. It was elegant, discrete, and able to provide for the needs of officials and visitors. Harriman frequently invited Meiklejohn and his mother to join him for dinner at the Mayflower.

Clearly, this was a time of transition. The next month would provide them with opportunity. Washington DC had its moment of flair.

* * *

There was daytime work to do in Washington. The month opened with meetings between Secretary of State Cordell Hull; Harry Hopkins and the President at the White House, all of which required paperwork and attention by Harriman and his staff. In this environment, new thoughts about the war were coalescing.

In the taxi on his way to a luncheon suddenly, Harriman turned to Meiklejohn and informed him that the job of Ambassador to Moscow was to occur "in all probability." He said he had not yet had a chance to determine the terms with which he would take the position.

As a post-war world was taking shape in their minds, Harriman's mission in Moscow would supersede the traditional role of diplomatic and Armed Forces representation at the Embassy; the role of commerce was now his to manage as the *greater* priority. This was the deal he struck in Washington DC.

Still, the scheduled time for departure was far from confirmed. Harriman suggested that he wanted to stop briefly in London, but that failed to materialize. This puzzled Meiklejohn who was not privy to information Harriman had received from

Kathleen in London. Something was troubling Harriman at this time.

Meantime, Meiklejohn knew that for the moment, their top administrative priority was to arrange for the three-way meeting between Stalin, Churchill and the President.

On the evening of September 3rd 1943, on his way to deliver papers to the Mayflower Hotel, Meiklejohn got word that his brother David was to be First in Command of the Combat Information Center of his ship.

Later, Harriman affirmed that they too were likely to be going to Russia "shortly." The situation now seemed firm, pending political confirmation.

The Harriman staff were accustomed to long hours and hard work, but they were unaccustomed to waiting on the nuances of politics in Washington. In large part, this came from having been in control of their operations in private industry and having autonomy over their Mission overseas in London. This became a waiting game of political appointments as they cancelled flights previously arranged for London and adjusted to regular office routines. It was not an unhappy time.

The Nation's capital quickly engulfed them. During the next few days, Meiklejohn took his mother and some family friends to the Army-Navy Country club where, in the hot humid temperatures of the city, they enjoyed afternoon swims followed by dinner and summer nights out.

The waiting, for Meiklejohn, was filled with domestic affairs. Meiklejohn and his brother discovered friends in their military community. Two girls were added as friends to the family parties, and nightly they gathered for dinner and dancing. Sunday's luncheon occurred regularly at home in Arlington of the Meiklejohn's.

As the evenings served entertainment, parties and dancing at the Carlton Hotel in large crowds followed by starlit socializing on the rooftop of the Army Navy Club, David announced his engagement. He asked for help buying a suitable engagement ring for his finance, Dorothy Bradley. This he wished to do before leaving for duty.

Washington was preparing for the end of the war.

For Harriman and Meiklejohn, the news of the surrender of Italy on September 8th arrived while they were making arrangements for one of Harriman's luncheons, their impending mission advancing steadily through the political system.

Harriman attended to matters of commerce and trade, especially as they related to the war. For those engaged in industrial and commercial activity, Harriman was a beacon. He met with business leaders continuously in Washington. In his role as Business Advisory Council of the Department of Commerce, he sponsored a dinner.

The dinner was held at the Mayflower Hotel to honor those who did much to enable production for the war effort in the US. Guests included Mr. Deupree, Chairman of the Council and President of Proctor & Gamble; Gano Dunn, head of J. G. White Engineering; William Batt head S.K.F Industries; Will Clayton Fleming, President of the Riggs Bank. Amongst them also was Mr. George Mead, his personal distress acknowledged as he grieved for the recent loss of his son in the Philippines.

By September 16th 1943, with the city still was hazy with unmitigating heat and humidity, preparations were made to proceed for travel.

Harriman and Meiklejohn were scheduled for cholera and typhus shots for overseas travel. Later in the day while in the car en route to 1600 Pennsylvania Avenue, they recognized a friend on the street hailing a cab. They stopped, picked him up and gave him a lift – all on the way to the White House.

If still in the grip of languid summer vacation, Harriman and his staff filled the hours with concept planning and substantive objectives shaping the outcome of the war for America.

Yet it seemed surreal. Following the pressure of London, the Harriman staff found Washington a place to regroup strategically. So deeply were they engrossed in matters of the war that when logistical procedures augured their impending departure, they were taken by surprise.

Lt. Colonel Bond of the Air Corps presented himself for duty. His job was to provide for their disposal a Liberator bomber converted for passenger comfort and airborne conferencing. Awaiting instructions, he said. Unprepared, they stared at him, papers in hand.

They were on the move again. Harriman was to fly to New York on Eastern Airlines. He advised Meiklejohn to bring his Navy uniforms to the Mayflower Laundry service since none other would get them pressed in time.

By the last week in September, David Meiklejohn appeared in Washington DC to say farewell to his family and friends. His ship, the USS CANBERRA was deploying for duty. They spent several last days together, all enjoying outings at the Carlton and Statler Hotels for dinner and dancing.

On October 1st 1943, Meiklejohn noted "Announcement of Mr. Harriman's nomination as Ambassador to the Soviet Union finally appeared in the newspapers. Got my promotion from Lieutenant, Junior Grade…in the Naval Reserve to full Lieutenant. My promotion is definite. WAH's [Harriman's] is subject to confirmation by the Senate."

Two days later, they were packing their suitcases. . Strangely, Meiklejohn's Navy uniforms were not pressed and ready for travel due to a disruption of service at the Mayflower Hotel Laundry service. He would have to travel without them. He asked his colleague Nelson, who worked at the White House, to deliver them to London next week when he flew out to join them. "It's not often your laundry gets delivered to the White House" wrote Meiklejohn.

Meiklejohn would have a sense of humor that would serve the Harrimans well in the years ahead.

* * *

Kathleen was in uniform as a member of the American Press for Newsweek in 1943.

Her return to London in September after her voyage on the QUEEN MARY placed her amongst familiar friends and acquaintances. Or so she thought.

An unfortunate situation had developed.

Beaverbrook, excluded from the trip to America on the QUEEN MARY, may well have behaved like a miscreant and targeted Kathleen as retribution.

In her mid-September letter to Mary, Kathleen told her sister that she spent the weekend [her first week back] at Lord Beaverbrook's estate, Cherkeley, with Pam Churchill. "Max [Beaverbrook] is very dreary on the subject of the war. Guess that's 'because he's got no hand in its running anymore."

Kathleen noted that Louis, brother of Harry Hopkins, was there as a house guest. He told her that he was "amazed" at Beaverbrook's proclivity for serving drinks to the assembled group and making them "pie-eyed after about six rounds of drink. Result, conversation became exceedingly lewd as it invariably does under those circumstances..."[148]

Embarrassed, and freshly returned from home in New York, Kathleen had been plunged directly with Pam Churchill and exposed to a disrespectful display of lewd drunkenness by Beaverbrook as his house guest. She left the premises abruptly Sunday and was entertained instead by General Eaker for "some tennis and what have you…on a level that makes me feel more at home."

Certainly, the matter was of some concern to Harriman in Washington DC when he confided to

Meiklejohn that he was considering a quick visit to London and back for two weeks. This sudden suggestion was met with some concern since Harriman had "cleared his desk" in London before leaving for the Quebec Conference weeks earlier.

Without Harriman present, London was not necessarily an appropriate place for Kathleen. As the American representative nourishing allied progress, Harriman was at the center of a political maelstrom in London. British frustration with the war's progress, now in its third year was eroding confidence in the leadership.

In London, there had been hints that Harriman's career was altering course, even as the Harriman Mission was ending, its start-up effectiveness indisputable.

Disparagement and disaffection had surfaced.

A storm had been brewing.

* * *

Less than six months prior, in a report to the U.S. Senate, the Truman Committee found that the United States had failed to build sufficient escort vessels to sustain supply. Enemy U-boats were sinking a million tons of shipping a month in the Atlantic.

Harriman had for two years prevailed upon Churchill to reveal to American authorities intelligence about British shipping losses and British reserve stock. Harriman considered the information essential to better serve the resupply.

Churchill resisted. The Admiralty regarded such information as highly secret because if leaked, such knowledge would only aid the enemy.

Harriman had long felt that the United States had not been fully apprised of the critical nature of British stock positions. Such estimates were fundamental to fulfil the UK Import Program.

Not only had the information leaked, but the true amount of British supply was now critically inadequate to win this war.

Harriman took this very seriously. In March, Harriman ordered the US Army service of Supply ETOUSA; Ministers of Production and Food to prepare an analysis of British stock positions. He wanted a realistic list of available principal commodities: The goal was to inform the Americans precisely what was needed for production and distribution "to develop agreed figures on revised consumption." Without it, planning was vacant.

Furthermore, it became Harriman's aim to optimize efficiency on delivery systems to minimize exposure and demand on Shipping by the United Kingdom. Staggering losses at sea were to be amortized, supply lines of provision to overcome enemy strikes at this vital artery.

While his assignations resulted in committees to review the "packaging [stacking] of products," it generally became known as "conservation" methods of delivery. The Anglo-American Conservation Committee was then a subcommittee of the Combined Raw Materials Committee.

Thus, whereas the war was everywhere visible but nowhere quantifiable, it became the preoccupation of Harriman, a seasoned industrialist familiar with mobilizing large-sized logistics and government stock and operations, to meet this need.

The report on the stock position of imported materials to Great Britain was a fundamental essential. Especially since it related directly to plans for the invasion of the Continent.

Not only was it necessary to establish the build-up of the necessary invasion forces and supplies, but the information also allowed them to provision for "feeding and supplying the civilian population of the areas to be liberated." Especially since it was evident that supplies for liberated areas must come largely from the United Kingdom.

Harriman had set up the infrastructure for a complete survey of Allied requirements. The result of that intelligence was considered the single most important task of the London Harriman Mission.

The legacy of support and infrastructure established at the Harriman Mission was passed successfully to its successor as it attached to the American Embassy to became the "Mission for Economic Affairs."

In that Roosevelt picked his leaders, it became abundantly clear that Harriman was the man best suited to this task. His accomplishments as an industrialist were appreciated, even as other events came forward. His reports to Roosevelt, moreover, included acumen about the political landscape.

One event of some urgency was created by Admiral Standley, US Ambassador in Moscow. In the Spring of 1943 the matter raised a storm of protest in America. At a press conference in Moscow he asserted that only "limited information had been given the Russian people by the Government-operated Russian press with regard to the magnitude and character of American and British Lend Lease assistance."

In fact, it would color the nature of the Allied relationship with the Russians, if not seed a cold war.

Later, Harriman would concur that the Russians held a "complete lack of comprehension of the naval and air warfare carried on by their allies." The Russians, he said "thought primarily in terms of the movement of large land armies such as their own."

It became clear that such policy - including the paucity of resources made available to returning men of war from the front, revealed the Russians had never thought (or planned) for Supply and Provision in the same way as did the Allies. Such abysmal disparity amongst Allies clouded the end of the war. To many, it re-weighted the yolk of sacrifice made by the Russians, especially with regards to negotiations for reparation.

Lend lease, if not post war partitioning would be viewed with increasing skepticism between Allies, and no easy task to negotiate with any sense of parity. [149]

* * *

Kathleen was maturing and stepping up as both a reporter and family to her father's ministerial position, perhaps at the envy of others. Some of the London based staff might have shown more consideration for her young age.

Kathleen was careful not neglect her role of courtesy expected by her father. She developed new acquaintances and a firm grasp of the situation. "I met the new head of the Eighth Air Force Bomber Command, who is a hellova guy. The most human operational general I've run into yet." Nor did Kathleen complain.

Kathleen lapsed into her duties as Reporter. She did not miss the appointment of a Press luncheon with the Polish Prime Minister, Mikolajcayk. Her role in London as a Media representative of the American press for Newsweek was noticed.

The Press event was set up by Ed Murrow and Stan Richardson of NBC and AP Bureau. Kathleen met both the Polish Minister and his Minister of Information. "Lunch found me struggling to think what the hell I'd talk to the P.M. about. He asked all sorts of questions about American production, none of which I couldn't answer. So I decided I'd better get the lead and do this questioning myself."[150]

"Mikolaicheck is very pessimistic on possibility of any Russo-Polish rapprochement. He figures a war vs. communism inevitable and it will be provoked by a combination of Russian encroachment on Anglo-American interests in Persia, Russian Balkan policy, and Russian pro-Japanese policy, and lastly Polish Eastern frontier difficulties"[151]

She added information about a growing dilemma, as if by signaling a new turn of events: "He says no Polish government in London will or could agree to the idea of Poland being given Eastern Prussian territory in compensation for Lvov-Vilna being taken by the Russians."

Considering the context of strategic information that Kathleen was exposed to, it is clear that she was keeping her mouth shut in public, but nuanced for her father's intelligence. "He is puzzled by the apparent German strategy of reinforcing southern Italy. He's figured that they'd just reinforce the North and fight hard there only."

Kathleen was careful not to tip her hand about her father's appointment. "To get back to Russia, he [Mikolaicheck] says the recent Soviet overtures to the Orthodox Church show that the Soviets have decided to use the church instead of the Communists to win favor from Eastern European countries, particularly the Balkans (also Eastern Poles who primarily are bound by their religion, rather than the government). He figures the Germans will continue to retire until they reach the Dneiper."

Kathleen was cautious about her information. She took a swing at the heavy hitters in the Press, instead. "That's about all. As we walked out, I suddenly thought what a chance he's missed not inviting Bill Hearst to the little gathering. His was food for thought for any anti-Russians."

* * *

Averill Harriman returned to England with a new career ahead of him. The Harriman Mission in London was to come to a close.

In Washington DC, the United States Senate had unanimously confirmed Harriman's new appointment October 5th, 1943. Six days later, Harriman was at the American Embassy in London officially taking the Oath of Office as the new US Ambassador to Moscow.

Harriman was replaced by his Deputy Philip D. Reed and his office, now attached to the American Embassy, was renamed "Mission for Economic Affairs."

A Farewell cocktail party was given in his honor. Attending were five US Ambassadors, including Winant the resident US Ambassador to the United Kingdom; Biddle for the Governments in Exile and Phillips, an Ex-Ambassador to India and Harriman himself, newly appointed Ambassador to Russia. Present were five US Generals; two Admirals and a Commodore, all toasting to Harriman and his daughter. Harriman's departure, it was noted, came after a successfully executed mission for the Lend Lease Agreement of American supplies to the Allies: It laid a solid footing for the ground war in Europe.

As the final travel arrangements coalesced, they prepared to take off October 13th, 1943 on a C-54 plane specially outfitted to transport a large attached party including Generals Deane and Vandenberg, Colonel Bond and Mr. Leverich of the State Department – all sent from Washington for the Foreign Ministers' Advance Talks.

Travelling from London was the attending group comprising of Kathleen, Harriman, Meiklejohn, Llewellyn Thompson (a Russian speaking Foreign Service Officer); RAF Squadron Leader Morris and Samuel Spewack of the Office of War

Information for Public Affairs who was also to become in Moscow Kathleen's "boss" in her capacity as a reporter.

On October 13th, 1943 less than ten days after his appointment, Harriman and his official party assembled at Prestwick Airport in the dark to depart for Moscow. Their travel itinerary would take them into the hot zones of the equator and back up the latitudes to Moscow as if flying to another planet.

The moment of departure upon them, a few came to see them off - some from the Mission, some from the Embassy. Amongst them was Pam Churchill who called it "a dark, dark day."

The transition to Moscow, for Kathleen was a giant step. It would take her suddenly away from London and into a milieu of high level diplomatic engagements. Even if London had prepared her for it.

In Europe, if cast somewhere socially between the daughter of an American minister and a member of the working American Press Corps, Kathleen had enjoyed the spirit of the season with colleagues and professionals alike. She had reported on the condition of the war; its impact on Great Britain; Europe's need for American aid; the oral accounts of exiled sovereigns and the growing threat of an unrelenting enemy. She had performed her duty, contributing to the war effort.

More, she had developed a professional niche for herself as a writer of necessity for the young American lives now pouring into Europe. This gave her an intellectual currency of deep value and sensitivity.

Finally, as part of the bigger picture and being on mission with her father, she had been exposure to top-level decisions.

Now Russia was key.

For Kathleen and for her father, nothing could be more urgent or compelling than to prep Russia as the vanguard. No hour, day or personal convenience could arrive soon enough to propel the mission forward. If it meant hike-as-you go, day or nighttime to stem the horrific unfolding of this war, Kathleen showed readiness.

Kathleen had been notified by her father that she was going to Moscow on October 4th, 1943, about one week before the expected departure date.

Armed with a fashionable fur coat for good measure, Kathleen Harriman became de-facto the First Lady and Consort to the US Ambassador to Moscow.

* * *

Kathleen never looked back.

From the porthole of the C-54 bomber leaving the shores of England below, she could see precipitous cliffs and sea surging against its rocky crevices, bays and coves laced with beach and white seawash. England might well have stolen her heart - even through two crisis-strewn years. Yet with only one week's notice, here she sat, preparing to touch-down at St. Mawgins Airport, the launching place for all military flights south to the Mediterranean. While fueling up, Cornwall was viewed as a highly fortified training facility for flight cadets preparing to assault Europe.

They dined on Lobster at the officer's dinning quarters before climbing aboard their C-87 on a full moon, the wind blowing.

Once back aboard, Kathleen changed into her ski pants, the plane cold. It was almost midnight when they lifted off for the Bay of Biscay, the hour chosen to avoid enemy detection and flagrant misinformation by the enemy.

If Kathleen had come to England a young woman off the ski slopes of Sun Valley as a privileged celebrity merely 22 years old, she was now a working woman with full knowledge of a professional world and a diplomatic role ahead.

* * *

Harriman had pressing matters to manage.

The logistics of arranging for a personal meeting between Stalin and President Roosevelt was now paramount. The President had wanted a private and personal meeting if possible, but in concert with Churchill if necessary.

Such a meeting was scheduled for October 1943 but only if preceded by talks between the three major Foreign Ministers in advance of the three Heads of State. The Advance Foreign Ministers' Meeting was to take place in Moscow 18th October, less than four days away.

U.S. Secretary of State Mr. Cordell Hull was to represent the United States, Harriman officially attached as a member of his delegation while also arriving as US Ambassador to Moscow.

They would all rendezvous, gathering members from their various posts along the way to Moscow. Harriman was to host the working assembly at his new quarters in Moscow.

Thus, with his appointment as Ambassador only just confirmed ten days ago by the US Senate, and his credentials not yet presented to the host country, his team were fully engaged in logistics, if not substantive issues of the impending meetings.

If sleep came with some difficulty on the plane, the morning of the 14th October brought them flying over the port of Rabat where military tracks had scarred arid landscapes between clustered villages and open desert along the Atlantic Ocean to Morocco.

By noon they had landed at Maison Blanche Airport, some forty minutes away from Algiers. Greeted by Mr. Royce of the North African Economic Board; Commander Butcher of General Eisenhower's staff, and Brigadier General Sidney P. Spalding of the Lend Lease staff at Moscow, they were whisked away in car transportation.

Harriman and Kathleen had lunch with General Giraud, and they were accommodated at Eisenhower's residence overlooking the harbor.

The harbor was full of ships, most of them damaged and semi-submerged. The scene, azure and expansive, could only have been a morbid reminder of the present state of Pearl Harbor.

Secretaries Morgenthau of the US Treasury and Cordell Hull of State were expected to arrive the next day. Others arriving included General Joyce, and Admiral Duncan, Naval Attaché at Moscow, who had been attempting to catch up with Harriman on analogous military flights.

Eisenhower's villa was nothing less than a glamorous mansion of the Moorish Mediterranean style. Highly decorative colored tiles adorned walls, porches, sitting rooms, dining room and fireplaces. There they gathered, an evening of talk and drinks into the night before leaving for Cairo. One guest, Prince Poniatowsky, a Major in the French Army had come calling on Kathleen.

Before leaving for Cairo the next day at noon, Kathleen was taken to the Post Exchange store for military personnel, which carried a full stock of items for recreation. She found skies and ice skates – something for which there would be plenty of time to enjoy in Moscow.

The Harriman staff discovered Algiers to be a modern European colonized town filled with palm trees, eucalyptus, pepper trees and bougainvillea terraces overlooking the sea. And it was teeming with military traffic.

The gathering Delegation parties now assembled at the airfield tarmac and took off in two planes, a C-54 bomber and a C-87 plane prepared for their flight mission. The decision was made to fly south to Biskra, then eastward, rather than cross the Gulf of Sirte – a route considered to be too close to enemy control.

Passing over the Quattara Depression they saw the lines of battle demarked. Next, the Pyramids; the Nile River; Valley of the Kings, everywhere the desert sands white hot and hazy.

They finally landed at the American-built "Kilo Eight Airport" outside Cairo, Egypt. It was October 16th, 1943. Just thirty six hours away from their scheduled rendezvous in Moscow for the Foreign Minister's Advance meetings.

Greeted by Special Envoy Alexander Kirk; Major General Royce; General Cheves; General Paymonville and General Michela, Harriman, Hopkins and Secretary Hull were taken directly to Mr. Kirk's townhouse for consultations.

Kathleen was to be entertained by Embassy wives.

Walda Pasha, Garden City on an island in the Nile was where the working party had assembled. The site, it was told, had belonged to an Egyptian prince who declared himself a pro-Axis advocate, yet sent to a concentration camp.

In Cairo, a luncheon was hosted by the British Minister of State Mr. Casey and his wife for top officials, Kathleen included. But time was pressing with urgent work to do.

Talks continued at Kirk's place. Here they framed thoughts of their upcoming meetings were formulated. Dinner was served to the leaders gathered as support staff waited, some entertained by Embassy personnel.

Kathleen was shown a tour.

They departed at pre-dawn the next day, if the calendar had slipped, their resolve had not. Their mission pressed on with definitive and substantive objectives now formulated.

The flight to Tehran took them across the Suez Canal and across the Dead Sea. They passed over Lake Habbaniya and Baghdad on the Tigris River, now bronzed by the dry season.

Kathleen, Harriman and Meiklejohn, the London trio, may have peered through the portholes with wonder and trepidation.

The flight climbed into the jagged gorges of the mountain ranges rising two thousand feet from the desert floor in sheer cliff walls. At thirteen thousand feet altitude over the Elburz Mountains, they put on oxygen masks and passing over Hamadan, a broad plateau for Tehran.

They saw the capital city of Iran with its main streets, asphalt highways, green parks and European houses as the ancient heart of Persia.

Chali Morghi Airport was largely held by Russians. The Reception committee included Major General Connolly; Brig Gen Scott, and Colonels Brown, Lewis and Stetson.

Major General Kargin, Victor Migunov and others were Soviet officials in attendance.

Driven off in U.S. Army cars, Harriman and Kathleen stayed at General Connolly's place, others stayed in officers' quarters at the Amiribad Barracks.

If the ancient city was defined by kiosks, bazaars and caravans of camels carrying straw, here was the unmistakable footprint of a military depot. Vehicles, Russian droshkies, American trucks, US supplies and transport convoys were in motion; troops, both Russian and American, moved about without incident, many of them removed from the desert action of the Persian Gulf. Here, much of the U.S. supplies were passing through to Russia.

Few noticed the walls of center city compounds hiding lavish houses and verdant gardens, all cistern-fed by underground water channels of mountain-dug wells.

According to Meiklejohn, visiting such a place evoked notions of Arabian Nights and Persian treasure. For Spewack of the War Information – this was a place of mystery and wonder for the world to see in subsequent Hollywood movie productions.

On October 18th 1943, the American parties going on to Moscow realigned for the last leg, departing Tehran in three C-54's and one C-87, including Secretary Hull's plane.

Over the Caspian Sea they wore oxygen masks, then descended to avoid icing conditions over Baku. They flew over the Volga River and the frozen ponds to approach the Russian Kalmuk Steppes marked by evidence of Army supply that had provisioned Stalingrad.

Onward past Kamyshin northwest, the soil now blackened and freshly plowed, they were on an endless journey that progressed over scattered forest, farms, and windmills then over the Oka River near Tula.

Thickening forests spread beneath them, and Moscow was at last on the radar. Suddenly, they were flanked by four escort fighters.

They landed at Moscow Central Airport after eight hours of flying from Tehran and were greeted by an assortment of dignitaries, including Anton Molotov, a senior advisor to Stalin, plus a full Guard of Honor.

No less than 75 pieces of luggage were unloaded for Harriman, Kathleen and the staff. Meiklejohn oversaw the movement of their luggage himself.

The American Embassy was a building on Mokhovaya Square in Moscow.

They drove past the American Embassy building and on to "Spaso House," the official residence of the US Ambassador. For the next two weeks they would be sequestered here at Spaso House, Harriman entertaining Secretary of State Cordell Hull; several delegates plus their staffs for the tri-party Moscow "Advance Foreign Ministers" Conference being held prior to the Tehran Conference of the three Heads of State.

Kathleen, unpacked and lodged in adjoining quarters – in a "little house" close by to allow for the Conference was already playing hostess for all that taking place at Spaso House.

Since the recalling of Admiral Standley by President Roosevelt, the routine affairs of the Embassy fell to a career Foreign Service officer Maxwell M. Hamilton. He was Acting Charge D'Affairs. Harriman let him continue with the affairs at the American Embassy as he turned exclusively to his own mission at Spaso House.

They set to work around the clock.

Later described in Harriman's book called "Special Envoy to Churchill and Stalin" the Foreign Ministers' Meeting was to set the stage for the major agreements of the three leaders, Stalin, Roosevelt and Churchill.

Immediately, a picture emerged that shaped the interests of each party.

Whereas the Russians remained solely focused on a planned cross-Channel invasion of the Continent by the British and American Armies, the US Delegations were primarily concerned with crafting some early understandings with the Soviets about the *post-war* world to follow.

Stalin would get his cross-channel invasion commitment in November when the Heads of State were to meet in Tehran. But there was more.

Secretary Hull achieved from Stalin a promise to join the United States; Great Britain and China in a fortified "Declaration on General Security" - pledging the four powers to cooperate in the post-war period.

Also established was an international organization for the maintenance of world peace and security that would become "Open to membership by all nations, large and small." This would become the United Nations - a policing authority omitted from the Resolutions of the First World War.

Kathleen used her time accommodating those in residence. Fourteen guests attended dinner nightly - all served by a Chinaman and Russian major domo called Mike who served nothing but caviar, soup, chicken and rice with peas.

Secretary of Hull's staff filled the place with officials pacing everywhere in ante rooms; sitting rooms and office suits/ as bedrooms. For support staff, temporary accommodations were made for stenographers, generals, diplomats and others, many of them phasing in or out of Spaso House while packing for flights back across Siberia; Cairo or destinations elsewhere.

Breakfasts included open buffets. Banquets and refreshments served caviar, champagne and vodka. Spaso House, Kathleen's new home, operated like a ship at sea.

Harriman's staff looked forward to getting out of Spaso House and into the official American Embassy offices.

For now, no one was going anywhere. The routine was rigorous.

From a political perspective, Harriman had his head full of possibilities for negotiations. He behaved like a task master and roused people out of their sleep at 6.30 A.M to start an early day of work.

The Russians had raised the subject of the "Second Front." They were asking for military cooperation. For the Americans this posed as opportunity for negotiations.

They crafted policy and advanced American interests. All this, while several thousand miles from home, and in preparation for an imminent Conference. It was hard work.

Moreover, there was an ever-present concern. Security. Harriman was on foreign soil in a house unsecured and serviced by local domestic staff.

According to Meiklejohn, Official Cables, sent in code over special cryptographic equipment brought with them on the C-87 plane, were dispatched to the President. Only after that task was completed could everyone - generals included, be dismissed from Harriman's entourage at 1.00 A.M.

Sleep was elusive. It was all Kathleen could do to keep up with everyone's demands, and to assist where needed.

Cables were classified, many containing details of battle fronts - much of those details intended for the eyes of the President only.

One lengthy cable strayed into the hands of regular staffers in Secretary Hull's quarters, and they read it.

Harriman was furious and met with Hull's political advisor to make a clear understanding as to who should be Keeper of the secure cable traffic: It was to be his Aide, and his Aide only, Lt Meiklejohn. The Secretary of State may be under his roof, but Harriman's communications went *directly* to the President.

Meantime, Mr. Molotov officially received Harriman and accepted his formal credentials as US Ambassador. On the way to delivering them to the President of the USSR Mikhail I. Kalinin, Harriman was asked to lend one of his planes to rescue Donald Nelson whose plane had been damaged at Sverdlosk, near the Ural Mountains. Harriman agreed.

Harriman arrived at the Kremlin with twenty members of the US Military Mission, the Russians shooting cannon to celebrate the recapture of Melitopol.

Soon on amicable terms, the Russians came to appreciate Averell Harriman as an able statesman.

Fifteen items as goals had been established during the Advance Meetings.

Work now turned to drafting details for the upcoming meeting between the three State leaders. Amongst them were the proposed peace terms for the Axis countries; strategic plans for the ground war in Europe; details of the bombing offensives.

The work routine had been rigorous.

At midafternoon daily, a conference session of the British, Americans and Russians took place at Spiridonovka House, the British location where Beaverbrook had hosted the earlier Beaverbrook-Harriman meetings in 1941.

In preparation for the afternoon session, Secretary Hull would meet with his staff in Spaso House at 10 o'clock AM.

Harriman began his work very early in the morning so as to be prepared for Secretary Hull's 10 o'clock staff meeting.

In clandestine fashion, they worked behind closed doors. Nothing was left to chance and every precaution was taken to proceeded quietly, quickly, and under tight security, all of them knowing that servants might turn over anything they found to the secret police. With methodical care, they placed all working papers in combination safes; held briefcases locked and guarded; saved carbon papers, scraps and drafts for burning.

Following the afternoon sessions, everyone returned to Spaso House between 7 - 8 PM where Kathleen would receive all in the dining room for dinner, she and her father seated at the head and end of the table.

After dinner, the day's progress was dictated in code for cables to President Roosevelt by Army, Navy and State cable clerks. In the West, the day was only beginning.

All the while, activities of Spaso House were under Soviet guard. Mainly described as being for their own protection, this was described as a "way of life here."

As the Ministerial conference came to a close, new challenges arose. Secretary Hull received a cable from Roosevelt saying that he expected to leave Washington that day, Friday 29th October for North Africa in progress to the Heads of State meeting. For secrecy, the whereabouts of the President of the United States was not named. The destination was assumed to be somewhere between Basra on the Persian Gulf and Tehran.

Harriman and the Chinese were to attend the Heads of State meeting. This meant preparing his staff at Spaso House to travel immediately and to have all Advance Meeting Agreements and briefs in readiness to sign and ratify.

The conference ending, Kathleen sent out invitations for a Farewell Supper Party to the Conference Delegates of the two visiting parties. Food was laid on with supplies from the Diplomatic Store. Molotov, Maisky, Eden and several generals and admirals were to come.

She was pleased with her arrangements, making everything suitable for the occasion, but nervous about attendance. Still, she must take management under her control. With her chin up, she marched into the kitchens.

To the utter consternation of the cooks, they were instructed to serve caviar – yes, plus duck, chicken, salmon, sturgeon, Boston baked beans, spaghetti, chocolate cake, coconut layer cake, stewed apples and pears. One hundred and fifty people attended. The occasion affirmed her as a big success within the diplomatic colony at Moscow.

The next day, US Secretary Hull achieved his Public Communique on the Four-power "Declaration on General Security," including post-war relations promised for Austria and Italy.

Cordell Hull thought he was done and planned to leave the next day. But he was informed that on that night, the British delegation were giving a reception for three hundred and fifty people, followed by an invitation to the Kremlin given by Stalin for all the leaders, including Kathleen!

An Opera at the Bolshoi was scheduled to bring the occasion to a close.

The question of where to meet the President remained outstanding. Secretary Hull discovered that Stalin was reluctant to travel any further than Tehran, and the matter of the upcoming conference was still unconfirmed.

* * *

With her father officially installed as the new Ambassador, it fell upon Kathleen to introduce herself to other Ambassador's wives. This she attempted to do with a courtesy visit to each.

On November 1st, Kathleen and the British delegation were treated to a tour of the Kremlin, home to the Czars.

Kathleen saw segments of the structure originally built by Ivan the Third in 1487, she noted. Guided through rooms in which her father and Beaverbrook had crafted early Agreement in 1941 for ratification, she found the Kremlin Palace to be a veritable wonderland decked out for Christmas, complete with a Christmas tree weighing three tons and decorated with silver and gold ornaments.

That night Kathleen recommended the visitors of Spaso House all attend the "Nutcracker Suite" Ballet.

At dawn, the Foreign Ministers Delegates prepared to leave Moscow.

It was snowing.

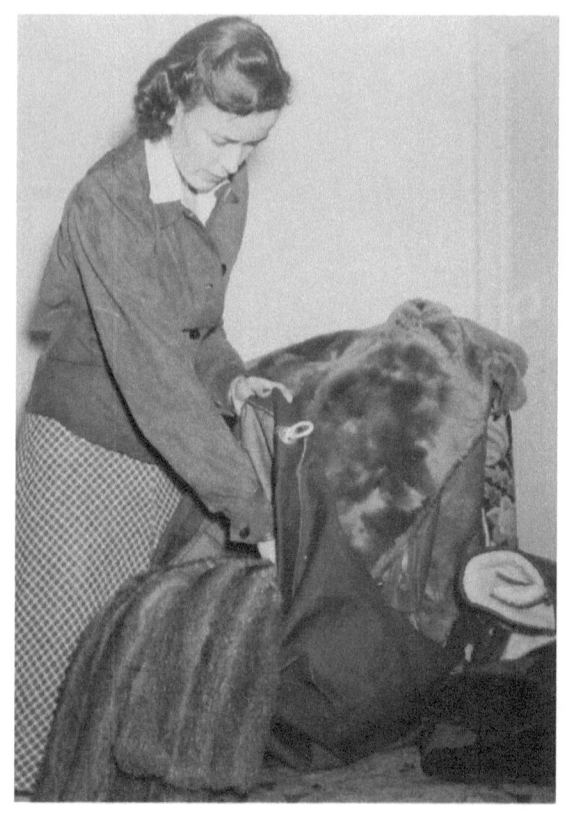

Kathleen, preparing for Moscow with Fur Coat. 1943

Courtesy Library of Congress

Kathleen (above), Harriman (Below)
Tehran, October 1943, London to Moscow

Courtesy Library of Congress

Cordell Hull, Secretary of State (L); Victor Molotov (R).
Moscow October 1943.
Foreign Ministers' Advance Meeting, preceding Heads of State.

Courtesy Library of Congress

7.

With the departure of the Secretary of State from Moscow on November 3rd 1943, the mission of the Foreign Ministers' Advance meeting was completed. Remaining now was ratification of those Agreements by the three Heads of State at their official meeting.

Harriman had been designated as a Minister to participate in both of these meetings. For the first he was to attend to the Secretary of State; for the second, the President of the United States. The responsibility of achieving a successful meeting for President Roosevelt at this Conference was his.

Having arrived in Moscow with the Secretary of State's party to work exclusively on the Foreign Minister's Advance meeting, Harriman had barely a chance to acclimatize to his new surroundings as Ambassador. For him, his staff and Kathleen, Spaso House was home, if center of operations.

Spaso House was a large, commodious and formal mansion able to accommodate large parties in multiple quarters serving official capacities.

They had unloaded their gear from the long flights to Moscow on military planes including all manner of secure equipment; safes; stationary, seal and franking devices and communications. Meiklejohn described the supervision of his unloading 75 piece of luggage (bussed by Russians) as having coding machines. "They were mercifully unaware of what they were lifting."

Kathleen reclaimed her room just vacated by Conference staff, a luxury suite measuring some twenty seven feet by twenty five feet. Large guild mirrors adorned the walls, gold chandeliers hung from fifteen foot ceilings clustered by baroque ornamentation of plaster sculpturing and paintings.

There were ante-rooms adjoined by French doors; balconies and porticos through double-door fenestration, the walls easily one foot deep. Occasional pieces of imperial furniture decorated the suite; her bathroom comprised of a bathtub the size of a small pool crafted from "cement."

She added her toothbrush, pleased with herself. Had she done well, she wondered.

There had been a staff of housekeepers to get to know at Spaso House: Chinamen to cook, serve and clean. Guards, servants, porters and maids.

Formal events were hers to oversee, including parties for Soviet greetings; introductions; representatives from all military official quarters; ministers and other diplomats. Spaso House was the social face of America. This was now her responsibility.

Spaso House itself had been the center of an ongoing official conference, filled from the first day with Delegates of Foreign Ministers - each requiring a small staff in support. Everywhere, there was equipment, baggage, communications gear spread out; office tables rearranged, desks and chairs dispersed. Upstairs there had been needs for laundry, bedding, bathrooms for accommodations. Then food to manage.

Added were guests coming to Spaso House from other delegations weaving in and out, including Russian Ministers, interpreters and their lieutenants.

Further, there were administrative matters, official titles to learn, names, offices, special assigned events to recognize. She had to decorate interior spaces, reshuffled for large cocktail dinner parties – all catered by the kitchen staff and managed by Kathleen at Spaso House.

Finally, the logistics of transportation for conference events, planning and coordination of the delegates, including table placements; tags and passes for the assembly going Bolshoi Ballet, the Tour of the Kremlin. Even bedtime snacks and drinks.

Moreover, it was Christmas and Spaso House was made to look beautiful.

Amongst her responsibilities in Moscow as consort of the US Ambassador, Kathleen not only interacted with her counterparts within the diplomatic community, but she was learning to speak Russian.

Professionally, she was still a working reporter and she had tasks to perform for the Office of War Information. She and her boss Sam Spewack had "an impermanent office in the chancellery."[152]

* * *

Harriman turned his attention to the Embassy while finalizing critical plans and agreements for the meeting of the three Heads of State. Official translations and copies had to be in order; negotiations still pending, and Tehran logistics to arrange.

The American Embassy and Chancery was located on Mokohovaya Street near the Kremlin. He found it woefully inadequate for his needs.

Six stories high, it was next to the National Hotel, one block from Red Square. It held offices for Embassy affairs, its upper floors dedicated to residences for some staff.

The accommodations of the Embassy, while spacious and ornately formal, were older, having the patina and furnishings of a traditional era. Upgrades were necessary.

After London, arrangements were made for modernizing the premises, especially for the pace of work that the Harriman team was accustomed to. A source of much frustration was communications.

All telephone calls came in, unscreened, directly to one desk - Harriman's!

Meiklejohn made a humorous account of what happened. A Navy electrician installed a filter buzzer, an old fire alarm bell, to warn Harriman of incoming calls. But it failed. As Meiklejohn explained, they improvised with new "signals" like kicking the wall three times, or opening the door a crack, to indicate who…

Military and Naval Attaché offices also occupied the Embassy building offices. They were supported by autonomous secure Communications code rooms; clerks, typists, secretaries, officers plus their own Heads of Mission.

A Commissary was available for stores and supplies, the Embassy Mission was designed to be as self-reliant and cross-disciplined as possible.

The Ambassador's offices were on the third floor. Adjacent to the Ambassador was the Minister-Counselor Mr. Hamilton, Chief of Staff at the Embassy, his title Charge D'Affairs. Hamilton had served in the Far Eastern Division of the State Department and spoke Chinese. His office was assisted by two young Aides, Smith and Cohagan.

One addition known to them now was a new man appropriated from the Hull Staff, stenographer-clerk Nelson Newton who had served under Ambassador Crew, Ambassador to Japan at the outbreak of the war. He spoke Japanese.

Harriman achieved his obligatory phone calls to other Moscow Ambassadors, something he considered a drain from his time at the moment. For the present, he made it clear that the Embassy would have to live with shorter office hours of attendance from Harriman and his Aide. What was historically a routine mission overseas was now a war-time imperative, and Russia a new ally.

Further, he had an ongoing mission at his Ambassador's quarters, Spaso House. At least until the Documents' Safe and Cabinets were officially taken to the Embassy, he would make Spaso House his office.

In addition, there was another purpose that he held there as a political appointee.

Harriman's Commercial authority had been negotiated with Roosevelt. It was to be of higher purpose for negotiating a future with Russia. This mandate had a superseding imperative, a mission that surpassed the traditional quasi-military authority of the Embassy. This, he would continue throughout his tenure there.

* * *

Spaso House was now populated by Harriman, Kathleen, Meiklejohn and a few lingering staff from Secretary Hull's party. Other guests included Sam Spewack, playwright and friend of Harriman, now head of the Office of War Information; John Melby, Third Secretary of the Embassy; and Hamilton was ever welcome.

Naturally, the Moscow US Embassy presented him with its mission requirements, including diplomatic representation at the host's military parades through the Red Square. Mandatory attendance to events like celebrations of the anniversary of the Soviet Revolution at Spiridonovka were a draw on Harriman's time.

Further, there were social invitations. On one invitation, it said "White Tie" as dress code. Dress was something for which the Harriman's had given little thought under the circumstances. Kathleen, while running around trying to assuage them with possible solutions, encountered the British Ambassador asking the Second Secretary of the American staff if he could borrow a boiled white shirt. Harriman threatened to fire his Second Secretary if he gave his shirt to the British! Spaso House filled with laughter, something for which Kathleen's presence was often responsible.

On the 8th November, the British Embassy Foreign Office hosted an official party for the diplomatic corps of Moscow to welcome the American Ambassador. Five hundred people attended. It was a vibrant event with some drinking and much outspoken relief at having the Americans. According to Meiklejohn, the British Ambassador apparently made one toast too many and landed in the punch bowl, bringing the table of food down upon him. His military staff so quickly closed ranks that nobody noticed. Harriman and Kathleen tactfully avoided any Vodka-induced hubris by leaving early. The next morning however, Harriman was searching for seltzer pills to quell his hangover, and Kathleen was drinking "buckets of water" – "for just a few sips of [vodka-laced] punch"

Still, in Moscow the pressure was never far beneath the surface, even if much was ascribed to a proclivity for bluntness by the Russians.

For Harriman, the work was relentless. Nightly at Spaso House, he and Kathleen gathered in Meiklejohn's suite where they kept their office equipment including code machines and a radio in the lounge area. They listened for the BBC news at 11.00 PM by the heater, even if clear transmission was irregular. The war was never far away.

It had snowed all night and accumulated to two inches the morning of November 9th, 1943.

Kathleen had an announcement. With the help of the U.S. Army, she was having skis made for all the staff by the Red Army. They would be laminated wooden skies with steel edges, Kandahar bindings, plus boots. The skis would cost ten dollars. As she stood there explaining her project, the mood of Spaso House was entirely brightened.

Meanwhile, Roosevelt and Churchill sent a cable to inform Stalin that they were meeting in Cairo. Stalin returned a cable saying that he would travel no further than Tehran. In fact, the staff were uncertain if he would leave Russia. The location of the impending meeting was beginning to create tension. Roosevelt and Churchill insisted on Cairo.

Harriman made the necessary arrangements to settle for a date. He suggested 11th November, 1943.

Stalin made his position clear about the meeting place. Tehran, and he would be accompanied by Molotov.

The next days for Harriman were filled with cables, logistics and coordination. Neither was the war going well, nor was the President adequately supported by the White House for his meeting. The hours passed with difficult periods of waiting, delayed information and uncertainty.

On 15th November, a cable arrived in Moscow from the President dated 13th November. It said he was on his way. Presumably, he was at sea.

Harriman arranged to be leaving Moscow in four days, Friday the 19th November. Preparations were made for a flight in the C-87 Liberator.

* * *

Harriman was rushing through Spaso House, the clock ticking, a crisis developing. All arrangements for a Presidential delegation at Tehran were inadequate!

From Moscow, Harriman was too far distant to help. While he hoped that much of the planning for a Head of State meeting had been considered in Washington, it become clear that insufficient preparations had been made for the President. Harriman must fill the gap!

The venue of the meeting to take place – its identification only lately revealed without advance arrangements, was insufficiently provisioned for the President to serve the task at hand. It was a situation largely beyond his ability to solve. Thus Harriman prevailed upon the military staffs in place for office support at the location where the meeting was to be held. Tehran.

Moreover, for Harriman greater policy questions remained outstanding, and he was concerned.

If approved "in principle" by the Soviet Union at the Moscow Conference, too many issues remained unresolved.

Since the Advance Meeting, much had transpired. Or rather, failed to transpire as follow-up confirmations, including the Cross-Channel invasion promised offered by the Allies. Clearly, it had become the source of discontentment by the Russians, if not creeping impediments to the upcoming Agreements.

If Harriman harbored any hopes of assistance or follow-up overtures made by the US Embassy in Moscow, he was disappointed. There were none. He was alone with his liaisons with the Soviets. This, he would have to explain later.

The Soviets, being a military autocracy, respected little other than decisions brought forward by the Heads of Embassy Military branches.

For now, the first issue and most important for the Allies, was that the Soviet Union make available on its territory airbases for American bombers to land, refuel, reload and shuttle back to their home bases in the Mediterranean "hitting German targets as they came and went."

The second was to allow for the Russians and Americans to exchange critical weather information, and for this purposes, improve their signal communications.

The third was that the Russians and Americans were to open up more travel and transport opportunities to the West.

As later reports filed by Harriman would show, there were reasons why the Russians had failed to comply and open up.

Their need to insulate their citizen population from exposure to the West was political. As a government, they had made no economic progress, and they were unable to deliver goods and services as promised under Communism. Hence the resistance to expose their disparities.

Meantime, the matter of winning the war was at hand. The President was on his way to Tehran. The day for departure arrived.

Kathleen had breakfast with her father at 5.30 A.M at Spaso House on November 19th, 1943. Also present were Mr. Hamilton and "Chip" Bohlen, First Secretary. Harriman was leaving instructions in the event of an emergency. There was much to deliver in the files of his briefcase and miles yet to go before meeting with the President. Contingency plans, should anything go amiss, were to provide for the safety of Kathleen left behind in Moscow.

Clearly, the wellbeing of Kathleen was of supreme importance to Harriman as a statesman serving the President.

Two hours later, Harriman took off on their C-87 Liberator plane kept at a special hangar at the airport and piloted by Charlie Bond.

With him were Australian Captain Holship as Interpreter; Lt Meiklejohn also now serving as a member of the US Military Mission to Moscow. Other passengers included the British Ambassador Archibald Clark Kerr, Lt General Martel; Major Birse Interpreter, and Captain Bolton, Aide to the British Ambassador.

The flight intended for Baghdad landed at Stalingrad because two engines showed high oil pressure.

Touching down, the weather temperatures had dropped so drastically that they were looking at a deserted air field, parked fighter Yaks and Aircobras in revetments. They opened up the hatch and were met at gunpoint. Only later did the soldiers discover who the party onboard this plane represented.

A few Russian DC-3's at the airfield allowed for scrounging by Russian mechanics as the Americans huddled in four underground rooms, waiting. There, they were told that the airfield had been the center of combat, if it now served as a relay way-station for winterizing planes.

Harriman checked his watch, observing the time for Tehran.

Cars appeared to take them to lunch - three miles up to a local municipal building. There, they met the chief of the Stalingrad Defense

Council, Alexi Semenovich and chief of the Stalingrad County.

The Russian hosts spoke of their recent defense of Stalingrad, citing ninety-one thousand Germans captured, followed by another ten thousand emerging from hiding after the official surrender. Many were said to have died on the short march to the prison camps, mostly of malnourishment, including Von Paulus, the German commander. Their hosts recounted how demoralized the Germans were, and that only five thousand Russians were left to guard the ninety-one thousand prisoners whose main fear was not the Russians, but the Romanians who assaulted them.

A tour of Stalingrad followed. The Americans were shown the destruction of the city, fifty thousand homes demolished, leaving three hundred and fifty thousand people quartered in small wooden huts and stone buildings pending reconstruction. Their power plant, badly damaged but still serviceable, must have had over five hundred artillery shells fired upon it.

The Harriman party, if taken aback by this unscheduled stop were courteous. There was little they could do but observe, and wait at the hands of their hosts.

Roadsides were littered with abandoned track vehicles and airplane fuselages. One area had the remains of twenty five hundred German planes. Slowly, the Americans saw a devastation that was endless, one food grain elevator pierced like a "colander."

They drove past the demolished Red October Tank Factory and passed a group of German prisoners under guard. They were fed the same rations as Russians if they worked, the guides told them. Tales of civilians, young Russian boys laying mischief were told, even as they were shot.

As per the rules of engagement, it appeared that the prisoners were properly maintained. Here, the Americans saw a harsh reality of this war.

Their plane was not ready. They spent the night in a makeshift Intourist Hotel in Stalingrad, their hosts trying to accommodate them.

Dinner was laid on and the occasion brought out the Mayor of the city; the Vice Mayor and members of the Defense Council. The owners of the hotel effected some translating while making for them a cultural event of Russian food and hospitality. Vodka was in plenty, and so roused was the singing contest that only when the Americans sang "I'm tired and I want to go home" did the evening close.

Cold and primitive facilities sent them early back to the airport before light. To Harriman's chagrin, they had more waiting to do to fix their mechanical problems – most of the party now nursing Vodka hangovers and fatigue. Harriman finally had them lift off the tarmac at approximately 9 o'clock AM. That night, they landed at Cairo.

President Roosevelt had landed in Cairo by plane Monday November 22nd 1943, near Thanksgiving Day. The President brought with him Navy cooks who had milk, cream, butter – ingredients needed for a feast. They procured bread and pies from the U.S. Army Camp at Heliopolis for the upcoming Thanksgiving Feast.

The pre-Tehran conferencing at Cairo took place at Mena House, a luxurious hotel at the foot of the Pyramids. It was attended by the British, American and Chinese who gathered with President Roosevelt, Hopkins and Churchill. The Russians were absent, and Harriman urged the President to invite Molotov or a representative of the Soviet General Staff to join the Cairo talks. Apparently, the Russians disliked being confronted "with Anglo-American decisions already taken."

Churchill objected, hoping instead to solidify his position with Roosevelt before progressing to Tehran, and he entered an official letter saying so.

Stalin, who heard that Roosevelt had also invited Madam Chaing Kai-Sheck and the Generalissimo to Cairo, refused to engage, especially with regards to drawing plans for the defeat of Japan.

Still, the meeting was considered successful since it was agreed by the Chinese that the Burma Road over the Himalaya Mountains would be opened as a means of sustaining the Chinese front against Japan. Chiang left Cairo November 28th for Chungking pleased with his new relationship, and Roosevelt considered the demands of the Nationalist Chinese Government met in full. Together, they posed for a photograph.

The pre-Tehran Conference proceeded across the Thanksgiving Holiday with a mandatory Church service at the Cairo Cathedral of the Church of England. Then Cairo was enjoyed by everyone, especially those who had travelled under difficult circumstances.

Harriman and Hopkins sequestered themselves and proceeded with planning for those states whose displaced Sovereign leaders were caught up in the war of Europe.

There were critics. Dismissed as "a reductio ad absurdum" it was implied that these men were making decisions in the back rooms – including Hopkins "Harry the Hop"; Harriman the "brains trust" wielded too much power. But with a war raging daily they decided that critics-be-damned, urgent decisions had to be made for the prosecution of the war against the Axis. They began formulation of the terms of peace for an Allied victory.

On November 26th 1943, at 5 o'clock, the sky still dark, the parties took off from Payne Field for Tehran to meet Stalin. The Delegations flew in several planes, including a C-54 for the President.

* * *

The President's plane landed first.

The Tehran Conference was to further the elements discussed at the August 1942 Moscow

Conference where Harriman had participated for the President, and to allow for a meeting now between Roosevelt and Stalin, face to face.

Here, Roosevelt had kept his delegation small, wanting to deal with matters on a personal basis for future relationship-development.

The British had brought a small army of personnel, as had the Russians. Great Britain was represented by Anthony Eden, the Soviet Union by Commissar Molotov. Roosevelt had from the Department of State Charles Bohlen, an interpreter.

Harriman immediately took "personal responsibility for the organization of the President's party"[153].

Harriman prevailed upon the Army Sergeant typist-clerks of the Persian Gulf Service Command for support. Meiklejohn became responsible for all the official White House record and following documentation from Tehran. [154]

Roosevelt stayed at General Connolly's quarters, a walled-in enclosure shrouded by trees. It was fortified, but due to new Intelligence, considered unsafe. He was invited to share the Soviet Legation accommodations across town with Stalin. Special telephone wires on Iranian telephone poles were rigged for extra security.

Roosevelt gave a private dinner party that evening. The following day, token ceremonies of trust occurred between the leaders wherein an honorary exchange of a sword was paraded.

On the second day of the sessions, discussions between Stalin, Churchill and Roosevelt were productive.

There were other matters, small but significant. The new young Shah of Iran found Harriman in the corner working with his Aide. He wanted to chat. Meiklejohn said he was suddenly kicked in the shins and told to stand up to say "Hello."

The President was invited to review a display of gifts available for purchase by the Shah. Roosevelt did inspect them with interest, but graciously said he could not under the circumstances buy a single item at taxpayer's expense. Perhaps later he would buy a small memento for himself, he said.

Before leaving Tehran, Harriman sent out for a little shopping. He was to find boots and an Astrakhan hat for Kathleen. A Russian official who specialized in supplies joined the shopping because he "knew his furs." Picking through dozens of skins they seized upon a winner for Kathleen.

A party was arranged for the British Prime Minister's sixty-ninth birthday. The politicians stayed on, but military representatives had to fly back to Cairo to further confer on matters of the ground war. Thus, President Roosevelt had time with Stalin in calm and quiet circumstances. Stalin wanted to know who would command the cross-channel invasion.

Harriman had the only set of conference documents, leaving only one copy of the official Agreements for the President to take home with him. He and his staffer Meiklejohn had hosted the event as the American delegation for the President, and all arrangements went flawlessly.

With decoy arrangements designed to confuse potential spies, the President managed a well-publicized photo opportunity tour of the local barracks and hospital before leaving 2nd December, 1943. Harriman had made it all look effortless.

Within days, Stalin received a personal cable from Roosevelt "It has been decided to appoint General Eisenhower immediately to the Command of Cross-Channel Operations.   ---   Roosevelt"[155]

Harriman stayed behind to clean up. He formally thanked those who helped them fill the gap at the Tehran Conference. Especially the Army Sergeant typist-clerks of the Persian Gulf Service Command.

The results of the Tehran Conference may well have colored the atmosphere in which Kathleen and Harriman lived in Moscow. Stalin gave the Americans the utmost respect.

Roosevelt's solicitous back-door diplomacy with Stalin sans the concurrence of his other Ally, Britain, was a source of worry to many however. Certainly, Churchill and he had their differences. Even American official diplomats found Roosevelt's style alarming, particularly as he advocated a UN Trusteeship liberating Indochina (Vietnam) from France. Or as he encouraged a Soviet-styled reform from the bottom-up for the "solution of the problem of India."

Discussions had ambled on, if some of the rambling controversial. But in terms of substantive issues, neither did it go unnoticed by the Americans that Stalin, from that point on, become wary of the Polish leadership sitting in London, nor did Churchill remain silent on the topic.

If Roosevelt had strayed somewhat from the Allies' agenda in his negotiations with Stalin, he was not found to be a mindless man. It is hard to imagine that he was not playing his jest-full hand to achieve his ends. So far, Roosevelt had not received any signed ratification from the Moscow Advance Foreign Ministers Conference of October. (Neither had Deane nor Harriman achieved it at Moscow.) Thus, in his private meeting with Stalin, Roosevelt handed him Harriman's Memorandum outlining the American proposal to allow for an air base in the Soviet Union, and to have the Soviet Union sign on as an ally against Japan. Stalin said he would take it home and study it.

Neither was Roosevelt finished. He explained to Stalin that in his quest for re-election in 1944, he would need the vote of six to seven million Polish American voters. Thus, even if he privately agreed with Stalin's aspirations for shifting Polish and German borders to the Oder River, he could not "publicly take part in any such arrangement at the present time."

Again citing his upcoming election to achieve the votes of American citizens of Lithuanian, Latvian or Estonian origin, Roosevelt was pressing upon Stalin the convention to hold plebiscites along with liberation of those states

- with "self-determination", even if the people "would vote to join the Soviet Union."

In the end, the principal outcome of the Tehran Conference was a firm Anglo-American decision to carry out a cross-Channel invasion of France in May 1944; plus a diversionary invasion elsewhere, and the appointment of an American Supreme Commander of the Anglo-American invasion forces.

There was also an outlying document, one that promised to reward the Shah of Iran's government for allowing Allied supplies through its territories. It was signed quickly at the end by Stalin and Roosevelt, both aware of its potential in a future peace.

If Stalin, a man of strength and head of a powerful Communist Regime observed a President sitting in a wheelchair talking about his next election voters, he must have surely marveled at the population that supported him. It was exactly the perception that Roosevelt sought to achieve. Russia must open up!

At dawn on December 3rd 1943, the remainder of the Harriman party arrived at the Tehran Airport for departure. They were delayed by a caravan driving a herd of camel, followed by more delays because of weather closing in on Moscow. Of course Harriman was disappointed. He was holding Kathleen's boots.

The following day, another attempt to lift off from the airport was frustrated when the only landing destination option was Stalingrad.

A third pre-dawn departure attempt to leave Tehran was made on the 5th December 1943. They lifted off successfully, if exhausted. But the weather had so deteriorated that even with an agreement by all to avoid it, they were unable to locate even Stalingrad. Thus, they landed some two hundred fifty miles south of Moscow. Radio contact with Moscow hailed them to proceed, which they did by landmarks alone. Finally able to land their craft on hard-packed ice and snow, they touched down skidding to a stop.

Kathleen was there to meet them with cars.

* * *

The day after Harriman's return, Kathleen was confined to bed at Spaso House with the Mumps.

Ten inches of snow fell upon the city of domes, spires and wide streets. All the Embassies settled into a quiet wintery existence of rest, comfort and calm under a white Moscow snow.

Kathleen's condition of the Mumps enflamed one half of her face so badly that she could not open an eye. At Spaso House, a non-contagion food relay was performed through a series of trays passed on by Meiklejohn – who already had measles – from the Chinese cooks through his suite antehalls into Kathleen's quarters.

Gamely, Kathleen stayed in bed and made light of it as everyone kept their distance.

Fatigue, work, stress and uneven schedules was taking its toll. It soon became clear that influenza was making the rounds in Moscow. The senior Commissars of Russian Foreign Affairs; the diplomatic staffs of other Embassies and most of the Americans were afflicted, such that when the British Ambassador went to the US for his holidays to be with his wife, the British Embassy was left to Harriman to manage across Christmas.

Still, Christmas at Spaso House turnout out to be splendid. Kathleen had set up a 24 foot tree and made the place shine. They would host a Christmas Eve party for all the diplomatic colony, wives and children, she insisted. The party was to include a buffet of Christmas treats, and local musicians played for entertainment.

So successful was the festive event that it was all they could do to unburden the house after the celebration. Meiklejohn delighted to tell of the vodka punch that led many to retire "well oiled" – that is, discounting the plane crews who called themselves "The Sixteenth Air Force" – who had to be politely evicted. But that was not all.

At 2.00 A.M in the morning Kathleen, the Ambassador, General Donovan and a few others from Spaso were discovered in the card room "putting the [musician] performers through their paces for a private party." Kathleen was clearly the life of Moscow.

Christmas morning it became obvious that Kathleen had been busy for days. Harriman gave his Aide Meiklejohn a gift of "skis and boots" with a note of appreciation for all his good work and efforts.

Moreover, the Ambassador gave every Russian on the staff a case of canned milk. To the household staff he gave woolen shirts for men and sweaters for women - all bought in Cairo. The gifts were received with great pleasure.

Finally, Christmas day presented Spaso House with no less than three different parties as Moscow drifted slowly through the festive season under a grey sky of soft falling snow.

Only one incident marred the festive days. It was the eviction of the Swedish Minister by the Russians. He was accused of being a spy. For a neutral country, the Russians found it deplorable that sensitive information had found its way to the Germans through Swedish communications.

Meiklejohn reported that an unexpected peace overture made the rounds amongst the Allies. It came through a Swedish businessman. Himmler and a German military officer sent word to the Allies to ask what was mean by Roosevelt's "Unconditional Surrender." A reply was sent back that it meant what it said.

The next day, a German battle cruiser SCHARNHORST was sunk.

* * *

If the year had been long for Harriman's efforts, elsewhere it closed with multiple advances by the Allies.

In the Pacific a two-pronged strategic offensive against the Japanese agreed to at the TRIDENT Conference in Washington was successfully executed. New Georgia Island was taken by Admiral Halsey in September and October; and the capture of New Guinea by MacArthur's forces occurred in November. By December, 1943 MacArthur's forces landed at Cape Gloucester, and gradually, the major Japanese naval base of Rabaul was neutralized.

In the Central Pacific a successful campaign was launched in November against Makin and Tarawa Island in the Gilbert Islands.

The British, who attempted to clear Burma of the Japanese but found resistance had regrouped for another offensive.

In Russia, if unresolved were the post-war boundaries of Poland and the treatment of Polish prisoners, at least the recognition of the sovereign exiled Polish government in London was on the table.

Administratively, the American military and strategic personnel were now fully installed in Moscow at the Embassy. They were digging in for end-of-war planning.

* * *

If New Year's Eve was lively in Moscow, at Spaso House they chose to stay in and cozy up to watch the movie "Casablanca" with Humphrey Bogart and Ingrid Bergman.

New Year's Day 1944 would start with a rowdy contingent of Navy personnel had come to pick up Kathleen and her staff. They were all going skiing.

The ski slope down the Arbat was a few miles from town. The road that passed by Spaso House was the same road that took Stalin to his dacha – the Kremlin's country house. For that reason the pavement was well sanded and maintained in icy conditions.

Some eight Navy personnel and about a dozen Army people came along, including a few from the Embassy staff. Not all could ski, and most were falling over happily, but they found the slopes open and gentle across a little valley that ended at a stream. The ski party of New Year's Day was on its way back to Spaso House just as General Connolly and his "crowd" arrived from Leningrad.

Kathleen fed them all a buffet lunch. That evening, a performance of Russian Folk Dances, called "Peoples Dances" was held at the Tchaikovsky Theater. The next day, they went skiing again.

In an odd circumstance of mixed messaging, a small misunderstanding occurred between Harriman and the Russians.

Harriman had offered his plane, the Liberator, for the convenience of his staff. General Donovan, Chip Bohlen and Sam Spewack were leaving for Tehran. General Donovan, when in Washington, was head of the OSS, Office of Strategic Services. As an agency of intelligence, this office would later become the CIA after the war. Donovan was carrying with him sensitive material and key coding machine equipment. Clearly, they held considerations for security.

It was early morning January 4th 1944 when the American party was settled into Harriman's plane waiting to take off.

Without warning, they were denied permission to take off.

The Soviets insisted they leave on a Russian plane, a DC-3, standing by. They asserted that only the Ambassador himself could use the Liberator.

Harriman was furious. His planes were for use at his discretion. Harriman went to the Airport to see it off with his party, but again it was denied permission to fly. The Russian DC-3 finally took off.

Permission to fly involved safeguarding the plane's passage across Russian defensive lines with advance warning.

Harriman's Liberator plane did take flight on January 6th, 1944 with Donovan's party on board. But not without words of protest from Harriman. From then forward, the Liberator was hangared at

Cairo and touched down in Moscow only for special passage on demand.

The incident passed, and only after the heads of Russian Intelligence came to Spaso House for a Dinner - an evening with Kathleen in attendance.

* * *

Intelligence was changing the face of this war.

In London there was growing concern over the discovery of a German secret weapon, the rocket. Quarries were identified in the landscape of Pas-de-Calais territory. Generals Deane and Eaker realized they were set on large catapults, aimed at London.

For Harriman there was a growing suspicion of a different kind.

The Russians, perhaps too steeped in a Communist regime bereft of critics; intellectual thinkers or competing constituency representatives, might now be an Ally with an emerging agenda of its own.

The case for Harriman, a man of commerce whose mission superseded the two military missions of the American Embassy, and who had been sent to cultivate trust and commercial liaisons with the Russians from his position at Spaso House, was alerted to a diplomatic shift.

As head of the Embassy, it fell upon him to differentiate between Russian national interests, and wholesale Communist territorial expansionism.

* * *

Life in Moscow settled into a seasonal rhythm of winter activity by January 1944.

The Russia Opera production "Rigoletto" was Saturday's entertainment for the Americans, sandwiches laid out at Spaso for their return at midnight.

Snow fell gently, the temperature dropping, hovering around freezing. Spaso House was not holding its heat and everyone went about in their woolies. They began to miss the sun, even if cold, which had not appeared through grey clouds for a month in Moscow.

During the opening weeks of the year, things remained uneventful at Spaso House. With Harriman and Kathleen away briefly, possibly to personally view intelligence plans being laid out for 1944, the Cuban Charge D'Affairs came for dinner at Spaso House and was entertained by other American officials.

Embassy staff at Mokhavia thinned out, the building quiet, but not entirely vacated. On a quiet Tuesday evening, Harriman, Kathleen and Meiklejohn were invited to dinner by General Deane at his flat located in the upper floors of the Embassy building, alongside other apartments occupied by Army, Navy and other military personnel.

They enjoyed a good evening together in the cozy warmth of the apartment and discussions turned to the matter of the dispute with the Russians about Harriman's plane denied permission to fly. The affair still rankled; it was so unexpected and had clearly cost Harriman some political capital.

General Deane regaled them with accounts of US inter-military wrangling over rank; planes and landing priorities. Such things, he said, could often lead to disputes, as was once the case between General Marshall and Admiral King who would not speak to the other for ages over a landing strip! They laughed. It helped.

Life returned to measured routines at Spaso House. They went to the Circus, and Harriman came to his Office Desk at the Embassy for the first time in weeks.

By mid-month, Kathleen had them all skiing at "Lenin Hills" with a steeper slope. There, they found themselves in company with Russians, Norwegians, French and others. The sun had come out over Moscow, and Kathleen invited them all to a lunch buffet at Spaso House.

Never alone, they were vigilantly covered by a body of Russian security personnel. Relentlessly, the Harrimans were accompanied everywhere by this detail of bodyguards. Either for their protection, or for observation, it had the mixed effect of annoying the Americans while at the same time coming to know the Russians.

Harriman was kept abreast of development with constant communications. However, a moment of surprise came when, suddenly, it came across the radio BBC news that Secretary Hull announced the opening of relations between the Russians and Polish "through the American Ambassador in Moscow who had presented to the Soviet Government the offer of good offices by the US."

To make this post-dated news incident effective, Harriman tried to reach Molotov but discovered he was out of town. Two days later they caught up, and Molotov said he heard it first through the BBC news.

The world was in a freefall, it seemed, the ground war developments leaving little room for imagination or vision. One speculative report issued that Washington was making plans to print Occupation currency for use in Germany. It was resolved by Harriman to double up on his planning for a post-war peace plan.

* * *

On January 20th 1944, The Russian NKVD Chorus, a men's choir of the policing agency, performed a recital and the Americans attended. Kathleen noted that the event was held at their headquarters building, with "good dancing acts."

The following morning, Kathleen and John Melby joined several news reporters for a three day investigative field trip. Supervised by the Russians, they went to Katlyn Forest near Smolensk to view evidence of a mass grave. According to propaganda information issued by the Germans, it was said the dead were Polish Army officers, men supposedly massacred by the Russians in the spring of 1940. The Russians asserted that the massacre occurred at the hands of the Germans in the late summer of 1941. [156]

Here, Kathleen acted as an investigative reporter. She interviewed many Poles, sometimes in groups. Generally, it was understood that the Germans did the massacre. However, since the Russians were conducting the investigation, nothing was conclusively determined.

Kathleen returned Sunday night to find that her father had been out skiing at the Lenin Hills all day.

By the end of January, Kathleen's name was on a secret telegram sent by Harriman to the Secretary of State for the "Eyes of the President and the Secretary".

"Kathleen and members of Embassy staff have returned from trip to Smolensk with American and British press. They were shown evidence being assembled by the Special Commission to investigate the circumstances of the shooting by the Germans of the captured Polish officers in the Katyaski forest near Smolensk."

It was the start of a long investigation. Over the years, it would question the veracity of the Russians; the history of Soviet Revolutionary tactics if not the legitimacy of the Communist Regime. Kathleen's only involvement was that she was present on this visit. She was never required to testify, nor was she involved with the developments. However, her name and image appeared in newspapers at the discovery site. Kathleen had stood there on that visit with the Press in bright colors against a dark background for the world to see.

Later called "A Special Commission to Establish and Investigate the Circumstances of the Shooting by the German Fascist Invaders of Captive polish Officers in the Katlyn Woods," the matter would become the topic of an extensive Intelligence Report delivered by the State Department in 1951.

Time Magazine would give the details of the "Political Circumstances of the Katyn Graves" and uncover the motives of the principals at the Russian Investigation; asserting by the unfolding of events in real time accounting that the Russians were trying to cover it up.

The Senate investigation unearthed key revelations about Soviet arrests of key Polish Military Personnel in 1939 including their segregation into Special Camps (1939); liquidation of the Special Camps (April May 1940); evidence of the Railway journey where eyewitness saw the officers alive; the Polish search for their own missing officers, and the discovery and revelations of the Katyn Graves by the Germans in (April 1943).

Before the Internal Military Tribunal of 1946, the investigation would also examine the Polish and German reactions; the Soviet's own Investigation in 1943, and the Katyn questions that remained.

A German Account was offered; as was a Polish appraisal of the German account presented. A Soviet Explanation of Katyn was entered, as were other Polish questions.

* * *

At Spaso House, the winter days were marked by close communications and movie production reels when they arrived by mail pouches. The shows were the featured source of Embassy entertainment. Some were shared.

Harriman, Kathleen, Melby and Thompson had a private showing of the movie RAINBOW, a story based on a novel of Nazi occupation of a peasant village finally freed by Soviet partisans. While courteous, the production, they thought, was nowhere equal to American stories that had human interest. Hollywood, they felt was only just getting started.

Toward the end of the month, a funny domestic caper developed. They were served Pork Chops for dinner. The chops arrived in the kitchens of Spaso House under unusual circumstances. A routine consignment of fresh meat had been delivered to Moscow by one of the American convoys for the Army-Navy staff. The Military office management decided to donate one chop each to the Harriman mission - an Embassy mission of a different nature with economic overtones. It had never been done before. The feast was enjoyed by Kathleen and her father at Spaso House, and the military mission delighted with their feat.

Shortly after that, a party was laid on by Harriman for Roosevelt's birthday. They had invited Russian officials and, in particular, their wives. Kathleen did the arranging, with strict admonition to the reporters and staff not to get drunk. It was a great success.

* * *

Harriman's frustration was surfacing. He reported in cable traffic that little progress in Moscow had been by the Russians on promises made in Tehran.

By the last day of January, Harriman asked for a meeting with Stalin. He was granted a meeting for the following day. They had worked hard, noted Meiklejohn as Harriman returned while Kathleen and her staff were at the dinner table. Harriman wore an expression on his face of the proverbial "cat who just swallowed the mouse."

The meeting with Stalin had been successful.

Harriman, whose later record "Special Envoy to Churchill and Stalin" explained the details, had pressed for resolutions wanted by the White House on matters agreed to in Tehran. They were approved.

Stalin had his reservations about offering an airfield in the Soviet Far Eastern Maritime Provinces for the use of American bombers in connection with air raids upon Japan. He said he did not want to provoke the Japanese who had large standing armies in Manchuria. Especially since the Soviets were unable to prepare themselves for any retaliation. Stalin explained that he had long ago signed a peace accord with Japan.

In his meeting with Harriman, Stalin promised that an air facility would be provided for the use of three hundred or more U.S. heavy bombers.

Further, Stalin agreed to an exchange of intelligence regarding Japan with the United States.

Also, three airfields in the Ukraine were promised for the Allies to use against the Germans. Both Stalin and Harriman agreed that "daylight bombing can penetrate more deeply into Germany if American Bombers from the UK and Italy were permitted to land regularly in the Soviet Union" Harriman noted that it helped if Americans did not have to "fight their way back, often in a crippled condition, through swarms of [] interceptors" [157]

For the Allies, this critical mission was to be code-named FRANTIC JOE.

Over the next four months, the Russians made prodigious efforts. Three airfields were completed in the Ukraine, including runways; hangars and service facilities for American bombers, and provided with manpower needed to run operations. No defense was needed.

The next day, Harriman, Kathleen and their staff went to a party hosted by the Navy doctor, Commander Lange. The event was for two doctors, one was Dr. Hastings arriving from the U.S. Office of Scientific Research and Development; the other a British physician Dr. Fleming – who was the first to use the new antibiotic, penicillin. They would share notes with the Russians.

Later, Harriman received a visit by the Ethiopian Minister and his Secretary. It was a diplomatic courtesy visit, and the Harrimans entertained them graciously at Spaso House.

* * *

Springtime. Unseasonably warm temperatures started to melt the snow.

Embassy mail, delayed by months, showered upon them with back-letters; newsreels and movies. Spaso house settled into a routine that brought relaxation with milder temperatures. Harriman himself seemed to more lighthearted, his dinner table-talk included boyhood reminiscences and family laughter.

Spaso House remained his mission office quarters after all. He did not frequent the Embassy, necessarily, the "spread of 'flu following his return from Tehran" a continuing drain on staff and their tasking. For Harriman, strategic moves on all fronts of the war gave him initiatives that required consistent administering. Change was decisively in the offing.

Harriman worked late, often in synchrony with U.S. time in waiting for response cables. He would have breakfast in his room, rarely dressing for business before noon. He would work quietly in his bedclothes, often drafting a cable for the President, or in consultation with one of his Military Ministers who knew his quarters at Spaso House.

By lunch several Couriers showed up from the Embassy prepared to take back material to the code office produced by Harriman and typed by Meiklejohn. There the cables would be encoded and sent.

Or as needed, he would dictate cables for delivery to the Embassy by car from Spaso House. By 2.00 PM they were again listening to the BBC news for progress on the war.

Afternoons were spent by a warm fireplace sitting in arm chairs where Harriman dictated further correspondence and communiques for other officials and agents in Washington. Those cables were also often rushed to the Embassy by Meiklejohn in the Ambassador's car.

Meiklejohn said that when he arrived at the Embassy, it was there that he received tea, biscuits and attention in abundance, "if it weren't for tea I would starve before dinner time..."

Dark in Moscow by four o'clock in the afternoon, the days moved swiftly through the paces of the war and its progressions on all fronts.

* * *

Kathleen had flourished. She was fit, engaged, and her spirits high. The nights of February had passed quickly, dinners occurring around eight thirty P.M.

The evenings were spent cheerfully. Harriman, Hamilton and Melby might play "bottle pool" in the sitting room of Meiklejohn's quarters where the heater and office machines held domain. Kathleen, always present and accounted for, watched and enjoyed. Card games, radio broadcasts and staff gatherings often passed the hours into the night at Spaso House, even as they waited for cable replies and official directives back from Washington DC.

Frozen pipes burst at Spaso House. They would go for a drive to get out, but remained unimpressed, said Meiklejohn, by the steel-cold blanket draped over the "wide and empty" colorless boulevards of Moscow.

But the winter was moving on for Kathleen. On Sunday February 20th 1944, Kathleen went skiing at Lenin Hills. There was a competition underway, so she signed on for the women's division, slalom only. Ten women joined her, later about sixteen men. Kathleen finished Fourth, but due to one penalty, her place moved up to Third place.

She noticed that an Army brass band played for the presentation of awards and that there were spectators - hundreds of them! Harriman showed up with his interpreter, and the event was turned into a public relations opportunity by the Americans, all done with a contingent of Russian NKVD Intelligence security detail following, if not holding their coats and hats. They discovered later that the competition was the Moscow Skiing Championship.

* * *

The war was moving forward, and during February, the Embassy received a few "feelers for peace," expression by enemy camps making overtures to the Allies for ending aggression. First came the Fins and then the Bulgarians.

It was encouraging, if uneven the landscape.

The last week of February took them to a social party at an apartment in their Embassy building on Mokhovaya where a Navy officer entertained a Russian friend on her "Name Day." Everyone at Spaso House attended. Still, the censure of city life; the curfews and limitations of opportunities for young professionals cast a pall.

As the weather improved, invitations arrived for dinner and theater from other Embassy staffs, including one performance to be held at the Gypsy Theater. Noted Kathleen, they spoke a particular dialect, and their play was based on the morals of the heart over the morals of society.

Military plans were progressing. Two days later, an American Flying Fortress bomber with combat crew and equipment landed to bring three Army Air Force Colonels to Moscow. Colonel Jack Griffith, Colonel Paul Cullen and Colonel Kessler were all three from the Eighth Air Force. They would stay at Spaso House and handle the shuttle bombing operations from Russian airfields.

* * *

There were other issues outstanding. Harriman went to speak to Stalin about the Poles. He made no progress on the issues developing, and he was much frustrated at their reticence.

By mid-March, Harriman wired Stettinius at the State Department to arrange for a London conference. He had hoped to get to Washington, he felt he was not making much progress in Moscow.

In April, Harriman left with Admiral Olsen, Commander Tolley and Stevens of the Embassy for

Murmansk to deliver to the Russians the USS MILWAUKEE, a light cruiser ship loaned to them in lieu of Italian warships promised in Tehran. In the eyes of many, including Churchill, such a promise by Roosevelt was of little value since the warship could have been used either against the Germans or the Japanese. It was used eventually, said Meiklejohn, as a training ship. Especially in the post-war Soviet Navy build-up.

A growing sense of urgency permeated the atmosphere of the Moscow Mission. While lesser tensions arose, reconnaissance and bombing missions leading up to the great invasions of Europe was underway, even if with a mild awareness of emerging Soviet technological advances in radar recognition. Harriman asked about it.

According to Ray Ellis, their development and competition in radar was catching up and equal to the very best that the Americans had. Harriman arranged to take a special trip to Novosibirsk in Siberia to visit a factory there.

The Ambassador returned mid-April from Murmansk, and as usual was greeted at the airport by Kathleen.

The rest of the month passed with small events conducted in-house for local Russian interests. Also for staff, including a party at Spaso House for the clerks and non-commission personnel of the Military and Embassy Missions at Moscow. It was the first of its kind, and Kathleen had arranged it. Chocolate cake and ice cream was served in such abundance that their supply of butter was depleted for the month. Still, it was a wonderful evening, Sergeant White, nephew to the President of Western Union of which Harriman was Director, attended the event and led the party in a round of singing at piano.

The mood at Spaso House was upbeat, their diligence and hard work everywhere recognized. Frivolity came from visiting Army Generals and staff with jokes about war-time uniforms and civilian life, especially directed at Meiklejohn who was in US Navy uniform – having no Navy to oversee at Spaso House, they teased.

Good Friday April 7th 1944 brought snow storms. Kathleen went skiing with a number of staff at Lenin Hills. Easter Sunday was passed at the Army Mess serving Ham, pineapple, potatoes and vanilla ice cream. This, they liked enormously.

The following Sunday was the Orthodox Easter Sunday service at the Cathedral in Moscow, and many on the staff attended. The Cathedral was estimated to hold three thousand souls. It was filled with a mix between traditional ritual worshipers wearing ceremonial vestments; foreigners and local populations. "There were real story-book Russian types in the audience and among the priests" wrote Meiklejohn.

Kathleen and Melby attended a different church and then went to the Russian flat of a local employee on the staff of the American Embassy. His place was filled with art. He had been a leading authority on Russian Icons, and a lawyer.

On Sunday the 16th, an event took place at the Embassy Dacha, a country estate some twenty miles outside Moscow. Three acres of manicured grounds with a main house, a cook house, a sauna and a caretaker's house presented them with a wonderland retreat. Two feet of snow lay on the ground, and with Kathleen in the lead, they built a snowman.

By the end of April the snow had all but gone, filling the air with spring birdsong. A number of foreign Ambassadors and their wives came to Spaso House for lunch, Kathleen seated between them as hostess. Included were invitations for Ethiopian and Afghan ladies now appearing in Moscow.

* * *

Harriman was increasingly uneasy with Russian posturing. He detected ruptures within their administrative networking, if not insufficiencies that might become unacceptable to the Allies.

Further, in a move to improve notice of the American effort, he arranged for a Press Conference.

He informed American reporters about the delivery of the ship USS MILWAUKEE.

He used the occasion to ask about the city of Odessa, recently liberated. At a port on the Black Sea, fabled for "catacombs" beneath the city, partisans had reported that thousands lived underground prior to the Soviet Liberation. It was now rumored that the Romanians had rounded up fifteen thousand Jews in the fields and killed them in a brush fire. Harriman allowed the Press to probe.

With plans imminent for the final invasion, Harriman felt impelled to go to Washington and advise the President about the end of the war. He made his request known, and it was answered when word came in from Stettinius' office that he wished to meet with Harriman at Marrakech in Morocco. This suited Harriman who would be making his to Washington via London. At Spaso House the news was joy, and they brought up "Becky" their Liberator plane from Cairo for the trip.

At pre-dawn on April 25th 1944, with Hamilton, Page and Melby to see them off at 3.30 A.M., Kathleen's journey began on "Becky" with only her father and his Aide for company, plus one staffer to be dropped off at Cairo.

The itinerary listed the flight as departing from Moscow for Teheran, Cairo, Tripoli, Caserta, Algiers, Marrakech, Casablanca, Newsquay, London, Prestwitch, Stephenville, and finally Washington DC.

General Ira Eaker, former head of the Eighth Air Force and head of the Middle East Air Forces at Caserta, was waiting for them. They had intended to make a direct leg in the trip to allow for an over-stop with him.

However, after eight hours of flying time, they faced fierce weather in Tehran, a sandstorm so violent as to be a danger to airplane engines. They approached the Russian airfield but found it too windblown to land. Circling, they moved to the British airport sheltered by a land-buffer embankment and managed a safe landing, just as a Fortress plane crashed on the Soviet runway.

Harriman pressed on. They refueled quickly and continued to Cairo. Six and half hours later, they spotted the runways of Cairo and landed in the dark.

General Giles greeted them and they gathered at Shepherds Hotel for a dinner of steak and potatoes. The party was joined by Colonel Ritter, Captain Ickes (nephew to the Secretary of Interior), Lionel Dregge and Lt. Bodgood; US Minister Kirk and Messers Jacob and Hare of the Cairo Legation. At midnight they retired to General Giles' apartment.

The flight proceeded early the next morning, passing over the El Alamein battlefield and skirting the sea along the coast to fly over Benghazi and across the Gulf of Sirte. They saw again those scarred landscapes of battlefields and trenches, abandoned vehicles, damaged buildings and barren terrain, then Algiers Harbor with its eight sunken Freighters. It was a grim reminder of what must end soon.

Picnic on the plane made for a modest lunch before landing at Tripoli Castel Benito Airport midafternoon.

Major Jones and Squadron Leader Ducket met them as the plane was refueled. With poor weather in Italy, it was determined that they should spend the night in Tripoli, and they messed at the Officer's quarters.

So anxious was Harriman to press on to Washington that an account was made by Meiklejohn of the events of the morning. It began at the Morning's Reveilles: "Waked at 7.00 AM by Major Jones who says that Harriman [had] got up at the crack of dawn, tore down to the meteorological office personally and convinced himself that we could fly on to Naples immediately. Then he discovered that he had lost the plane crew who, relying on the weather report of the previous evening, had gone to Tripoli and had not yet returned. By the time they were located and we were on our at 8.45 AM local time, he [Harriman] was fit to be tied. Some day he will kill us all with his insistence on flying no matter what the weather is." [158]

They left the coast of Africa by mid-morning and headed across the Mediterranean Sea. Kathleen, if exhausted, was without complaints. The flight proceeded over Sicily, passing Marsala, Palermo, over the mountain islands, Capri, and then westward from Italy into the Tyrrhenian Sea to approach Vesuvius before landing.

Within the perimeter of the Allies' largest base, they were accommodated in portable bungalows at the Palace of Caserta.

The splendor of the Palace was unmistakable. Dated from the 17th century, they saw a lavish compound equal only to the Palace of Versailles with its verdant grounds, water ponds and Roman statuary. Damaged, it was undergoing repairs by military personnel "to avoid hazards and mosquito infestation."

Harriman met with General Eaker at the Palace even as preparations were made for his return visit to Algiers and Marrakech. Preparations for the cross-channel invasion were clearly of the highest priority.

Kathleen had an agenda in Naples. She connected with family. She had cousins Henry and Gerry; her brother-in-law Shirley Fiske who had seen Harriman off from La Guardia in the spring of 1941. She also met up with her step-brother Captain Poole.

At 5.00 AM they taxied for take-off from Marcianise Airport in General Eaker's C-47 transport plane "Yarbird III," landing at Algiers four hours later. Harriman, Kathleen, her brother in law Captain Fiske assembled with Major Hormel, General Devers, and General Carl Spaatz for a short break before taking off again that afternoon for Marrakech, French Morocco.

Military airfields at landing were stacked with planes and personnel. Special action was preparing for B-29 bombers. Marrakech was located on a plateau of fifteen hundred feet and surrounded by the Atlas Mountains, which rose another fourteen thousand feet. It was a major communications center to the Far East, an eerie corner of the planet from which to affect world peace.

The dignitaries were driven to "Taylor Villa," now under Air Transport Command – where both Roosevelt and Churchill had stayed. Surrounded by olive groves, orange, lemon and vine orchards, Taylor Villa was once the home of an American.

Attending were Undersecretary of State Stettinius; Freeman Matthews; John Pratt; Bob Lynch; Dr. Bowman and Philip Reed, new Director of Harriman's former Mission in London.

Here, seated together on stone porches surrounded by wood-carved ceilings, paintings, pillars, ironwork, marble floors and blue-tiled pools, they planned for a post-war world. Before them was the blueprint of a political and economic landscape in reconstruction.

Meiklejohn noted that staff were taken to the Mamounia Hotel, a place famous for its French influence and Ottoman architecture.

Aware that these were critical moments, he welcomed the break, observing commodious European quarters; palm-shaded boulevards and tropical deluxe gardens. Medina, the walled city populated only by natives, was closed to all visitors.

A tour of the city was arranged, doubtless at the behest of Kathleen, and the party went.

Kathleen saw the man-made mud wall erected in 900 AD. They observed that it was some thirty feet high, surrounding structures barely allowing passage for a vehicle, the streets littered with small shops of working craftsmen and skilled laborers. They listed trades amongst peoples that had been intermingling for centuries. It was reported that there was a population of 220,000 in number.

The scene delighted Kathleen. At open squares, where markets and vendors gathered, storytellers held over fifty people captive with their tales. They saw snake charmers, knife throwers, musicians and entertainers, even as one snake-charmer came over to talk to them saying that he had been to the New York World's Fair in 1939! It was the thrill of a lifetime for Kathleen. For the Americans, it came as a breeze of refreshment.

The stop was brief.

Stettinius had a plane on hand- an older C-54 considered less than glamorous but reliable. Dr. Bowman, a Geographer who had aided President Wilson at the Versailles Conference in WWI was here as President of Johns Hopkins University. He petitioned to survey the land of the Sahara region.

Stettinius returned to Marrakech. A trip was laid on to proceed to Casablanca for Harriman, Kathleen and Reed's party where they would meet with others for a briefing at Villa Mas. By 9.30 PM that night, they were departing Casablanca in a ATC C-87 Liberator for the UK.

As for the secrets of the war, if Harriman and his party carried in their hearts all the plans, hopes and fears of a cross channel invasion pending, such strain and stress could not be shown: Also onboard that flight for passage was U.S. Navy Commander Burns with four German prisoners of war; two American Generals; one British General and two junior U.S. Army officers.

The flight was made in silence.

With window-portholes darkened to block viewing of recognizable landmarks, and the Harriman party seated far forward, there was little discussion between them. Exhausted, they dozed all the way to the United Kingdom.

Just before dawn, they passed over the Scilly Islands and began their descent to St. Mawgins Airport after 9 hours of flight.

It was 7.44 AM War-Time, May 2nd 1944 when they landed on British soil.

Greeted by Station Commander Colonel Plummer, they had breakfast while refueling. Refreshed, they took off for London in a Lockheed bi-motor transport. Relieved of prisoners, conversation onboard was now animated. They discovered that Commander Burns was an ex-New York City fireman who was developing techniques and response teams for incendiary events, even for onboard ships having fire blazes after bombing. He explained that while he had participated in other landings, he didn't know why he was being sent to London. Harriman and Meiklejohn looked at him closely, their mouths shut. Meiklejohn, knowing the briefs he carried for Harriman in his briefcase, wrote "He doesn't know why, but I do."[159]

Just before noon, they landed at Hendon Airport in London. Ambassador Winant, Commodore Flannigan and Major Bartlett were waiting.

They stayed at Claridges, and Harriman did walk through the familiar London Mission offices. More briefings followed, and two days later, they left Bovington Airport in a C-54 for Prestwick then on to Newfoundland for the last leg of the journey to Washington DC. At Prestwick, knowing that it was prohibited for woman to eat at the British mess, they went to a nearby American base which was teeming with personnel and aircraft preparing for impending action.

Only two others aboard, General Wilson from the Pacific war theater, and Colonel Flynn of the Atlantic ATC. Forward, they were able to sleep on bunks, all of them utterly fatigued.

Headwinds prevailed. The trip across the Atlantic lasted almost fifteen hours before landing at Newfoundland. The plane changed crews and was turned around to taxi-off promptly at dawn for a six and half hour flight to Washington DC.

Mrs. Harriman was in Washington for her husband. At landing, it was May 6 1944; Kathleen had just logged 94 hours of flying time.

Behind them was England preparing for a cross-channel invasion, an invasion that was to launch on the weather.

* * *

Harriman's offices were at the State Department, not far from the White House. There, he seemed to be remarkably free of work, or rather, encouraged to rest and refresh in preparation for the next phase of American strategic interests overseas.

He and his Aide did enjoy time off with family while on standby. Several flights back and forth to New York were posted by Harriman. During that period, he and his wife Mrs. Harriman were officially invited to dine at the White House on several occasions.

* * *

Kathleen was little in sight, off to her familiar haunts in New York.
She had left America in 1941; lived in London; returned for a fleeting visit in 1942 only to sail back by Christmas. Then, quite decisively, she had left London in 1943 with her father for a tour of duty at Moscow, Russia. Now, after a long flight through Europe, she could plant her feet freely on her own soil. She had been overseas for three years.
If Kathleen felt any remorse with her life, none was evident. On the contrary, she was having a wonderful time. As images showed her climbing in and out of planes, her face happy, her foot steady and her clothing fashionable, Kathleen was flourishing. Even as the events of war unfolded around her and the weather closed her in at Moscow, Kathleen's disposition was untouchably bright. The posting at Moscow gave her agency.
The day of departure to return to their posting did arrive. This, they clearly anticipated,

even as Harriman conferred with the President and others as to what lay ahead.

Judging from the gear to take back to Moscow, Kathleen had been on a binge. Her luggage, totaling some fifty pieces and weighing more than a ton, consisted of "a dozen duffle bags of assorted junk for Spaso House" included feature movies; a carpet sweeper, a tennis net, volleyballs, billiard cue tips, radios for the Office of War Information, tennis balls, mouse and rat traps, carpet tacks, spare parts for the Embassy cars, four dozen dance records and a portable victrola."

* * *

Ambassador Harriman and Kathleen,
Moscow 1943-1946

Courtesy Library of Congress

Kathleen, Hostess for the US Ambassador.
Spaso House, Moscow 1943

Courtesy Library of Congress

8.

June was D-Day for the cross-channel landing. Washington was too preoccupied to think of anything else.

Harriman, whose mission was already considering the conditions of the end of the war, there was much to accomplish. In his final report he gave insight about this period showing a tenor grave but hopeful. He was, after all, in Washington to receive instructions for his return to Moscow. America's position on issues coming up for negotiation would need to occur after the cross-channel invasion, and more importantly, after the Presidential Election.

"I was to explain [to Stalin] that the President could not take an active interest in the Polish question until after the election. The Curzon Line with modifications seemed to him reasonable as a basis for settlement, although he was still puzzled about Lwow. Stanislaw Mikolajczyk (Prime Minister of the exile Polish government in London) was coming to the United States in June on condition that he make no public speeches while in the country.

"The President would urge Mikolajczyk to drop General Sosnkowski from his Cabinet, with one or two others who were resisting a settlement with the Russians. He [Roosevelt] was still hopeful of finding a satisfactory solution to the Polish problem; Stalin could help by giving the Poles a break and carefully avoiding any step that would embroil the issue in the heat of the presidential campaign."[160]

There was a mixture of campaign rhetoric and policy direction. Once again, this was a President who spoke in populist terms and could capture metaphors from clouds. Diplomatically, the heavy lifting with Russia was still ahead. Harriman had a serious and difficult mission to accomplish.

Thus, for Harriman the US Ambassador; his daughter Kathleen and his Aide Lt Meiklejohn USRN, the return journey to Moscow began from Washington National Airport on May 23, 1944.

It was a happy send-off with family and friends. All their gear had been delivered the day before; weighed in, checked, and stowed properly by a Captain Ryan.

They were to travel in a C-54 twenty-six passenger Army transport plane. However, one hour before embarking, the Lieutenant got a call. The Victrola wouldn't fit on the plane!

Kathleen was aghast. Her record player, a Victrola musical gramophone, had been ordered from Army Special Services. For her, it was an essential item for Spaso House, a crisis.

They rushed to the scene of the loading. Inspecting the problem, Kathleen sighed. There had been a terrible misunderstanding: The Army had provided them with a Facility-sized large console weighting three hundred and eighty pounds! Too heavy for the flight, Army Supply office wanted to know if Kathleen would accept a regular-sized "portable" Victrola instead?

The crisis happily solved, they climbed on board. Kathleen wanted a portable victrola anyway.

Major General Walsh came aboard to join them. Officially he was to be the Air Officer for the Moscow Military Mission, but his command was over troops at the three air bases now in Russia as per agreement of the Moscow and Teheran Conferences. His upcoming mission was secret. He didn't know where his destination point would be. In fact, Harriman knew that the planned operation of his command, codenamed FRANTIC JOE, was to be a diversionary tactic from a major offensive elsewhere taking place soon…

The cross-channel invasion had not yet commenced.

Their plane, having lifted off about mid-day, landed in Newfoundland that evening, but there was engine trouble. It would delay them.

Harriman was put out. Time was of the essence. Another C-54 was discovered leaving that night. Thus Harriman, Kathleen and General Walsh proceeded to transfer their baggage to that cargo plane. That left the General's Aide Captain William Breese and Meiklejohn to follow later in the plane needing repairs - both of whom were to enjoy privileged quarters for the night "and a good night's sleep."

At the airfield, a maintenance crew worked all night, changing the engine altogether with a spare that was on hand. By morning, the plane was made ready for flight. It landed in London the next day.

The Harriman party had already reached London and immediately taken a flight to Caserta with General Eaker.

All parties re-united in Italy, promptly departing for Cairo in the Ambassador's C-54 on May 30th 1944. Traversing over the deep sheen of the Mediterranean Sea, the sky was open and blue. But suddenly, flying over Alamein they noticed a British Fighter plane flying alongside as escort. His presence was unexplained, his radio silent. They concluded he was looking at Kathleen.

Their baggage transferred to "Becky" in Caro, they were again delayed due to malfunctions and finally departed at 3 o'clock in the morning for a six hour flight to Tehran. Unfortunately, Russian defense of Moscow had closed their re-entry opportunity and they were advised to stay in Tehran. They might be shot down.

Lingering for some badly needed rest, they picked up fellow passengers Eric Johnson, President of the US Chamber of Commerce - with his party of two: Mr. O'Hare of the Chamber of Commerce and Mr. White, a newspaper reporter and son of William Allen White.

At dawn they left Tehran and by nightfall landed safely in Moscow. It was June 1st 1944.

Barely home, Kathleen was packing again for more travel. They were going to Poltava in the Ukraine to witness the arrival of the first American shuttle bombers, Generals Deane and Walsh with them.

General Eaker was the first bomber mission returning from Italy to land at a Russian airfield: The invasion bombing had begun.

The next day was June 5th 1944. Harriman asked the staff to keep the radio on and listen for any special news. The Second Front Offensive, along with the scheduled cross-Channel invasion was launching.

The weather was foul. News came that Rome had fallen to the Allies. The next day was June 6th 1944, D-Day.

As planned in Tehran by Harriman and the Allied parties, the announcement on the radio declared "Early this morning, the expected Anglo-American invasion began when air-borne forces were landed in the area of the Seine estuary. Le Havre harbor is being exposed to fierce bombardment. German naval forces are engaged in fighting with landing craft off the Saws."

The events unfolded. One hundred and twenty bombers and eight fighter escorts landed in the Ukraine at Poltave, Mirgorod and Pyratin new Kharkov. Only one bomber was lost.

The Germans, if puzzled when bombers did not return to Italy to refuel, were unable to disengage from the action that came at them from both the East, and from the UK. It was all they could do to maintain.

Operation FRANTIC JOE – the plan of using Russian airfields as negotiated by Harriman with Stalin, was a strategic success.

Spaso House was full of guests. Amongst them General Eaker; Major Parton (an historian); Major

Tex McCrary; Colonel Hull and his staff. Also Eric Johnston and his staff. Everyone listened to the news of the cross-channel landing, including the Russians who came over for a small ceremony of military Decoration.

The news was spreading and repeated on various radio broadcasts. Even the servants of the Moscow Mission staff came in to listen.

The mood grew lighter over the next few days. Reporters, newsreels and photographs were everywhere. Spaso House offered food and treats for all. It was a difficult ground war, they knew, the suffering of it all, incalculable. But the moment of relief was everywhere visible, many of them now having a clear view of the finish.

With reports improving, the weather pleasant, and improvements to Spaso House complete, Kathleen now spent time sunbathing on her balcony. Her pace was settling into a calmer life, her burden lifting.

The Victrola was put to good use. Evening dance parties improved the disposition of the staff. Nor was the work load heavy as cables reported only advances and territorial gains.

Kathleen felt that her father's hard work at the Conferences was finally paying off.

On June 10th, they were receiving gifts. Harriman received a handsome polar bear skin; Kathleen Astrakhan skins in honor of the Second anniversary of the signing of the Soviet American Mutual Aid Pact. Molotov hosted a lunch and toasted the Ambassador's return to Moscow. Stalin met with Harriman, cables sent to the President.

Vice President Wallace was on tour. Harriman suggested he meet with Wallace going to Tashkent and perhaps they proceed to Chungking, China. The mood was upbeat.

But Harriman had no illusions. He remained vigilant with his duties; his leads, his responsibilities. His diligence continued with care and details. If he had ideas as to goals for after the war, he noticed a significant absence of new directions from Washington. For now, he must wait.

Suddenly, a strange cable came in that left them cold. The Germans, evidently now feeling pressure, were taking hostages. They said they were offering to send Jews from Hungary, Rumania, Czechoslovakia and Poland to Spain and Portugal in exchange for essential commodities and supplies from the Allies, including ten thousand trucks and certain quantities of coffee. Alternatively, they would exchange the Jews against German prisoners of war at Switzerland. As a demonstration of their good faith, the Germans would even release five or ten thousand Jews before receipt of the goods. Failure to comply …would mean the utter "extermination of all Jews in those countries."

The Russians wanted nothing to do with the proposal of the cable. The Department of State tried to rationalize the logic and couldn't make heads or tails of it. Finally dismissed as entirely propagandistic, the matter was dropped. But it left a pall on Spaso House.

Harriman redoubled his efforts at ending this war. Time, he felt, was ticking. At mid-June, and without word from the President, he took off with Thompson in a Soviet plane for Tashkent to meet Vice President Wallace on a four day visit of Soviet Central Asia.

In his book, Harriman later remarked "Roosevelt did not want Wallace to talk with Stalin. Indeed, he thought that the Vice President's liberal influence might do some good with Chiang. But he [Roosevelt] was taking no chances of confusing Stalin about American policy." [161]

Domestic life had returned to usual at Spaso House. Kathleen was frequently out on the balcony with staffers, followed by outings to the Bolshoi Theater for "Sleeping Beauty". This, she described as long and tedious, if with resplendent scenery and costumes. In the spirit of modern commercialism, however, she stopped at the newly opened coffee-shop restaurant in the theater.

Next night came the performance of "Don Quixote" with remarkable feats of "acrobatics to music."

It was only now, with the quiet and growing acquaintance of city streets and houses along Arabat that the Americans ventured out. They noticed, through open second story windows, that the Russians were in various stages of economic decline and severe want. It surprised them since they were unaware of how far they had fallen behind Western standards of living.

Further, it was dawning on the Americans that the Communist regime, unable to deliver promises to people to improve their lot, wanted the citizenry to remain uninformed. Outside influence was heavily controlled. For Americans meaning to break new grounds for opportunity, the heavy hand of authority was a bad political omen. In fact, the Americans were now a threat.

On Sunday June 18th, Harriman returned from his Far Eastern trip in the company of the Chinese and Mexican Ambassadors to the USSR - all of them fatigued and irritable. Especially Harriman who gave the Russians a bad time for holding him over.

That night of his return he proceeded directly to work and sent for Hamilton from the Embassy to come to Spaso House so that he could send off cables.

A Press conference about the Tashkent tour was given for public information.

What remained unspoken however, was the child-like fixation by Wallace - a New Dealer, on Russian farm industry which he embraced whole heartedly. For an American to imply emulation of socialist farming labor methods was ill-advised, and Harriman put a lid on it.

Lieutenant Colonel Litvac, a movie producer who made "Battle for Russia," came with newsreels of the cross-Channel invasion. He was on his way to Poltava to witness the return of the bombers. Harriman invited him to stay for a party.

By the third week of June, while Harriman was engaged at a cocktail party at the Embassy, General Deane informed him that the airbase at Poltava had been heavily bombed by the Germans.

The report was bad. Finding no resistance, German bombers circled overhead for more than an hour to wipe out the airfields. One American, and over one hundred Russians were killed, including the woman-operated searchlight battery.

Harriman was now recognizing the disparity between Allied Armies and their defenses. He had to put out fires and could only imagine the disarray ahead as their Armies disbanded across Europe.

For now, he must remain steady. He gave the party at Spaso House for Colonel Litvac who would be one to expose such events through the movie industry.

At lunch the next day, Harriman and Kathleen entertained a witness to the event of the airfield bombing. Bill White, son of Willard Allen White had watched from a slit trench as American-parked bombers lit up in flames along the airfield.

He said "Damn it, they'll never send us home now after what we've seen here."

What was implied was the code of silence expected of foreigners with regards to the lack of Soviet protection of the airbases. There had been no defensible emplacements designated by the Russians for their Allies.

Bad enough that the Russians had failed to defend the posts of their allies, but with the assault on Pearle Harbor still ringing in their ears, Harriman did his best to keep this embarrassment from the general public circulation. The President was running for election.

The emphasis was on the Pacific Theater. In June and July of 1944 American forces in the Pacific moved from the Marshall Islands to the Marianas Islands, ending the use of Japanese naval bases at Truk and Rabaul on the Bismarck Sea.

The Japanese fleet lost 480 planes; three aircraft carriers, sustained damage to battleships, heavy cruisers and other escorts in the Battle of the Philippine Sea on June 19th. Further, the losses of Japanese tankers had left its fleet without fuel to operate much beyond range of the Singapore oil fields.

The Saipan battle were concluded by the first week in July, Tinian followed, and Guam fell on August 12th, 1944. That cleared the Japanese forces.

* * *

Harriman had long meetings with Stalin. Eric Johnston, reporter and friend of Kathleen, was with him for a spell, and he spoke to Stalin directly. He asked to visit the Urals and received full concessions.

A Press Conference followed, such that Harriman was set behind his schedule and worked around the clock to complete his cables to the President.

For this occasion, without going to bed, he and Meiklejohn changed their clothes quickly at dawn, had breakfast with White, O'Hara, and Calder taking off on the flight with Johnson, and only later had a cat-nap before attending an event by the British Embassy Navy and Army Missions in Moscow.

It was time to relax. The following day Harriman, Kathleen and the staff went on a boat trip up the Moscow River and Canal. It was an event hosted by the Canadians for the 77th Anniversary of the Confederation of Canada. Said Kathleen "…Feeling original, they hired a boat and we went tooting down the Moscow Canal."

Dancing on deck was allowed for some three hundred invited guests including all Ambassadors; Vishinski, Pulgunov (Head of TASS), some NKVD officers and several ballet dancers. Said Kathleen "The party started at 4.00 PM, and by 4.30 PM to my horror I found myself included in a select little party of bigwigs in a room up front, surrounded by glass windows so all others could look in as they walked around the deck. I sat between Tolstoy and the Vice Commissar of Foreign Trade, a very nice man who has lived abroad and speaks good English." [162]

Kathleen was one to mix and circulate. "…a few of us started dancing on deck to a piano alternating with a gramophone. It was quite genial but exhausting as the deck was sticky…"

The Harrimans were not unknown. "There was a big turnout of Russians…Ave's and my one advantage over most of the other members of the diplomatic corps was that we knew them all."

Like all other opportunities at the Moscow Mission, it was about engaging the American way. "I made one new delightful friend in the form of a minor Foreign Office official, Vishinski, a 2nd Interpreter, a young boy with a shaven head whose specialty is American slang! He danced abominably but was proud of it (I mean he thought he was good.) Assurance is something unique in a young Russian, that is, when he's with a foreigner."

The canal, surrounded by rolling countryside and lush woodland, revealed log-made farm houses of colorful carvings at the window sills. The waterway, teeming with an operational ferry service of river boats, ran late into the night with Moscow sunsets occurring well past after 10.00 PM. Even as it coped with a different world, Moscow made for a festive atmosphere as a grand old city.

"The party over, I progressed to the flat [at the Embassy] of one of our secretaries. Ave dropped in for a while, but tactfully left as it grew more drunken."[163]

From a commercial standpoint, and whenever possible, it was Harriman's brand to advance a lighter side to life for the enticement of free market thinking. This method suited London nicely, war notwithstanding.

In Moscow, he was introducing new concepts to diplomacy that had not been the case under the Minister of the staff, Charge D'Affairs Hamilton, nor his predecessors. At this time, many on the staff were being rotated from completed tours of duty. For Harriman, this seemed to be a relief.

When Kathleen and Harriman returned to Spaso House that night, they met Mr. George Kennan, Mr. Hamilton's replacement as Counsellor of the Embassy, Harriman put him to work at once. "Our new minister has arrived so Ave's thrilled. The other guy [Hamilton] leaves soon, his departure in the bag, he's brightened up considerably…"

July 4th 1944, Independence Day. Molotov, the Commissar for Foreign Affairs came to the American Embassy for lunch. It was a first, a sort of resumption of diplomatic relations between the two countries since 1933.

Other officials attended the luncheon, including the British Ambassador Clerk Kerr, Hamilton, Kennan, Thompson and Page. It was all Kathleen's doing. "Tomorrow's the 4th of July. Ave's having a party for Molotov here in Moscow and at the same time we're entertaining all Americans at the datcha – a picnic with baseball, etc., and beer. The number now adds to something like 150. A half of the arranging goes to me, plus the worse part of trying to think what others might have forgotten to do!..."[164]

Kathleen's party was a success and did much to lift morale. She managed the staff of Spaso House, then went to the Dacha to prepare for the celebration. There she set up for a Volleyball game with the help of Admiral Olson. Thus they lunched at the main house, migrated down to the River to be crossed on a pontoon for a softball game on the other side. Volleyball followed – now against the Russian drivers, and finally a hay-wagon style ride back to Spaso House with Kathleen "in an open truck with the Navy howling like banshees all the way!"

* * *

Celebration of Normandy Invasion.
Cocktail Party at Spaso House June 5, 1944,
"Bottoms-Up" for the Allies.

Courtesy Library of Congress

Ambassador Harriman with Kathleen 1944.
Taylor Villa, Marrakech Morocco.

Courtesy Library of Congress

9.

They found shadows, if cast long ago. On Tuesday 12 July 1944, a new Navy electrician came to Spaso House to check the wiring. He examined the switchboard and discovered something that he wanted to share only with Mr. Harriman.

There was an extra connection. The Soviets were recording all telephone conversation into the Embassy and the Military Mission. Harriman, according to Meiklejohn, expressed a few choice words about bad form and Russians needing to learn how to behave if they wanted to play a part in world affairs. But in fact they had all assumed as much anyway, showing discretion on the phone. Still, Spear the electrician was to check the Ambassador's rooms. That, and the knowledge that NKVD security guards were now snoops and never far away left a sour taste. Regardless, it went unreported as a matter of courtesy.

One thing became increasingly clear to Harriman. The cross-Channel operation behind them, Russia would now have to be made more accountable to her allies for her aspirations in Europe.

Harriman knew that he would soon need to step up his negotiations with the Russians. The President was approaching his re-election for a fourth term of office.

By mid-July, Harriman and his Generals were hosting formal luncheons at Spaso House, offering congratulations and conferring medals upon others including the Distinguished Service Medal to General Walsh by General Deane.

Others came to visit, like Major General Joe Cannon arriving from Italy to confer with the Russians about air support. It was asserted at Spaso House that the air war against the enemy had been won. There was little resistance remaining.

The next day, July 17th, a radio announcement was made by the Russians that some fifty seven thousand German prisoners of war from the White Russian Front would be passing through the city.

It was not a "Parade" – the word prohibited by the Geneva Convention. But it might well have been by the attendance on the streets as they walked through under Russian guard. Those at Spaso House went to Tchaikovsky Hall's balcony, and from there they watched. Harriman the US Ambassador went out of his way to show that the Americans were watching.

Some staffers went on ahead of the marching column and observed. They saw non-descript uniforms; dark facial features and uneventful body physiques, leaving them to conclude that only one fifth of the prisoners were likely real Germans. They were loaded onto to trains.

Generals Cannon and Dean visited the Eastern front and found Germans retreating in large numbers with quantities of equipment. The Russians were filling in behind them, moving into liberated areas, lining up the able-bodied men and bringing them to the Army to learn their trades. It was a method, they observed, to secure "constant replacements for their losses."

The battles against cities, while fierce, were brief. Once the Russians circled, there was with little resistance from the Germans.

By the end of July, many in the diplomatic colony at Moscow had left or were scheduled to leave on military flights. The war, it appeared, was coming to a close.

For Harriman, affairs of a post-war world was loomed; upcoming Conferences at London yet to be arranged.

Kathleen was to take a ride on the Liberator "Becky" bound for Italy, then on to London. Accompanying her was General Deane and Lt. General Burrows.

Moscow was firing cannon and rockets as victory salutes to celebrate cities liberated by the Red Army. The Russians, while showing their wings, diminished recognition of American aid. "The Red Army is certainly making history." To the Russian people, the American contribution to the war was lost.

Still, a certain degree of trumpet blowing was conceded. "They have lost millions in killed and wounded and even now are suffering losses many times anything that we and the British have ever experienced, and they [were] killing Germans wholesale while we were killing in retail…"

On July 28th 1944 another revelation surfaced. It came from an American reporter Jerome Davis who had made a number of trips to the front with other reporters, collecting forensic letters and diaries of the German dead. In his published article he said he found that amongst the German troops there was a sense of hopelessness, discouragement on the Eastern Front. Many were surprised at the new Russian offensives. German soldiers sensed a loss of control at the top of their commands and disliked the younger Hitler officers. Most of all, they spoke of the Anglo-American bombing raids.

* * *

Intelligence now superseded battle news. In London, information revealed a new German rocket weapons being readied for deployment.

The "doodlebugs" were doing damage. They were like drones, and whereas British fighters had been able to tip them off course, they were too improved to be deviated. The city of London was taking direct hits. Much around Grosvenor Square was still standing, Hyde Park was not.

Kathleen was in London.

The staff at Spaso House missed her, and parties on the lawn fell flat without her. Morale at Spaso House was low, even as her father hosted an exclusive dinner party at the British Embassy for Mikolajczyk, the Polish Prime Minister, Romer and Keenan. The Polish question was looming.

The next day, it was lunch at Spaso House to discuss the matter with the British Ambassador. They detected a different kind of war beginning to take shape.

Later that afternoon, an item of attendance was required. The former Shah of Iran had died, arrangements made at the Iranian Embassy. A courtesy book of condolences was to be signed at the funeral by delegates of various representatives in Moscow. Both the British and American Ambassadors were elsewhere preoccupied, and the book was signed by their chief of staff officers instead.

Formerly expelled by the British, the retired Shah was a Nazi.

* * *

While hopes were up and bets on for the end of war, entertainment at Spaso House consisted of movie reels and evening gatherings, including some of Kathleen's favorites. They served to keep the Military missions happy and out of mischief.

By mid-August, the offensive landing in the South of France codenamed "ANVIL" was taking place. This, as the Turkish, Belgian and Cuban Ambassadors came to dinner at Spaso House. Especially celebrated was the severing of ties between Turkey and Germany.

Still, the Polish question remained, and the situation worsening.

Polish Underground forces in Warsaw petitioned for anti-tank guns and ammunition against the Germans. Outside the city, Russian troops stalled as the Polish Underground remained under assault.

Mikolajczyk, head of the exiled Polish Government in London was under pressure to make a deal with the Russians. In his report, Harriman explained the situation.

On July 22nd, Radio Moscow announced that the Red Army had liberated their first large town in Poland, creating there the "Committee for National Liberation."

The following day, when the town of Lublin was liberated, the Committee was changed to "Lublin Committee." Autonomous, it was designed to oppose the political party of the exiled government in London.

Within a week, Marshall Rokossovsky's Army advanced three hundred miles to the Vistula River at Warsaw. A Russian broadcast called for the "Union of Polish Patriots" to rise against the Germans. "For Warsaw, which did not yield but fought on. the hour of action has now arrived. Poles, the time of liberation is at hand. Poles, to arms! There is not a moment to lose."

Word came from London that the Germans had planned to vacate troops from Warsaw ahead of the Red Army. Thus, General Tadeusz Bor-Komorowski, Commander of the Home Army who oversaw the Polish Underground, proclaimed a general insurrection for August 1st 1944.

On July 31st, Mikolajczyk arrived in Moscow to negotiate with the Russians about his reinstatement.

Stalin cited the insurrection, and insisted he make a deal with the Lublin Committee for the administration of a liberated Poland. Mikolajczyk met with the "Lublin Committee" August 6th, and on August 10th he returned to London thinking an agreement of collaboration had been reached.

* * *

With Kathleen absent and Spaso House almost vacant, Harriman received a visit from Prime

Minister Mikolajczyk on August 9th, 1944. They sat together on a bench out in the middle of the front yard - away from anything that might hold a microphone. They talked.

Harriman sent a letter to Molotov asking approval for an Allied air-shuttle mission to supply and aid the Warsaw insurgents; then to land in the Ukraine. It was August 22nd, and Stalin refused.

Roosevelt and Churchill appealed to him. He again refused. However, on September 9th, Stalin yielded to pressure from Churchill and allowed Allied planes to use Soviet air fields for supply drops into Warsaw.

Large drops were made September 18th, most of it falling now to the Germans. Two weeks later, the insurgents of Warsaw surrendered to the Nazi occupying troops. "The Soviets did not occupy the city till three months later" wrote Harriman. [165]

* * *

Notwithstanding their sensibilities about Freedom, Harriman had to consider the greater picture of American interests in dealing with the Russians.

A reception at Spaso House was attended by Molotov, Vishinski and assorted Soviet Colonel Generals to receive from the American Army some 198 medals for Soviet officers and men, a reciprocal act to those conferred upon Americans by the Soviets. Harriman's remarks were sincere and appreciative of their commendations.

The event was a great success, and Kathleen was doubtless present, conferring upon them her smile and applauses with as much grace. She had full confidence in her father's vision for the long term.

Meantime, visitors at Spaso House had shown full rigor. General Deane, Admiral Olsen and Captain Taylor and staff arrived in Moscow from the U.S. by way of Siberia, having flown around the world.

In August BBC news had announced the liberation of Paris, ascribing much of its success to the Underground Resistance movements. Celebration was everywhere. Embassy staff noted that this was a stark contrast to the Russian liberation efforts at Warsaw, an action that would deny the local resistance a future of their own.

On the same day August 23rd 1944, the Soviet radio announced that Rumania had accepted Soviet peace terms and made peace with the Soviet Union. The conditions were less than clear. It was decided that the Rumanians should send a delegation to Moscow to negotiate the final peace terms with the other two Allies present. This, in accordance with the terms of the Agreements made in Tehran.

A new Finnish government under Mannerheim filed for peace. They were instructed to do the same, as was next Bulgaria.

In principle, the efforts were well intentioned. But according to the records kept by Meiklejohn, the bureaucratic inertia of a cumbersome Russian infrastructure, combined with end of war fervor, resulted in local inter-Embassy misunderstandings; delays and frustrations.

Further, the media was less than accurate, if not under censorship.

Post-battle assertions, especially regarding the disposition of the German Navy - made for highly inaccurate accounts produced by the TASS Agency that dealt routinely with propaganda. Such distortions made the European liberations diverge drastically from accounts confirmed by the Allies.

Revelations were coming in from all quarters. Europe had been badly thrashed.

At the end of August, Dick Lauterback, a LIFE reporter came to lunch at Spaso House. His own report was shocking.

Lauterback set about the descriptions of his visit to Lublin. He told about the slaughter of Jews, Poles and others from occupied territories. The Soviet press also described the murder camps at Maidenek near Lublin in Poland. Public information was scant, even as all three Allies, including the Soviet press, tried to assess the numbers killed. It was described as a program by the Gestapo for "eliminating undesirables" brought in from all over Europe. One estimate said that two million had been killed. Another said the figure of two million was possible considering the camps' "capacity of the pace and the fact that it ran full blast for four years."

Lauterback told of others also reporting the awful evidence of wholesale slaughter by poison, then cremation. It was described as a neatly managed operation whereby all possessions were compiled and stored, sold or redistributed. A barn was seen in which piles, several feet deep, of personal items were stacked, including "used shoes – men's, women's and children's – and a warehouse with row upon row of shelves containing, neatly stored women's mirrors; children's toys; photographs; stockings etc., and a very large collection of gold teeth." [166]

The Soviet media focused on liberations of European cities, citing most markedly the efforts of the Red Army, especially along the Eastern Front.

Spaso House received special emissaries passing through on their way to Chiang Kai-Shek including Generals Pat Burley, Donald Nelson and Messer's Locke, Jacobson and their special assistants. When asking to do a little Moscow sightseeing "of which his nibs [Harriman] takes a poor view in wartime" reported Meiklejohn, they were ushered along.

For the Americans at the Moscow Mission, the war was still fully engaged, the pressure still on.

Over the radio, broadcasting from Berlin to the Pacific, the voice of the Axis Sal offered routine and persuasive talk that might lure away the hearts and allegiance of Allied troops. Said Meiklejohn "Most excellent jazz music, and the purpose of the program is to make the boys homesick and turn them against Prexy [the President] and his "Jewish" advisors for sending them overseas." [167]

* * *

Kathleen had gone to Italy to cover the war as a reporter. Hurley and Nelson were with her. She interviewed General Tito, if with Russian representatives about. She observed his expressions, personality and responses, if often delivered through an Interpreter.

Her opinion was rendered in a letter to her sister September 1st from Moscow. "Tito himself is small and heavy set. Very handsome with a strong face. Slit steel blue eyes that were cruel and hard looking but when he smiled or laughed, as he frequently did, his whole face lit up and made him appear less foreboding…What surprised me most were his hands…"[168]

Kathleen was speaking on more than appearances, if only by way of a letter, with "PS Many parts of this letter are indiscrete, particularly Para about Wild Bill. Please be careful what you show to who…"

Remarkably for Kathleen, she made a chance decision that was awkward, given the place and time.

While in Italy, Kathleen had set out to meet with Prime Minister Winston Churchill in Naples, unannounced. The guards at the door did not recognize her, and she was teased by him as a result. "He accused me of trying to pull a Virginia Cowles trick in coming down to Italy." (Virginia and Marty Hemingway both got caught trying to get to S. France illegally, some same tactics as they'd tried in Normandy, much to the annoyance of PROs. By the end of the war, they'll have been kicked out of every damned theater of war!)"[169]

Kathleen, walking that line said "he [Churchill] most cordially kissed me, thereby establishing my right to be there." When she told him "I'd arrived in complete innocence, he still didn't believe me!"[170]

"I wrote you after my first week in Italy, at any rate, before I could mention the fact that an invasion was coming up. The Naples harbor was filled with every type and kind of warship, troop ship, and landing craft. One day coming back from Capri, we saw a squadron of the LSTs sailing out to their rendezvous point..."

Not entirely a war correspondent, Kathleen was garnering news and information.

While on travel Kathleen was an invited house guest for the trip. "Bill Donovan gave a daytime party for Tito and another bunch of his officers the following day on Capri at Mme. William's villa." Tito, Kathleen felt, was setting himself up for a feature in the future of a Russo-Europe.

Kathleen returned from Italy after a three week absence, and within days, she was back on duty as hostess.

* * *

Drafting the peace was no small matter. There was much to align, and Spaso House was busy as ever with Kathleen entertaining guests.

Harriman had much to capture in his reports to the President. The Nelson party was preparing for China via New Delhi; the Rumanian negotiations were in progress. Luncheons, dinners and events such the official sendoff by Mikoyan filled the rooms and halls of Spaso House.

It was during the first week of September that Harriman detected something amiss in their liaison with the Russians, a subtle misrepresentation, if not a hidden agenda.

Molotov was handing documents over to the Bulgarian Ambassador. The Soviets were dissatisfied with Bulgaria since she had declared her neutrality against Germany instead of declaring war on the Germans. When asked, Molotov asserted that it was "the joint position of all three Allies...etc. etc." No such thing had been arranged by the Allies.

Meanwhile, family dependents were arriving in Moscow to join Embassy staff serving out their tour of duty. Wives, children and female clerks were welcomed at Spaso House, and by mid-September, events like boat trips, celebrations of national days and other functions had the place humming. It was a time of rotating civilian and military personnel.

Harriman, known for his endless work hours, defaulted on many social events and left them largely unattended. Kathleen had to take the slack of running affairs at Spaso House.

It was a transition period. With the war mainly behind them, there was much to do ahead. Yet closure had to be achieved on a number of fronts. Harriman remained vigilant, if not a little wary. His mission was to have long-term vision.

Still, small changes were possible.

On one afternoon, Harriman took a sledge-hammer to some brickwork designed to shield the basement windows from wartime bomb blasts. He, Kathleen and Meiklejohn all set to pounding, hauling and crow-barring at the reinforced battlement. Pleased with themselves, they played Badminton. An hour later, Prince Stirbey of the Rumanian Delegation came to pay his respects to the Americans. After he left, they turned to playing cards. Meiklejohn had to teach Harriman how to play Solitaire, and they enjoyed a breath of freshness.

Meiklejohn's quarters, which consisted of a suite with a Day room, arm chairs and office equipment, had become something of an Administrative social center. Here they gathered in the evenings, and relaxed.

One night, during a period of negotiations with the Russians, Mr. Crosthwaite, First Secretary of the British Embassy came to Spaso House at 1.00 A.M. with a cable. The Major-domo of Spaso House had gone to bed. Being as glass windows were no longer obscured as required for blackouts, the lights were out. Thus it was dark. Crosthwaite let himself into the House; "feeling" his way into the shadowy recess of the Foyer, then stumbled up the darkened steps to find the door to Meiklejohn's rooms. He opened and found Kathleen on the couch "painting her fingernails," Melby playing "symphony records on the Victrola," the Ambassador "sitting on the arm of a chair holding forth," and Meiklejohn "trying to type letters home." Crosthwaite found much humor in what he saw.

* * *

As the war was caused by military conflicts, by September 1944 a post-war Europe was taking shape.

Relief was within sight. The pace of activity by the leaders was picking up, even as fatigue took its toll and a heaviness of heart at the losses prevailed.

Harriman understood that from this point forward, the costs and reasoning would test even the best and bravest of men.

Moreover, for America there remained serious challenges.

Dealing with an Ally unaccustomed to procedures of administration and conventional communication was a bit like dealing with an alien Ally, they felt.

In his report, Harriman noted their differences in order to lay the groundwork for growing disparity. "Members of the American Military Mission were impressed by the Soviet effort to reduce their military problems to the simplest terms and to concentrate their efforts on the essential elements of their problems."

Harriman was referring to the Soviet military machine having few of the "extraneous activities" that the Allies had, such as multiple facets of organization, accountability and strategic advance planning. "They have no organizations comparable to our post exchanges…" This reflected on their responses. "this made advance planning extremely difficult and it is probable that their operations were on more of an opportunist day to day basis…." Without excusing their style, Harriman explains that with only one theater of war to consider "the Soviet methods proved to be entirely satisfactory for their purpose."[171]

But it was clearly unsatisfactory for a post war condition.

By the third week, and following the liberation of Paris, peace broke out in Rumania, Finland and Bulgaria.

Officially, the Armistice terms of Agreement had to be asserted, typed, translated, signed by the Allies and ratified. This required careful coordination, collaboration and public dissemination to spread the news of the new conditions.

The Russians pulled off the Agreements, sometimes long into the night with public information within a stone's throw, using the best of their official efforts as background props. For them, it was new.

The British and American Ambassadors were officially on hand to sign for their governments the documents of the Armistices in Moscow; including that of Transylvania. The process was long and tedious. The matters of reparations, boundaries, troop withdrawals, currency, security, economic recovery and rebuilding had to be hammered out. It was difficult and fatiguing.

Molotov, in weariness, was impatient with impasses and sought authoritarian solutions - in one case ending a debate abruptly between Maisky and Kristu by saying "I think we can consider this too hazardous to conclude."

When finally the documents and their translations were typed, if "messy looking" as treaties, they were official and legal. Said Meiklejohn "We finished the English text well before the Soviets finished theirs. They got into such a mess that Molotov himself finally grabbed the sheets and sorted them out [himself]"[172]

Following the Agreements, there was disparity about public dissemination and timing of media releases, some of it compromising of achieved negotiations. Added to the problem was Russian censorship of news delivered by Foreign Correspondents. As policy items, these releases became a matter of vexation to Harriman because it sent mixed messages back to Washington as if he were operating out of accord with State directives, let alone misinforming the general public.

Harriman asked to return to the U.S. for consultations. Harry Hopkins cabled him back saying that he didn't think it wise to come home while the Dumbarton Oaks Conference was underway with the Soviets. Already they were negotiating on a World Security Organization, Roosevelt's chief goal. Harriman should wait.

Increasingly, Harriman suspected that the Soviets were crafting their own post-war Europe.

* * *

Embassy events maintained an energetic level of activity. On the surface things appeared to be routine functions, such as the Mexican day of Independence party.

American shuttle-bomber bases at Poltava, Mirgorod and Pyratin were shutting down; the Army rotating nurses up to Moscow for a day of sightseeing before shipping out.

It had been a sore point amongst the Americans that the Soviets prevented the use of the bases to support the Poles in Warsaw. Again, they pressed for a concession to use the bases from the Russians at the Rumanian Armistice negotiations, September 13th.

But there was more. Harriman recognized the markings of a Russian policy taking shape. At the domestic level, the people of Russia were deliberately kept in the dark as to the joint contributions of the other Allies.

Further, he and the other ally were of the growing conviction that the Soviet Union, now demonstrating open infractions like disseminating inaccurate information, were showing small discourtesies of omissions and outward distrust towards Europeans. They might be harboring a hidden agenda of their own, the scope of it yet unknown.

Moreover, Harriman had his challenge. He was aware that the way to open hearts and minds to free trade and opportunity was through the use of public dissemination: His challenge for commercial competition might even cultivate a climate for a public forum for referendum.

Harriman arranged for an Anglo-American Joint Press Reading Service whereby the Soviet press was translated, much of it espousing propaganda "Socialist Emulation" as the model to follow. Designed for integration of school teachers into their program for the youth, it embraced the fundamental doctrines of Communism, itemizing societal differences that would divide the Russians from the West. Amongst other elements, it disavowed religion; disclosed "the laws of the development of human society revealed by Marxist-Leninist theory, dialectical and historical materialism." Harriman had unmasked their differences.[173]

The Armistice Agreements for the peace of Finland were signed by the British and Americans.

Harriman got word meantime, of the elements agreed in the second Quebec Conference of the British and American Heads of State that took place earlier in the month.

Permission was granted from the Soviets, due to the instigation of Harriman and pressure at the top, to drop supplies and aid to the Poles in Warsaw by bombers.

* * *

By 1944 it was clear that the war had taken its toll on the Allied relationship.

Since Stalin did not travel, it was the responsibility of the Americans and British to inform Stalin about the Conference in Quebec. On September 23rd they made a personal visit to Stalin in Moscow.

Harriman; the British Ambassador and his Aide presented the conference documents already signed by Roosevelt and Churchill.

The Conference conclusions asserted that at this stage, Hitler's downfall was assured; and that the Allied armies were converging on German territory from the west and east. Further details from the Conference showed an Allied determination to press on for Northwest Europe, including striking the Ruhr and Saar. Italy was decided to proceed with operations to eliminate the forces of General Kesselring and to clear the plains of Lombardy. The Balkans were to continue with military raids; and for Japan "we have agreed on further operations to intensify in all theaters the offensive against the Japanese." After the conquest of Germany, all efforts should focus to the Pacific theater.

As Ambassador, Harriman's presentation of military affairs was a deviation from his role as Minister of Economic Affairs at Moscow. More importantly however, was the relationship at hand with Stalin. And certainly for the Allies, these were the standing priorities to be pursued relentlessly.

Stalin reiterated his intention to join the war against Japan. He also allowed for the delivery of five hundred trucks with GI drivers to move across Soviet territory to Alma Ata to China for use there by an American Air Force.

Further, Stalin agreed to a Conference amongst the Big Three in the Mediterranean to address the matters of a post-war world. Surely, there, the interests of the Russians would be fully represented.

This was not an easy juncture for Harriman. As an American industrialist with a grand vision for commercial development; world peace and business opportunities, he might have felt his heart sinking.

Especially when Lt Col Ralph Olmstead, Agricultural Expert of the War Food Administration showed up at Spaso House drunk, and was dismissively denigrated by the Russians as a "drunk foreigner." Clearly, this did not bode well. Even as the Russian ploy of intoxicating diplomats for the purpose of ridicule was well known amongst the diplomatic colony.

Here, Harriman was observing not a forgiving and trustworthy Ally but a Soviet Union rooted in insularism and centralist suspicion. In utter frustration, Meiklejohn reported "The only way to deal with these people is to get tough. They simply don't understand courtesy and they think plying a visitor with vodka, women and ballets will make up for the failure to do the business he has come to Russia to do."

Neither was Harriman alone.

At the end of September, with everyone anticipating a trip home, Harriman announced that all was postponed. Churchill was coming to Moscow for a State visit.

* * *

Kathleen was giggling. She had a secret. It was October 3, 1944. The day would be busy and Harriman sent Meiklejohn to the Embassy at Mokhovaya to meet with the Admiral, requiring him to make special Navy uniform changes.

Harriman was a tough task-master. That night, Army movies were scheduled at Spaso House, and before dinner, the Ambassador was hosting a farewell cocktail party for General Fleming. Meiklejohn should make all the appropriate arrangements.

Midway through the movies moreover, Meiklejohn was called away for more work by Harriman. Meiklejohn arrived "in very bad grace." Suddenly fifty people jumped at him.

Presents piled up on him with "Happy Birthday." It wasn't just General Fleming's party at all, it was *his* surprise birthday party laid on by Kathleen and Harriman! On his cake was inscribed "Admiral Spaso." With them, all the American, British and Canadian young females were invited, and a dance floor for the occasion was set up using their "Special Services victrola" for music. Kathleen had made it a great success.

Meiklejohn wrote "There was a deep laid conspiracy to get me drunk that was quite hopeless to buck so I decided to humor and get it over with. Admiral Olsen and General Fleming were continually proposing "bottoms up" to say nothing of Kathleen, Melby and … [others]"[174]

…"The only serious boner I pulled was when in my ignorance I fell for the claim that a whisky bottle filled with vodka was 'Bleached Rye Whisky' and drank a healthy portion mixed with ice and water, which is no way to drink vodka.

…"Considering the circumstances, it is believed that I did fairly well and got upstairs, though in convoy, under my own steam."[175]

If Harriman and Kathleen knew how to have fun, the affairs of a war were still on.

The next day, while nursing a hangover, Harriman met with Stalin to present him with a bust of the President. But because it was so large, the decision was made at Spaso House to "lug the thing in the open rather than put it in a box for fear the Russkies would think it a bomb. Up to 2.30 AM sending cables to Prexy [The President]"[176]

Two days later, Harriman got an evening call from Molotov. The Hungarian Armistice was to be negotiated in Moscow following their proposal to quit the war and join the Allies against Germany.

Harriman had just spent all day Sunday at the Embassy with his Military personnel playing "War Games" to "indicate what might be the part the Russians would play in the Pacific war."

Within twenty four hours, Churchill and Stalin were to meet for a Conference in Moscow to further coordinate the efforts of the Soviet Anglo-American Allies. There had been some resistance to this two-party meeting because neither could such a meeting take place prior to the re-election of Roosevelt, nor could Stalin travel for such a meeting – by doctor's orders.

Churchill, waving aside elections, doctors or any other excuses insisted on conferring about concluding the war with two clear objectives. First, to bring Stalin into the war against Japan in earnest. Secondly, to achieve an "amicable settlement on Poland."

Churchill had lesser issues that included Yugoslavia and Greece. Plus a direct appeal to Roosevelt to use Harriman or Stettinius or Marshall to sit for a post-war plan. This was to be the agenda for the Second Moscow Conference.

Roosevelt responded by offering Harriman as an appointed "Observer" only. To Harriman, the President wrote "…Immediately upon the conclusion of the discussion I will expect you to come home. During the talks you will naturally keep me and Mr. Hull fully and currently advised."[177]

They arrived in five planes and were met at the airport by Molotov, Vishinski and others. The British Prime Minister; Anthony Eden and their staffs were also welcomed at the airport by the British Ambassador, Harriman, Kathleen and General Deane.

Stalin gave a luncheon for the Prime Minister. Harriman met with Churchill later in the afternoon, and the next day, he and Kathleen dined with him at their Embassy dacha.

Several Embassy parties followed in Moscow, one with Stalin in attendance -the lights outside indicating a celebrity within was tightly guarded. Security, Harriman noted, had increased substantially.

To deflect criticism for too much proximity between two allies, Harriman and Churchill played Bezique while Kathleen wrote letters to London, a fact easily reported.

Churchill, evidently, had handed Kathleen letters from London.

The record neither refers to a continuing correspondence held between Pam Churchill and Kathleen, nor does Kathleen's response to a letter from Pam brim with effusive greeting. Ever the

244

diplomat's consort, Kathleen shows good grace, if with a touch of frostiness.

Supposedly, there was a fast flight to London that could deliver mail. She opens with "Perhaps this letter will go off to you tonight. If not, Postman "Pug" [General Hastings "Pug" Ismay, Military secretary to the British War Cabinet and Churchill's liaison with his chiefs of staff] can take it, though not in five hours!"

In the absence of previous dialogue, Kathleen says "Moscow is such a nice place when friends come a-visiting. The past week, while Ave and the Big Wigs have been conferencing, I've been entertaining or been entertained by the Little Wigs…their reactions are so enthusiastic. Everything is so new to them."

…"Ave is thriving under the long hours of conferences and more conf. plus his own ambassadorial work…"

…"The most exciting thing as far as I'm concerned is that at last I've met U.J. [Uncle Joe, Stalin] I was beginning to despair of that ever happening. A couple of nights back a special program was put on at the big ballet theater…"

Kathleen adds with a touch of retribution "The first time I saw U.J.[Uncle Joe, a codename for Stalin] was your Embassy, he seemed …distant. But at the dinner he smiled, particularly by squinting his eyes – a good deal and seemed quite like a human being."

Not often did the British Prime Minister come to Moscow. Certainly they had heard of the liveliness there with the Harrimans at Spaso House.

Harriman shared Kathleen's sentiments. Kathleen was managing quite well on a foreign mission. "Of all horrible things, Ave figured I ought to make a toast in Russian, which the P.M.'s interpreter coached me on, so's I'd be sure to get all the right words sin their proper tenses."

Finally, Kathleen asserted her privileged position without further apology "Litvinov asking Russ re Look [Life Magazine] article it is true Ave has $100 million dollars. Russ said he didn't know.

Did he earn it or inherit it? 'How could a man who had $100 million … so sad!'"

Kathleen added, as if to make a point of her father's agency "Moore Crosswaith [British Embassy First Secretary] getting sore at Ave for making a big entrance for Cemanova [ballerina] at our party".[178]

Clearly, the Harrimans felt displeased with Pam Churchill, perhaps on account of her presumptuous and unsolicited insertions in matters of the war, politics, English interests and even American diplomacy.

* * *

Harriman was anxious to return to the United States. President Roosevelt was up for re-election. His participation was in every way delayed by his affairs here now in Moscow.

Molotov was hopeful in auguring for Roosevelt's reelection, and said so in his toasts for the President "May he have luck in October, in November and all the rest of his life."

Later in the day, Mikolajczyk, the Polish Prime Minister; Romer the Polish Foreign Minister and Mr.Grobski arrived from London on an urgent summons from Churchill in his final attempt to sort out a Polish peace solution.

* * *

Kathleen hosted a supper party at Spaso House for the Delegates of the Second Moscow Conference following an extraordinary theater performance at the Bolshoi.

The food was lavish. She arranged to have served on the buffet peaches, apples, grape and chocolate cake in abundance. The party was attended by General Ismay; two Brigadiers travelling with Field Marshall Brooke, the Prime Minister's Naval Aide, Commander Thompson, Miss Brite of Ismay's staff and a number of other staff. Generals Deane and Spalding attended, along with a former American Ambassador, Admiral Olsen.

Everyone was having a wonderful time. The event was such a success that finally General Ismay had to be taken aside and told that he should go home since no one of a lesser rank could leave until he departed. It was 2.00 AM.

The theater performance preceding the party was given in honor of the visiting British Prime Minister. The Bolshoi ballet and Red Army Chorus had put on a performance at the Bolshoi Theater. Stalin attended, as did Churchill, Eden, Harriman, General Deane and Kathleen, all of them seated in the Royal Box.

Harriman, for his part in the Second Moscow Conference. He gave a Press Conference in which he delivered a message that all three countries must continue to work together.

The next day, with state affairs behind them and the war still winding down, an exclusive Military Meeting of the Conference occurred between Stalin, Molotov, Churchill, Harriman and Deane. A second Military Meeting followed up on 15th of October, 1944.

It was Sunday, and a Farewell party was had been scheduled for the British legations at Spaso House. If less formal, it was just as fully attended "with enough military brass to fill the place" said Meiklejohn. It went on until the early hours of the morning, Kathleen arranging for dancing with the victrola. Once again, Harriman and Kathleen had made Moscow the center of a very palatable conference, noted Churchill.

The Americans had scheduled to leave Moscow immediately after the conclusion of the Conference. There were other matters pending for their attention. Planned for early Tuesday, the departure date was greatly anticipated.

Suddenly, Churchill took ill, and his departure was delayed.

Regardless, General Deane's farewell dinner for Colonel Bond took place the next night, Monday.

He was being reassigned State side, and many of his rank attended, including Kathleen and Meiklejohn. However, that dinner actually took place in General Deane's apartment, and it was Kathleen who brought everything over from Spaso House, sans the usual retinue of servants. They thought it lovely, and the word spread as to her efficacy…

Harriman "had to go to dinner with the Prime Minister." Their departure was delayed as Harriman attended an impromptu Kremlin dinner that would close out their conference negotiations on Wednesday. Here, Harriman had negotiated a key component of Roosevelt's agenda.

As he did so, they were packing to travel at Spaso House. Finally, with all business concluded and the conference completed, it was October 18th, 1944. Election day in America was November 4th

On the airfield at 6.45 AM, the Americans assembled to fly in General Wash's converted four-engine B-17 bomber, a Flying Fortress. Onboard were Harriman, Kathleen, Thompson (Secretary of Embassy ending his tour); Colonel Bond and Meiklejohn. Sent-off by a large party of military and diplomatic personnel, they taxied to leave Moscow.

Harriman looked out the porthole. Still stationary were three British York planes and three Liberator planes belonging to the Prime Minister's party. Those planes were to take off later in the morning, after the Americans.

"Proceed!" said Harriman.

* * *

A travel itinerary had been arranged in advance. The Americans landed for breakfast with the local Russian Colonel at Poltava in the Ukraine at about 10 AM before taking off again over the Dnieper River Crimea then Sevastopol on the Black Sea.

By afternoon, they were passing over Ankara, Turkey and arrived Cairo in the dark. General Giles met them and they had an "unbelievably tasty" steak dinner while the plane refueled. Back in the air by 10 P.M., Harriman and Kathleen climbed into their cabin bunks, all of them exhausted.

Kathleen awoke before dawn and offered her bunk for a couple of hours sleep to others. They landed in Casablanca at approximately 10.00 AM, finding Major General Walsh and his Aide to greet them. With luggage promptly transferred to a C-54, they took off for the rest of the trip home. One addition, Captain Robert Gerry, an Australian came aboard to join them. He was a relative of Harriman returning to the United States. However, while eating their lunch on board, and one hour into flight, the plane returned to the tarmac. An engine was out.

The problem solved, they were up again and over the Azores, airfields packed with military Transports landing or taking off for North Africa. The Harrimans stopped for two hours to refuel and dine - the weather threatening before their Atlantic crossing. This was to be a nonstop direct flight into Washington DC – their first.

Once landed on US soil, Harriman went immediately to see Roosevelt.

Matters of importance needed to be discussed about Russia. It became clear, as they conferred, that even with technology lagging, neither could America prolong exposure to this war, nor could America tolerate a Communist State as competitor. For now, to achieve the first objective, the second would have to wait.

Above all, the Allies needed to defeat the Japanese.

* * *

Roosevelt was campaigning for political re-election. It was not an easy campaign for him, and he might well have preferred to be retired at his beloved home at Hyde Park, New York. Instead, America was at war overseas; matters of state unresolved, and the nation needing new trade opportunities.

Harriman saw that Roosevelt's time was fragmented; his personal affairs joyless, and his health less than robust.

Roosevelt's physical disability was now presenting discomfort and personal indignity during the campaign - the weather getting colder and his public appearances out in the open. He felt that his public image had slipped, held up only by those around him. Most frustrating for him was that America's greatness had been challenged not only by a European adversary, but by a little known enemy in the Pacific.

Harriman delivered a campaign radio speech for the re-election of the President on November 3rd, 1944. On Election Day the voters spoke. Franklin Roosevelt was elected for a fourth consecutive term in office as the President of the United States.

Harriman had met with the President half a dozen times during his visit in Washington at the White House and home in Hyde Park. They discussed the Churchill Conference; the upcoming "Big Three" Conference and the Polish dilemma. Also discussed was the worrisome reconciliation of the Nationalist Chinese Government of Chiang Kai-shek with Mao Tse-tung's communist forces rising in China. Finally, of Stalin's position on Japan.

The war overall was progressing by plan, but closure had lost its momentum. What should have been a complete victory in the fall was now going on until spring. The Russians had greater success on the ground, liberating the Baltic States in the North; Rumania and Hungary in the South, and Poland up to the Vistula River.

The Southwest Pacific forces under General MacArthur had been a success, eliminating the Japanese forces in the Bismarck Archipelago; the Admiralty Islands and New Guinea. An invasion of the Philippines was ongoing with a landing at Leyte. Engaging now were the Central Pacific fleets and Air force. As a result, the Japanese fleet was finally being defeated.

More troublesome for Roosevelt was that the war had exacted much from America. Blow by blow, daily dispatches showed a drama unfolding in the Pacific that could not have been more offensive to a President seeking supremacy. America's symbol of might and glory, her naval ships of the line were deployed in action against an enemy of insignificant global standing still showing defiance and arrogance in the extreme. It rankled, and it was unmitigating.

On October 18th a confidential cable had told of Admiral Halsey's Third Fleet penetrating Japan's inner defense zone and attacking Formosa one hundred miles off the east coast of China. For three days Admiral Mitscher's carrier task force swept over Formosa. China-based airfields allowed for Bombers to add to the raid by the 20th Bomber Command, followed by super Fortresses.

It did damage. Of the 437 Japanese aircraft, 232 were shot down in combat and 205 destroyed on the ground. 100 ships were sunk. Radio Tokyo was outraged, and their opposition continued in defiance. American casualties were few.

On the 16th, Formosa was attacked by a large force similar to that on Okayama. A third raid on Formosa occurred on the 17th with fewer planes.

Radio Tokyo broadcast General Kuniaki Koiso declaring "the long awaited battle has begun. The battle against Formosa "augurs a bright future." The Domei dispatch said that "the distinctive war results achieved by our army and navy in annihilating the enemy 58th Task Force in the waters east of Taiwan have marked a shift in our position from a defensive to an offensive."

The publicity campaign was intolerable. Admiral Nimitz announced that no American ships were actually lost, neither battleships nor carriers. Only two "medium sized ship" were damaged by aerial torpedoes.

Still, the Japanese attack which had begun on the 12th October was that of small groups of aircraft repeatedly attempting to bomb or torpedo the carriers. In three days, over 200 enemy planes buzzed the American ships in "Japanese Kamikaze" style of attack. They were unrelenting.

On 16th October, 1944 the enemy attacks continued. Seaborne, waves of 16 units approached, intending to finish off the American fleet that was represented as "damaged." Finding the American force unimpaired, the enemy ships "avoided action and withdrew toward their bases."

Roosevelt would be long in the forgiving, especially now that he won the election. Serious action was needed. Options had to be considered.

"Chip" Bohlen, Colonel Bond and Meiklejohn's family were at the airport for the sendoff back to Moscow. As were Averell's wife Mrs. Harriman, and Mrs. Hill to see her husband off. Stettinius showed up at the airport for a last minute farewell to Harriman. He had information to share and the take-off was delayed by an hour.

Harriman, Kathleen, Meiklejohn, Brigadier General Hill and Sergeant Towsey finally climbed onboard for Moscow with five Army officers for a ride to England. They left from the new Transport Command Terminal at Washington National Airport. It was November 19th, 1944. Just five days before Thanksgiving Day.

* * *

Landing at Prestwick Airport in England after 11 hours of flying time, they expected to refuel and fly on to London.

Instead, they were greeted with the announcement that "train reservations had been made for continuing our trip to London, at which the Ambassador and the General immediately blew their tops. For an hour and half they argued and telephoned everybody in England except the Prime Minister for authority to either fly "our plane" to Bovingdon Airport at London, or to secure a C-47 which could land at Bovingdon or Hendon, but without success."[179]

Harriman stood there. The embrace of his wife still warm on his cheek; strategic war directives for Eisenhower in his briefcase; messages for Churchill with new technology warfare, and a mandate for Stalin from the re-elected President of the United States was his obligation. The discovery that his travel itinerary had been hijacked by someone - especially in the presence of Generals; daughter and staff, was nothing less than an insult, if not a threat to their security. He was outraged.

Kathleen opened her letter to Shirley and Larry with "…we arrived at a very damp and cold Paddington [train] station … morning at 5 AM...and found Beek (Beaverbrook] and Pam running down the platform to greet us. Beek had been "ordered" up to London, on business unknown to him. I guess he had a few bad minutes until he discovered why…" [180]

Pam Churchill was at it again!

They were accommodated at the Claridges for two days, that evening dining at No 10 Downing St in the company of the Edens; the Prime Minister, his wife, and Mary Churchill.

With Harriman fuming at the impropriety of Pam Churchill, Kathleen noted changes she observed while in London in a letter to her Mary in New York. Especially, she recounted the affair of a prominent London war correspondent who had sent his wife to the countryside under the pretext of safety while he remained in London to see another woman. Kathleen's dislike of the duplicity resonated with the harm of having Pam around, saying that this fell even below the standards of two failed friends - Pam and Beaverbrook - now described as a team. [181]

As if acerbated by the matter, Kathleen added that the P.M. had just come back from a "long and tiresome cabinet meeting, was in an unserious mood (Much to Ave's annoyance.)"

Kathleen marginalized Pam in an informational way "...full of work at her club, Baby Winston was sick in the country so I didn't see him. We [the baby and she] had a chat on the phone though... which wasn't too productive!"[182]

While in London, the Harrimans were taken on tour to witness V-2 bomb damage. Kathleen showed resoluteness. "I stayed awake one night - for about an hour waiting to hear a buzz bomb…I went out and looked at the result of one, the next morning. A very deep hole (a church was cut in half (a small Church) and not as much blast effect the VIs."

Kathleen had a heart for London still. "I felt like a skunk standing there idly watching - just sightseeing - while the people who had been bombed out rummaged around in the debris for their bits and pieces that were left…Jesus but the Londoners have had a hard time - for four years now, and they look just as hard and placid as ever."

On Saturday, they took off for Paris in their C-54 with a few passengers and stayed at Hotel Raphael on Rue Kleber just off the Arc de Triumph. Kathleen and Harriman were lodged in the Royal Suite, and they witnessed a post-war fashionable city in full sway.

Teeming with bicycles, taxis and horse drawn carriages, Paris was also buzzing with jeeps and military trucks. One convoy was of tanks and tank transporters. "I didn't anticipate all hats to be as extreme as those pictured in Vogue - but they certainly are. The females are fantastic - bicycling along skirts way above their knees, full sleeves and skirted coats and huge high turbaned hats..."[183]

She explained. Since the Germans had rationed cloth for clothing articles, they had failed to consider hats. Millinery trades therefore took to "piling all the material they could into hats". It became a symbol of resistance. Kathleen added "God help us if the N.Y.C. milliners take up their Paris style!"[184]

Staffers enjoyed some nightlife in Paris while the Harrimans had the company of Ambassador Murphy and Colonel Boettiger, Roosevelt's son-in-law. Sunday, Harriman left for General Eisenhower's advance headquarters at Rheims.

There was much to discuss, especially coming freshly from the President and Stettinius, such that they stayed an extra day in conference. Harriman drafted the account of his meeting for the President.

Eisenhower had given him "the detail of his strategy and tactics of what he hoped to accomplish by Xmas." To Harriman he made it clear that coordinating with the Russians was critical "He told me what he wanted to know from the Russians, and I intend to ask this of Stalin on my return." [185]

The ground war of Europe at that moment was up for grabs. "He [Eisenhower] was interested to know what was thought about him and his job at home. I told him that I thought the fact that General Marshall and the President had talked to me at length of what he was doing and their determinations to give him support above all other theaters gave him the best assurance of their confidence, and that there was no question the was doing the utmost that could be done…" [186]

Harriman informed Eisenhower of plans for the Pacific, and of the conditions of the tri-party cooperation between the Allies. He asked Eisenhower about his post-war plans and found that Eisenhower was not harboring any political ambition. "He is dedicated to the conceptions that we must work thing out in cooperation with the British; be alert to future danger of aggression; maintain not only a substantial military force but also intelligent control of strategic points, and keep an effective industrial production available for military requirements. He sent me down to Nancy where I met Patton who took me to the headquarters of the 4th and 26th Divisions…" [187]

Harriman got a tour from Patton. "Particularly interesting was the West Line where the Germans had built…Patton's Third army consist at the present time of nine divisions. H hoped to get two additional divisions shortly. He said he was using up his ammunition fast that it would last….He hoped to get to the Rhine by then. This would take him four days after he broke through the Siegfried Line. He described his tactics…He and General Wood both explained how handicapped they had been by the swollen rivers which normally were a few hundred yards wide and now is in some cases a mile wide. The high water was a record…."[188]

From Eisenhower's headquarters, Harriman was driven straight to Orly Field to board their C-54 plane bound for General Eaker's headquarters at Caserta Italy. Kathleen and the staff were waiting for him.

A general war meeting was assembled at Caserta attended by all but Kathleen. By Thursday morning they were on the plane again bound for Cairo where "Becky" their Liberator was waiting for them. At her request, Kathleen and Harriman tore about town for some quick shopping. Their cargo was itemized as a thousand pounds of movie projector equipment; communication equipment and other necessities for Moscow, and they left Cairo for Tehran December 1st 1944. There, the Harrimans stayed with General Connolly – the rest stayed at Camp Amirabad. Snow postponed their flight departure to Moscow.

10.

Russia was to participate in the war against Japan. As arranged in the October conference with Stalin, a secret accumulation of supplies to the Maritime Provinces of Siberia was underway.

For this, there was much to coordinate. General Roberts, Colonel Ritchie, Colonel Bogart and Captain Maples converged with C-54 plane at Tehran to join Harriman's flight into Moscow.

They left before dawn on December 5th, the flight crews of other military planes still grounded by weather. Harriman gave the pilots a "flight talk" and the plane climbed to 14,000 ft. off the Caucasus Mountains, collecting considerable ice as it headed northward. His aim was to avoid unscheduled stops before Moscow on account of weather.

Emerging from the clouds and skimming the surface at 300 ft., they landed at Moscow where a fleet of cars from Spaso House met them all. "Becky" their Liberator had followed safely and would be landing shortly.

Back in Moscow by December 6th, the Harriman staff resumed work with some improvements of personnel and facilities. Nelson Newton was moved into Meiklejohn Administrative Day Room for extra work; a kerosene heater had been installed - if without a chimney, and general upgrades made for a smoother operation at Spaso House.

Kathleen returned to Moscow to discover that her duties as a correspondent for the Office of War

Information had been changed by her boss Joe Phillips. He seemed to have altered them significantly, if not terminated her services, such that the dual lives she was living - one a diplomatic consort, the other a correspondent, was decided. She was to remain the diplomatic First Lady of her father's posting in Moscow. To her sister Mary, she complained bitterly in a letter dated December 9th 1944.

Meantime, General De Gaulle was in Moscow negotiating a post-war Franco-Soviet treaty. Stalin invited Harriman to join them for dinner at the Kremlin. The C-54 was offered to De Gaulle for his return trip, but the weather had so deteriorated that he left by train to Baku once his Treaty was signed.

It was Sunday. They felt like they were home. They went skiing at Lenin Hills. Kathleen had made improvements on their equipment, including Sun Valley ski-boots that fit Russian ski bindings.

House guests staying at Spaso House were General Hill and Brigadier General Frank Roberts to make joint plans with the Soviets for the war in the Far East.

Another guest, Lillian Hellman, was at Spaso House. A well-known American playwright, she had been invited to the USSR by the Soviets. Finding the National Hotel too cold, she was now staying at Spaso House.

The winter weather closed in and temperatures plunged. Unlike the previous winter in Moscow at Spaso House, this was a deep freeze. Suddenly the building filled with smoke and fumes. The kerosene stove in Meiklejohn's room threatened to explode. They laughed, Meiklejohn's source of heat had to improve. Toast, in the mornings, was made in make-shift ways with Kathleen and Hellman having fun at the breakfast table together.

Kathleen was busy hosting dinners. Guests included the New Zealand Minister and Swedish Minister, both staying for movies at Spaso House.

The following Sunday, they all went skiing as a group again.

On the 14th December, 1944 Harriman met for a working meeting with Stalin. They discussed various military and political matters.

However, December left Harriman with doubts about the Soviets willingness -or abilities, to follow through with their promises on Japan.

* * *

Meiklejohn noted that Kathleen, who had brought back some candles, insisted that they dined by candlelight. In the spirit of domestic harmony, Harriman agreed. However, he loved blowing them out when she wasn't at dinner and then would switch on the overhead lights so that "he could see what he was eating!"

Christmas at Spaso House began with a whirl of gift wrapping. Much had been brought over from the US or purchased in Cairo by Kathleen.

Said Meiklejohn, Harriman was to give all his Embassy staff a bottle of bourbon. Kathleen, "out of the kindness of her heart, decided to wrap them up pretty."[189]

"Newton and Kathleen did most of the job, but anybody that happened to come to my room that day got roped in. Taylor, General Deane's Aide snipping off the requisite lengths of Scotch Tape, while waiting for [Harriman] to approve a cable, and even the Army courier took time out to wrap a couple of bottles on each of his several trips to Spaso. It was all very festive if a bit distracting to serious business."[190]

Kathleen was a meticulous manager and took her duties at Spaso House very seriously.

"Every bottle had a personal card on it with the name and, in the case of the military, the rank of the recipient. We found out that of several score military there were only seven corporals and no privates, so we arbitrarily promoted the corporals to sergeants, and I found out afterward that the gesture was very much appreciated."

Neither did Kathleen neglect those of the cloth. "We sent three bottles of booze to Father Braun, the Catholic priest here. The car left with the bottles at three o'clock in the afternoon, and neither car nor driver was heard of again until noon the next day when the car was found wrecked on the outskirts of the city. [Father Braun however, received his three bottles intact]."[191]

Kathleen strayed neither far from the traditions of her upbringing nor the mission of her father the Ambassador. She decorated the Christmas tree at Spaso House on Christmas Eve. "It was eighteen feet high, with lights and ornaments sent from the United States."

The tree caused awe and admiration from the locals who brought their children to view the lighted tree - one Russian doorman was given the privilege of blowing the lights out.

Kathleen hosted the large Christmas party on Christmas Eve, a Sunday. It was for the American staff of the Embassies and counted over two hundred guests. She had managed the kitchen staff at Spaso House - working them to roast turkeys, bake cakes, pies and cookies. It was a formidable spread, such that when Kathleen presented the cook, everyone applauded. The cook cried.

After the party, one joke was delivered by Hellman about a drunk being carried off, his body jackknifed between two Colonels who inadvertently rammed him against a door-jam when a General walked in. The General saw him and said sadly "Yes, that's my Aide."

Of the military personnel in attendance, many had just been promoted and informed as they passed through the receiving line to shake hands with General Deane. This, they all said, was a courtesy appreciated at the party. It was Kathleen's idea.

For entertainment, Kathleen procured a Soviet dance orchestra; plus a small chorus of Army enlisted men and officers to sing Christmas carols. At the other end of the house, a smaller group of

Gypsy entertainers danced and sang their heartfelt songs of country tradition.

The party of Christmas Eve at Spaso House on December 1944 was a great success. The next day, Kathleen had her father and his aide distribute gifts to the House staff at noon. From his boss and Kathleen, Meiklejohn received a collar stud box [cuffs and links of gold] inscribed with his initials.

Clearly, these moments of insight reflected a happy relationship amongst the Harriman staff. Yet it would come at the most difficult times of the war in Moscow.

Kathleen, her touches of thoughtfulness and dignity gave them all balance.

* * *

Kathleen, waiting at Yalta Conference, February 1945

Courtesy Library of Congress

On New Year's 1945 the war was still active, but the world changing.

Kathleen persuaded Meiklejohn and another staffer to go to a small New Year's party at an apartment shared by two Embassy bachelors, Richard Davis, Secretary at the Embassy, and Joe Chase of the Navy Mission. There was music, dancing, a few girls and the event passed cheerfully.

At Spaso House, Meiklejohn was held in the highest esteem. At a luncheon he was invited to share with Harriman and their company his opinions about politics, morals and money. He had after all, supported Harriman on missions of the greatest importance; administered and crafted cables to the President; proofed protocols and agreements of every fashion at all hours and travelled dutifully through traffic, weather turbulence around the globe with Harriman. He wrote of that luncheon, "I have never seen so many people whose political and moral views were at such variance with their own ways of life – i.e. most conservative in practice, and liberal, not to say loose, in principle."[192]

They had turned the corner on the New Year, sobered by the realization that the war was lingering; its mission getting fragmented and its message messy. Extraction presented a whole new set of contradictions.

Harriman himself had a difficult time adjusting to the Moscow routine. Perhaps it was the sight of seeing his President win an election against many odds – or, seeing his health failing and his will showing disenchantment.

The American view of the war was shifting.

Present and new realities were setting in. Having inserted himself as Ambassador to Russia as a Minister of Trade, there was clearly no "winning the hearts and minds" of the Russians under a socialist regime.

Even the reporters, as they entertained guests with party-skits, came up with a parody of Churchill's famous line. "Never in the history of human endeavor have so few kept so much from so many."

It was well known that the Russian infrastructure wished to keep their people in the dark about capitalism, yet here was a war about liberation; free market economies, and independence from tyranny. This presented a dilemma for Russia that the leadership of the West well understood, and perhaps made allowances for. The recent history of socialist Russia could not be rewritten, they knew. Still, if there was any hope for a different outcome, here was the chance. . .

For Harriman, the situation was worrisome. Autocratic Russians operated in bold strokes, he knew, unlike the refinements of Western diplomats. Were they too entrenched, their aid now achieved from the West to win this war? How to read the threat? How best to proceed on Europe?

Most corrosive were reports coming in from American bomber crews who had been downed behind enemy lines. They were being turned over to the Poltave airbase in the Soviet Ukraine. Who was in authority there?

Poland, invaded first by the Germans in 1939 was the reason for which England entered the war.

Reports came from Lwow, a place where "people were well dressed in the latest Paris models." Surveyed as a mixture of Ukraine partisans, Communist Lublin Poles, resistance fighters, London Poles and deserters from the Soviet Army they all held the consensus that there was little hope for liberation.

Complicated as the regional history of Poland was, and difficult as it was, they hated the Russians more than they hated the Germans, they said. Germany was an enemy that wanted conquest; Russia an overlord that wanted their culture.

To the Americans, this presented a problem. If the Poles found the Germans as being "Certainly more tolerable than they will have under their Soviet liberators," what were the intentions of Russia, their ally?

Harriman was daily assessing. For now, there were other priorities. First, the upcoming meeting between Roosevelt and Stalin. Secondly, the outstanding business of the Hungarian Armistice.

* * *

The Heads of State of the two Allies had been scheduled to meet November. However, since the British had come to Moscow last October for an official visit, and Presidential elections in America had been the chief preoccupation in November, Harriman had a hard time fixing on a date with Stalin for the next conference. Stalin refused to leave the Soviet Union.

Yalta, a resort on the Black Sea near Sevastopol was finally the chosen spot for the next conference of the Heads of State. The date was settled for February 2nd, after the President's official Inauguration on January 20th, 1945. Roosevelt would travel by ship to Malta, then fly to Yalta. He would bring Harry Hopkins, Secretary of State Stettinius, Chip Bohlen and the Joint Chiefs of Staff.

Meanwhile, the Hungarians were still waiting for a reply from the Allies as to the terms of the Armistice. Russia had Resolutions. Britain and America had issues.

The terms of the Armistices Agreements with Rumania and Finland had been altered and was a matter of grave concern for Americans. Crafted in Moscow, the terms for both countries had attained the consensus of both Britain and America when signed by Harriman and Kerr, Ambassadors for Britain and America.

In interpreting that Agreement the Russians had defined the amount of reparations owing to be in dollars of a previously determined gold standard. But then deducted in-kind valuations using deflated prices of 1938.

Moreover, while insisting on oil deliveries from Rumania, the Russians were seen taking equipment from American-owned refineries in Rumania citing it as booty. A steel mill was scheduled for dismantling by the Russians, if without success.

Most offensive to America and Britain was the order by the Russians to the Rumanians - handed down in writing, that they turn over all persons, men, women and children of German origin in Rumania to be deported to Russia, including provision of five thousand freight cars for their movement.

No such provision in the Agreement had been signed to that effect by either Harriman or Kerr. The fate of those Germans from Rumania was not known.

Such a directive by the Russians aggrieved the diplomats in Moscow. Finding no merit and being outside the mandate of the Agreements, even if intended as a logistics solution, the leaders of the British and American delegations were deeply troubled. Was the face of Russia changing? What were the underlying intentions?

Meiklejohn's record was reflecting a slow creep of hostility. In Bulgaria, the Russians were delivering unauthorized orders in the name of the Allied Control Commission. "In consequence, the people are led to believe that we are a party to atrocities by the Soviets that bid fair to be of the same character as those committed by the Germans" he said.

Harriman's primacy of Economic Affairs was regressing into Military Affairs. He showed calm, attending dinners; skiing at the Kennan's. Moscow was under snow, draping over them like a blanket. But Harriman was clearly frustrated.

The situation was deteriorating and tension rising. One poorly timed news report revealed how the Soviets prevented the release of one hundred thirty interned American flyers who force-landed in Siberia after raiding Japan. The reason cited by the Russians was that such a release might cause trouble with Japan. This, after an agreement by Stalin in Tehran to enter the war against Japan. For Harriman, these signs were not good.

Spaso House would see one of its working staff leave suddenly. Nelson Newton, who had arrived in Moscow with Secretary Hull in October 1943 and stayed on to help Meiklejohn, was recalled to Washington. Newton had served under Ambassador Joseph Crew when both were interned in Japan, and he could speak Japanese. The President had just appointed Joseph Crew as Undersecretary of State, and Crew cabled Harriman to allow Newton to join him as his Executive Assistant.

Kathleen arranged for an appropriate Farewell, allowing for Harriman to offer his thanks. For assistance with administrative work at Spaso House, Newton was replaced by a Miss Arlene Jacoby.

By mid-January Lillian Hellman was leaving and given a Farewell party by Kathleen at Spaso House. The party included the "cultural elite" of Moscow. In her letter home of January Kathleen wrote "We entertained in a big way last night a farewell, thanks party for Lilian Hellman – all the people who entertained her, plus some members of the cast, directors and what have you, of "The little Foxes" and "Watch on the Rhine"[193]

The locals however, were observed to be in a deplorable state of neglect. Kathleen went on to describe the event of a painter who had painted two portraits of Harriman in water colors. He was elderly, of a small stature, and asked to see where the portraits was hung. Kathleen showed him. "They were in Averell Harriman's room. He wanted to sign his name. Could he say "hardly"? She said No.

"Would 'love' be alright? I still said no and then volunteered that 'best regards' might be appropriate." Being unable to write English, she gave him the words to copy, "unsuccessfully". [194]

In this letter Kathleen also wrote "Can't remember or not if I told you that Tex McCrary [Head of Army Information Services] in all seriousness offered me a job… the letter arrived about Xmas time and the job was to start Jan….As far as I can figure out, he and his General don't agree on many subjects – "[195]

In January United Press Reporters returning from Poland came to Spaso House and much information was being exchanged, and much to report on.

The ground war was over.

One month prior, mid-December, the Germans had advanced through the Ardennes Forest to cut off the Anglo-American forces from their supplies in France and Belgium. It came to be known as the "Battle of the Bulge." At Bastogne, the Americans were relieved on Christmas Day by General Patton with his Third Army from the South.

Also at this time, the weather had allowed for a flying air attack by the Allies, pushing back the Nazis to their original lines. Further, Allied forces advanced to the Rhine, and in gathering other forces, made a final advance to occupy the heart of Germany.

On the Eastern Front, with the Polish question still unsettled, the Soviets finally entered Warsaw after stalling at the Vistula River for three months while watching the Nazi's put down the Polish Underground Army.

Without advance information of this move, the Anglo-American alliances were getting alarmed about the motives behind this Warsaw propulsion. Eisenhower sent his Deputy; the British Air Chief Marshall sent Arthur Tedder to Moscow to inform the Soviets of plans and to garner from the Soviets their intentions.

Tedder arrived on the 15th of January and was met by Ambassador Harriman and General Deane. Generals Bull and Betts arrived by train. Harriman wrote "the Soviet winter offensive on the central front had already started when Tedder saw Stalin on his first day in Moscow." [196]

Stalin and Tedder exchanged information on a number of issues, including the timing of the joint assaults on all fronts to conclude the war. "Stalin said the Red Army had concentrated a force of 150 to 160 divisions for a drive of two months or more, with the ultimate objective of reaching the Oder River."[197]

It left more questions than answers.

* * *

By the third week in January 1945 everyone was preparing for the Conference at Yalta.

Kathleen was going too.

"Becky" their plane was unavailable. So they were to travel by the midnight train tracking across Russia, beyond Orel, then on to Yalta over the mountains by car.

The party consisted of Harriman, Kathleen, Ed. Page, Mrs. Balfour (wife of the British Minister travelling with them) and Meiklejohn.

They had three adjoining compartments, NKVD guards occupying the far end of the car.

Their accommodations were less than ideal, mentioned Meiklejohn. Though adequate, maintenance and management were wanting. A "bucket in the commode in the cabins" served as sanitation facilities. Only at the far end of the car was there a crude toilet and washbasin. The Americans were transported on a freight train.

They remained in their quarters. "3 compartments for the 5 of us." Kathleen suffered from bed- bug bites, and had her bunk fumigated.

They ate their own picnic food -including Kathleen's eggnogs "doused heavily" with Bourbon. "We had to take our own food as Soviet trains don't have Diners, but our cook did well by us – turkey, cold ham, loaves of bread, and we 'have hot water out of the samovar at the end of the car."

The miles logged on. "We saw enough war damage to last me a lifetime. My God but this country has a job on its hands just cleaning up."[198]

They passed moving freight trains loaded with American trucks. One, had Soviet armored vehicles with turrets affixed for assault.

Across the tracks they saw a variety of freight trains of different manufacture; railcars belonging to Germans; Finnish; French and Italian

Companies – all of them idle and docked in the yards of Soviet depots.

Three days of travelling in their cabins showed them the vast landscape of a snow-covered Russia. They passed Kursk, Kharkov and Zaparozphye, then over the narrow strip of land east of the Perekop Peninsula that connected the main with the Crimea.

The train stopped. They were at Jankol, uncertain as to why they had stopped. Slowly they proceeded to Simferopol. From there, the journey was to proceed by car.

Soviet NKVD generals and Foreign Office representatives advised against driving over the mountains now. There was a heavy snowfall.

Harriman would not be deterred. Unaccustomed to such protracted and uncomfortable travel, Harriman was angry with his hosts. He insisted they proceed. They were fifty miles from Yalta.

At the foot of the mountains, the convoy of cars set off in a procession. The ladies, bundled in fur coats; gloves and hats sat together in the rear seats, the men variously distributed.

The roads, covered with mixtures of slush, ice and snow suddenly climbed into steep-sided twists, turns and switchbacks. With caution they proceeded, window-shield wipers beating with ferocity in diminishing visibility; side windows sealing up with accumulating ice crystals. They gained altitude.

Finally peaking over the mountain ridges, they felt their descent down the other side of the mountain following sharp inclines and steep drops, the sea before them. Slowly, the procession weaved its way down to the Black Sea coast.

Nobody was more relieved to arrive at Yalta than Harriman. Officials of the NKVD hosted a "respectable meal" for them and the party moved to Livadia Palace which was to be the American headquarters for the Yalta Conference. Here, the President would stay.

Livadia Palace had been newly built by the last Czar Nicholas II on the site of an older palace. Kathleen would write of it. Redolent with the opulence of a world long gone, the premises were lovely, if teeming with Rumanian prisoners cleaning and pruning the grounds and shrubs. The three story structure, complete with roads and driveways overlooked the bay of Yalta from a peninsula. The view was stunning. Two hundred and sixty Americans were anticipated. The place was guarded with Red Army Guards, each holding rifle and bayonets.

Close by was Vorontsov Villa, an estate of equal stature which was to host the British Delegation, including Prime Minister Churchill.

For Kathleen, this was a new meeting with the Prime Minister. She was no longer a London guest in his country. She was in the company of her champions. "At Chequers, the P.M. holds forth and everyone else listens, but here there's just general conversation as far as I'm concerned no sweating and wondering 'What the hell shall I talk about next.'" Later she added "The most fun night was when Marshall and King dined instead of some of the usual political hangers-on. As you may have gathered, I've taken a great shine to Marshall."
[199]

All seemed in order, except for the commodity of bathrooms. Only one bathroom was available per floor. So for personal grooming, they asked for pitchers; water buckets and wash basins for each room. Harriman's suite was so filled with sunlight that he insisted it be reversed with the room reserved for the President whose quarters were along the darker parts of the palace with less view of the sea. They made the switch.

A Russian, Mr. Chuvakian presented himself for accommodation within the Palace. As a Soviet Foreign Office official assigned as liaison officer, he insisted on being housed amongst the Americans. They agreed, finally assigning him an annex – a room in the midst of their own American Secret Service personnel.

The Americans, feeling less like they were in the trustworthy arms of an ally than an adversary, took all precautions and anticipated any eventuality. Preparation was ample and in fully supply.

Signals and Communications were set up using an American electric generator plant so that they would not be dependent on the Soviets for power. A Radio teletype circuit was set up to the U.S. Navy communications ship CATOCTIN at Sevastopol, which would transmit to Washington.

On January 27th 1945, two cars drove up to take Mr. Harriman; Mrs. Balfour and Meiklejohn to Saki airfield. The second car was full of NKVD. They stopped briefly to inspect Simferopol, a possible rest stop for the President en-route to Yalta, then all proceeded to the airfield.

There stood "Becky" their plane, ready for duty to Malta. Besides her was the President's C-54 also waiting to transport them to Malta to join Roosevelt and Churchill in pre-conference meetings.

Kathleen would await the return of all parties to Yalta for the Conference.

In a letter to Miss Marshall from Yalta, Kathleen wrote "We left Moscow about 10 days ago to come down here to Yalta and get things in order for the conference. Ave's now left to join the big wigs and I'm just sitting, relaxing and enjoying myself."[200]

Kathleen described the palaces at which each of the delegations were staying in the poetic vein of memorial vistas. "Pre-revolution Yalta was the resort spot of Czars and Grand Dukes. So palaces were plentiful…The palace where the Pres. Is to live was built by the last Czar –overlooks the sea, with high snowcapped mountains behind. Beautiful old tress and grounds…All the Moscow hotels have been stripped of their staffs; furniture and plates, china, kitchen utensils to look after us. I wonder what the poor folk in Moscow are doing…"

Referring perhaps to the big picture, she added "I never quite realized that so many things could go wrong so many ways."[201]

* * *

The President's plane "The Sacred Cow" touched down. Harriman and his party were onboard - its accommodations vastly superior to anything they had travelled on. The flight from Yalta lasted eight and half hours, avoiding Cyprus and Crete, (still under German occupation and firing at airborne craft), and landing at Luqa Airfield at Malta in the evening.

Staff and crew were taken to RAF quarters. Harriman, to the surprise of everyone, hopped over to Caserta, Italy, and returned the next day in General Anderson's B-52 with Anthony Eden. He stayed with the Lt Governor of Malta and Mr. D. Campbell. There, British and American Joint Chiefs of Staff began consultations on war strategy on January 30th 1945.

The Harbor was already full of ships. Mainly American and British, they counted amphibious ships and submarines. Within the next seventy-two hours, Malta would receive three additional U.S. cruisers; two British cruisers; a British aircraft carrier, destroyers, landing craft and merchant ships. The airport was piling up with C-54s; British Yorks and other transports bringing in admirals, generals and dignitaries for the Conference.

Meiklejohn quartered on an LST 602, and was entertained ashore by her officers at the home of Marchesa Scicluna, at her "beautiful villa."

The next day, January 31st, Lt Cmdr. Meiklejohn went to the ship HMS SIRIUS and was piped aboard. He was stunned. He had worked for Harriman continuously either indoors, underground; in transit or *Incognito* for the tight security that attended the position of his boss since the days of his hire by the Union Pacific, and here he was piped aboard! More importantly, he was informed that waiting for him below decks was Harriman; Stettinius, the Secretary of State; Hopkins, White House Chief Bohlen and others of the President's staff.[202]

Later on the SIRIUS, Meiklejohn received a cable from the wife of the Captain of the USS CANBERRA. It came through the office of Secretary of State Stettinius informing him that his brother's ship the USS CANBERRA had been torpedoed and the stern blown off. It was in dry dock in the Admiralty Islands, his brother had survived and would be returning home for three months.

* * *

On February 2nd, 1945 President Roosevelt arrived at Malta on the USS QUINCY and was met by Harriman. Determined not to fuel suspicions that the British and Americans conferred without Stalin, Roosevelt left immediately for Yalta.

Stalin arrived at Villa Koreis, Yalta on February 4th1945. Also of Czarist era, the structure was located close by.

The Yalta Conference opened to a wide range of press and representatives including Major Tyson of the State Department delegation, and others. It was to mark a new era.

Photographed amongst Clark Kerr and Harriman was a Russian General Gromyko.

Another man, an American, was listed as Alger Hiss.

The Conference progressed calmly, with the three leaders conferring amongst themselves, and the Joint Chiefs making strategic plans for the end of the war.

The evenings, in cool weather, were beautiful under bright blue skies. The delegations variously talked and rested at appropriate times for comfort and convenience. Visually, the Heads of State looked calm, if fatigued, their faces drawn and resigned.

* * *

At Latiava Palace, Kathleen and Mrs. Boettiger were dining with President Roosevelt almost every night in an informal way.

The President, though clearly pale-faced, appeared to be happy to have them participating. The pace of the conference was steady.

By Friday however, the meetings jolted into full swing – each group taking notes as if in duplication. The work of recording all that was agreed escalated to a feverish pitch, such that only Meiklejohn's documents remained complete as official communiques. His documents alone became the formal Protocols and Agreements of the decisions made at Yalta.

Clearly, accountability was the primary objective, implying that these Agreements were binding commitments by each nation.

This time, there was a high degree of preoccupation with making the Agreements: They should be specific and remain within the confines of their intent; they should leave no doubt as to what should and should not be understood from them. Most importantly were the stated authorities behind the Agreements. There would be no bending of the understandings or local "addendums" like the appropriated Armistices of Rumania...

Dinners and courtesies were arranged by each of the delegations for their leaders: Roosevelt's dinner was scheduled for the 4th at Livadia; Stalin's dinner at Koreis was hosted on the 8th; and Churchill's came later at Vorontsov on the 10th.

Roosevelt, his political election won, needed Russia to enter the war against Japan. While the matters of Europe were still before them, he used the experience of his recent re-elections to express how Americans, comprising of an inclusive culture of immigrants, would be expecting accountability of their kin and assets in Europe. Clearly, there was more on his mind now.

Kathleen and Mrs. Boettiger attended most of the official dinners, as did the Prime Minister Winston Churchill and his daughter Mrs. Vic Oliver. In London, they had become acquainted, and Kathleen was now her friend.

Other occasions had quiet dinners. In her letter to Mary from Yalta, Kathleen wrote "Well, I've at last had my wish and met the President. It seems sort of odd it would be in Russia…. He's absolutely charming – easy to talk to with a lovely sense of humor. He's in fine form, very happy about accommodations all set for the Best."[203]

Kathleen observed "In true Soviet fashion, he [Stalin] sat in the middle of a long table with the Pres. On his right and Churchill on his left, Molotov Eden and Stettinius opposite. At times, Stalin just sat back and smiled like a benign old man, something I'd never thought possible." [204]

Before the end of the official dinner however, even with Anna and Sarah seated at the great table, it fell to Kathleen to deliver a toast of thanks in Russian.

"All are going home very happy. By tonight only the political people will remain and it looks as though all 'round it's been a good conference – a hellova long one too. Nerves have not become frayed, which is amusing." [205]

Generally, there was a glowing feeling that there had been solid resolutions. The Conference ended with all three Heads of State signing blank documents for media photographers while official papers were typed and properly prepared for signature.

Translations, corrections and small details to effect continuity amongst the three nations and their Heads of State required meticulous paperwork. The task was copious, and it fell largely upon Harriman's staff to accomplish the job.

The gatherings dispersed Monday 12th 1945. The President's plane left at about noon to join the USS QUINCY in Egypt with an escort of planes. This conference that was to define the terms of concluding the war came to be known as the Yalta Conference of the "The Big Three."

Stettinius' C-54 plane was next to take off with his party flying to Moscow for a day. On board with him were Harriman and Kathleen. "Becky" their plane followed with the rest of Harriman's staff;

both planes arriving in Moscow at about the same time. All but the clerks would be staying at Spaso House for more work.

In all, the Yalta Conference had been exhausting. Especially for Roosevelt. His party went home elated, putting a positive spin on what had been achieved.

The Far East Agreement was considered a success by Admiral Leahy. Harry Hopkins, the President's chief of staff who had been ill much of the time, thought the meetings meant a victory. Stalin had agreed to join the war against Japan.

Ambassador Harriman and Joseph Stalin
"Have we got a deal?"
Yalta Conference, 1945

Courtesy Library of Congress

Harriman was not so sure. He considered the Red Army's offensive through Poland nothing less than a de facto settlement.

He had arrived at Yalta early, worried that the President was unprepared for the gravity of what was unfolding. It was agreed that he, Hopkins, Stettinius and Roosevelt would talk in Malta. But the President had other ideas.

Moreover, Harriman was excluded in Yalta from the discussions on Poland. The Curzon line was the main issue. Roosevelt asked Stalin to modify it, Churchill concurred. Churchill held for the exiled Polish government still in London.

Harriman was less concerned about territorial lines than he was about establishing a legitimate government in Poland, even if an interim government was to hold up until elections could be accomplished.

Stalin, when confronted with this at Yalta, had taken a recess. When he returned he declared that the London Poles were a military threat and were unwelcome in Warsaw. He said an interim government was ridiculous. The session ended abruptly, the tension not lost on Harriman.

Three days later, Stalin agreed to an amendment of the borders, but insisted that the Lublin regime remain in place.

Harriman drafted a counterproposal in favor of giving the Underground Poles in Warsaw some agency, extending later to include the London Poles. It would be a provisional government, and it could include Russians.

Nothing came of it after hours of discussion. They could not agree on attendance of Talks, let alone representation by non-Lublin regime approved candidates. Especially for Mikolajczyk sitting in London as head of the former Polish government - a man popular and recognized as a political candidate in Poland. It was "hours of unreal, repetitious wrangling" offered Kennan in his Memoirs. Harriman suspected the Russians had an agenda.

"The Yalta Agreement, Molotov insisted, had mandated a government built upon the regime [Russo-Lublin] already in Place." [206]

Without a provisional government for Poland acceptable to Molotov, invitations to Yalta for the London Poles was considered futile.

Harriman returned to Moscow frustrated. As the Anglo-American sections in Moscow pursued the matter with the Russians, relations broke down gravely, quickly, and with little regard for Lend Lease which had supplied them - treating the Americans more like a malevolent than an Ally.

Roosevelt was left with a political indication of chilling premonition, and he instructed Harriman to acknowledge the US Military Missions of Moscow above those of Economic Affairs.

Harriman immediately complied. He did so with ceremonial Commendations to the US Military Chiefs for their effort at the Embassy, a gesture that the Soviets did not fail to observe.

* * *

A new coldness took over.

Kathleen, getting the gist of things wrote to Mary February 16th, 1945 "…It seems odd now to be back reading all the news stories about the Crimea Conf. I'm beginning to wonder was I really there?"[207]

The Russians shut the door on Poland. They broke their promise to repatriate American war-prisoners freed in Poland, even as several U.S. Army Air Corps officers who were released Prisoners of War showed up in Moscow after hiking 600 miles. Harriman was outraged.

Harriman asked the Russians formally for the use of American planes based at Poltava to pick up liberated prisoners. Stalin refused, and denied others from visiting, or checking on them.

One medical officer was allowed entry into Poland, but he was restricted to Lublin. At this point, Harriman informed Roosevelt that not only was Stalin preventing aid and assistance to liberated Americans in Poland, but that the *numbers* of Americans behind those enemy lines had been misrepresented. Roosevelt appealed to Stalin. Stalin refused. [208]

A retaliatory order was given to Eisenhower to restrict the movements of Soviet officers in France assisting Red Army soldiers liberated from German camps.

Now a stream of escaped prisoners showed up at Spaso House. They were sleeping in the Billiards room; Kathleen shifting furniture about to accommodate the various needs of the house. Many of the prisoners coming in held reports on what the fighting Fronts were like, and Harriman saw to it that they were shipped out of Russia on "Becky" their plane, even as the temperature in Russia plunged to below zero.

Soviets on the Fronts had no clear instructions about dealing with American prisoners. They were being taken to other collections points and held, then deported.

At Roosevelt's prodding, a Mr. Flynn was sent to Moscow to "persuade Stalin to make some friendly gestures towards religion." In America, the concept of sending aid to Russia where religious toleration was denied had critics.

The Soviets had made an effort to reinstate the Orthodox Church, even creating a new Patriarch. But like all else, it was sponsored by the state and named the Commissariat of Religion, with a Soviet Commissar in charge.

Harriman was uncertain about the future. Their war Ally, the Russians, were slipping away. It took its toll.

Kathleen noted ruefully "Now we're quieted down. A couple of nights with 12 hours and I'm all fixed up but Ave's laid low today with another attack of gypie tummy. We're entertaining tonight – the French – so I must get dressed..."[209]

* * *

Harriman's next directives was to set up the San Francisco Conference in April, 1945.

Following Agreements made at Yalta, the next item to accomplish was the creation of the United Nations. Designed to oversee peace and compliance of civil liberties, it would need the consensus of many Nations. Russia had agreed to be a participant, if with special privileges.

Roosevelt had been adamant. Wishing it to be his legacy and citing WWI Peace Agreements that failed to prevent WWII, he wanted to make a show of liberal democracy. At Conferences with Roosevelt, Stalin himself had lamented on the recurring ambitions of the Germans.

However, the Russians had expected a greater reward for the price of becoming a field Army Ally. They aspired to been perceived as a dominant power and they resisted the kind of non-exclusive participation that Roosevelt envisioned for this world organization. Invitations to participate were sent out to all liberated nations…

The creation of a peace-keeping organization for the upholding of civil rights worldwide might well have masked aspirations of deeper dimension, especially those nations with expansionism in mind since the turn of the century. The creation of a "United Nations" had its critics.

Amongst them France. France accepted the invitation to attend the Conference at San Francisco only at the very last minute. They had tried to achieve higher status, but their demands were dismissed by the Soviets. As far as Stalin was concerned, DeGaule had over-reached his mark.

In Moscow, the mood had chilled as the Russians turned increasingly to face domestic challenges. With an Army returning from war, Russia had to account for its enormous disparities, let alone accommodate foreign demands...

Harriman meanwhile, had practical matters of administration to tend to, and he lobbied with Vishinski for better housing accommodations for the American staff.

Further, there was outstanding work to achieve related to Yalta. Amongst other things negotiated at Yalta was a list of requirements from the Soviets in exchange for declaring war on Japan, as promised.

Russian decisions were now almost entirely preoccupied with their Army, their diplomatic posture outspoken and increasingly defensive. As an ally, they claimed, they had carried the greater burden of the war.

Neither did the situation on Poland ameliorate. On the contrary, the Soviets were allowing the Lublin Government to consolidate its position.

Citing critics as "fascists" the Commission on Poland as set up at the Yalta Conference insuring free elections would now have no sway.

In his nightly cables, it was all Harriman could do to warn Washington.

Spaso House, US Ambassador's Residence Moscow, Winter 1944

Courtesy of Library of Congress

March had its challenges as clear differences emerged on matters of doctrine.

In mid-March, a cable was received to share with the Soviets. Italy was ending resistance. However it fell short of the demand for unconditional surrender, especially since Field Marshal Kesselring objected. Unfortunately, the matter led to some acrimonious diplomatic exchanges between Stalin and Roosevelt, which Harriman later described in his report.

Further, the Americans observed that Dr. Eduard Benes, President of Czechoslovakia in Exile was in Tehran and scheduled to fly to Moscow. He had made a deal with the Soviets, agreeing to their "intervention policies" in the composition of his government in Czechoslovakia. That, plus the gift of Lend-Lease equipment given by the Americans! His instructions were to proceed to Czechoslovak to set up this government quickly before the end of March.

Kathleen, while not involved in matters of policy, was never far from the center of the activity at Space House and would add her touch of cheer.

Spaso House was busy with people travelling through. One was Bill Duncan, Labor Attaché at the Australian Delegation.

Whereas before he had endorsed the socialist revolution, Duncan now said he witnessed factories guarded by armed troops; farms operated by prison laborers under machine gun towers and he would return to Australia to apologize for his former "liberal" view.

At Spaso House they could only laugh in sympathy. "I wish Mrs. Roosevelt, Henry Wallace and the rest of the American "parlor pinks" could have the same experience" said Meiklejohn in his notes.
210

The Polish question lingered, Elbridge Durbrow arrived in Moscow from the Department of State along with a three American newspaper editors. Those liberals in America who had supported the war were at the forefront of questions.

It was Ed Flynn's opinion that unless a resolution was found of the Rumanian and Polish situations, the U.S. Senate might not approve the World Security Organization, Roosevelt's future United Nations.

Further, in Flynn's general recounting of the White House, he felt that the President was preoccupied with putting his house in order, his health less than fine. Establishing his place in posterity with a Library at Hyde Park and asserting the World Security Organization as the solution to lasting world peace was his priority.

For those in the Moscow Embassy, such notions, while understandable, were met with dismay. Their President was slipping from the scene. Harriman was getting worried.

Spaso House and the Embassy was crammed. The Soviets refused them bigger accommodations, even space in Hotels.

Meiklejohn's Day room became a main gathering place. Before the end of February, they had received a Thank You letter from Lady Frances Balfour who had travelled on the train to Yalta with them. "My dear Averell and Kathleen. What fun our trip was – I cannot thank you enough for all your kindness – it was a wonderful "grand finale". How I long to hear about Yalta and whether everybody was satisfied with their rooms and beds..."[211]

* * *

In her letter to Mary March 8th, Kathleen remained optimistic "The war is going wonderfully well again now, what with the offensive on the Western Front. Gosh isn't it exciting." [212]

However, Kathleen was not without awareness.

"But the news is slightly dampened here by our gallant allies [Soviets] who at the moment are being most bastard-like. Averell is very busy – what with Poland, PWs and I guess the Balkans."[213]

Meantime, Spaso House was having a snow melt. Snow on the balconies was shoveled off to prevent puddles and leaks inside the house.

Harriman lobbied for the release of Americans held at Odessa, a collection point for prisoners of war held behind enemy lines in occupied Soviet territories. One was Captain Richard Rossbach, son-in-law of Henry Morgenthau, Secretary of the Treasury.

Secretary Morgenthau arrived at Spaso House after travelling himself to Russia. He had toured the Front, revealing that the soviet front lines were not orderly or even property billeted. He described Russian troops having to find and forage for food nearby. Worse, many Americans were often robbed by beleaguered Soviets troops, causing Americans to simply disperse from Odessa, he said.

This was the cause of some embarrassment to the Soviets in Moscow unable to compete with the Allies' armies; and remained the reason for keeping them sequestered from intermingling.

Harriman called on the Red Cross to enquire about reports of returning soldiers. They too revealed disorderly conduct and warned of danger.

Mr. Shirk was called in to report from Odessa. The disbanding of Armies was now a menace.

Meanwhile, the situation in Poland was deteriorating to such a degree that in the minds of the Polish, the Americans and Soviets were already enemies.

This worried Harriman. Bad enough the report of friendly countries, how now would the Russians behave toward the defeated? This, while transportation, relocation and delivery of returning personnel caused log jams; flight delays; moratoriums and misunderstandings. The situation with the Soviets caused such duress that outward hostility between the Americans and the Russians was palpable.

"Ed Flynn is back from his Leningrad trip and due to leave day after tomorrow. He's delightful, not at all like what I thought a party boss would be. We gave a party, about 60 people for

Flynn last night, for him to return hospitality to the Russians and foreigners who'd entertained him. His list we padded nicely with genial people of other sorts and the result was quite a success."[214]

Kathleen's life was full, and she was without fear in Moscow. She engaged with the mission with greater support, sensing a failing trajectory in relations. "At the moment I'm involved in learning something about Russian history, which has always been a complete blank."[215]

On March 25th a meeting was arranged. The British Ambassador; Harriman and their military representatives went to visit Stalin with a message directly from General Eisenhower, Allied Supreme Commander in Europe: It was their hope that a coordination of the Allied and Soviet forces would work together on the closing drive on Germany. Eisenhower stated that he intended to by-pass Berlin and focus on the industrial Ruhr to end the war in Europe.

Eisenhower later informed Tedder and Prime Minister Churchill that Stalin should find some acclaim in the seizing of Berlin also.

In April, Mrs. Clementine Churchill, wife of the British Prime Minister came to Moscow. She represented the Red Cross. During her visit she had lunch at Spaso House with Harriman and Kathleen. While they found her purpose in Moscow somewhat incongruous, the Americans understood that it defined for the Soviets the clarity that they were being observed.

Two days later, Marshall Tito arrived in Moscow. He was given Yugoslavia to run in much the same manner as Czechoslovakia.

By now, with personal accounts of those who knew the members of the Embassy staffs, it was clear the Russians viewed the Americans and British with some inimical intentions.

Suspicion and defensive accusations of spying followed.

All the goodwill that had been achieved at Yalta was in shambles.

* * *

Previously, on March 20th, Kathleen had responded to a letter from Pam. It was all business. The world was now on a different footing, the lines well drawn. "We got a letter from you last night, plus a wire that you'd received mine, all of which spurs me to get some more news off to you."[216]

There was reference to a mutual friend. A letter was received by Kathleen from General Eaker from Headquarters Mediterranean Allied Air Forces.

Kathleen told Pam in patronizing tones "Ira was due to come here for a quick business trip, but while we were struggling getting his plane permission to come, visa etc., we got a wire from him saying that he was changing jobs … hence couldn't come. Our air general here figures that it's Deputy Chief of Air Forces in Washington. We know for sure that it's a Washington job, which, though perhaps a technical promotion, Ira will hate (unless he's recently changed his mind on that score). Such is life. … Spring hit us today for the first time and it's certainly…nice."[217]

Pamela's social world had included the Churchill Club, an informal place where people of importance intermingled and spoke freely, including those of the bomber commands. It was known that Prime Minister Churchill, aware of Pam's affair with Anderson asked her for information on key bombing strategies. This, she channeled through Beaverbrook.

Kathleen wanted to end old assumptions. "As you've probably gathered, the honeymoon after Yalta was short lived …We have a full house numbering 13 guests…I went to a manikin show the other day…Tonight Masaruk came to dine, just he, Averell and I and the two of them having talking, me sitting and knitting."[218]

* * *

Relations between the Anglo-Americans and the Soviets were deteriorating.

The Americans accused the Russians of failing to perform on their signed Agreements including consultation with the Allies in the case of Rumania and Bulgaria as required in the Declaration of Liberated Europe.

The "Commission on Poland" had rendered ineffective the establishment of a new Polish government.

Other complaints were lodged.

Americans were being denied liberation in Soviet occupied territories. No air base had been established in Hungary. No American inspectors were allowed into German torpedo experimental labs in Gydnia. No access into Germany had been allowed from the Eastern Front.

From the Soviets, the matter of attending the San Francisco Conference was refused by Molotov. The World Security Organization (United Nations) was to be created and the Soviets objected to its conditions.

Worse of all, Stalin told Roosevelt he was a liar; accusing the President and his staff of being traitors.

A media campaign ensued in Russia showing only Soviet victories without Allied help.

Harriman was deeply frustrated.

At the heart of the turmoil was the issue of entering the war against Japan. For the Soviets, their focus was seemingly only Europe.

April 12th started as a bright day at Spaso House, albeit a farewell party for John Melby who was transferring out and stationing in San Francisco.

The party was almost over when Kathleen walked in and took Harriman aside to the Blue Room. They came back together with a very "somber" expression. The music was turned off, the party closed, and everyone sent home. It was 1.00 A.M. and the radio announced that Roosevelt had died of a cerebral hemorrhage.

Harriman called the Soviets to inform them. Two hours later, Molotov showed up at Spaso House to express his condolences.

If there was one thing the Soviets had come to appreciate from Harriman and his President was respect. Harriman had cultivated not only trust, but sincere understanding of their ways, always showing respect, even as they diverged.

By 7.00 AM the next morning Harriman was seeing General Deane and Embassy Third Secretary Melby off.

Spaso House was besieged by a diplomatic colony calling and sending condolences. That evening, Harriman went to see Stalin.

He petitioned that Molotov go to San Francisco via Washington to show his support for Truman, the next American President of the United States. Stalin agreed, if Truman would invite him, he said in a conciliatory tone.

But the meeting revealed other matters.

In his Memo to the Secretary of State delivered on April 20th, Harriman recounted the events leading up to the San Francisco meeting when he visited Stalin in Moscow. "It was obvious the Russians after talking with …do not like the agreement with respect to Poland as well as they did at Yalta. This attitude is based principally on their belief that the Lublin Government could be kept effectively under Soviet domination, but that this would be difficult if any of the old Polish leaders had to be reckoned with. It seemed evident that Mikolajczyk and the other old leaders would be welcomed by the majority of Poles, and thus the Lublin group would be weakened."[219]

Spaso House held a Memorial service for the President. It gave the Russians an opportunity to officially present their condolences.

Within days, the American delegations from China descended on Spaso House.

Molotov was going to San Francisco, along with the Chinese. Harriman visited Stalin once again, and all made ready to leave for the United States.

Molotov was to take Hurley's C-54 to Washington DC via the Alsip route across Siberia and Alaska. Harriman was to stop in Washington then join them at the San Francisco Conference, and would return May 27th to Moscow. His planes were to fly via Bari, Casablanca, Azores and Stephenville.

Kathleen was going also.

"Becky" showed up at the airport, freshly buffed up. Kathleen loved the new look.

Also coming onboard were Elbridge Durbrown; Archibald Clark Kerr; British Ambassador with his Aide and interpreter. One Embassy wife was on board, as was a corporate member of the Columbia Broadcasting System.

The flight was uneventful but achieved record time for its transatlantic flight. They were met in Washington D.C. by a crowd including Mrs. Harriman; Meiklejohn's mother, Chip Bohlen and others.

"Becky" the plane, having achieved her maximum flying record, was to be retired. This had been their last voyage on "Becky."

11.

Iwo Jima in the Bonin Islands had been invaded. B-29 bombers bases were engaged in bombing Tokyo and the mainland of Japan. The battles of Okinawa in the Ryukyus Island was underway. In Washington, the condition was considered deplorably unacceptable.

By the end of the war, it was clear that inter-allied discrepancies were over. National interests, political doctrines and industrial ambitions were yet never far below the surface of victory. If freedom and liberations had been achieved, economic growth and stability were paramount. These were the next objectives.

Stalin was in the fray achieving the same purpose for the Russians, if for communism. A post-war world was about expanding national boundaries as well as advancing economic interests.

* * *

The Harriman staff were installed in the elegant office building of the State Department, off Constitution Avenue in Washington DC.

In honor-bound tradition, as required of all ministers and senior officials of a previous Administration, Harriman officially offered his resignation April 20th, 1945 to the new President of the United States.

His resignation was denied.

Harriman went to the White House on April 22nd 1945, and he was asked by President Harry Truman to return to Moscow as his Ambassador.

In the official Minutes of meetings at the Secretary of State's office, Harriman outlined the present position of the Soviet Union.

Harriman then left for San Francisco for the World Security Organization meeting. He took a commercial flight.

Kathleen had gone home to New York.

* * *

It was good to be home.

With his mother installed in an apartment just outside Washington, Meiklejohn was joined by his brother David coming in for leave. While there, he and his friends got together to celebrate at the Carlton Hotel. His date was Blanche Haring; his brother David and Dorothy Rutherford was there; Gay Melius and his fiancée, George Holderer and "Boo."

In Washington, Meiklejohn took David along to inspect the new plane assigned to Ambassador Harriman for his transportation. Built by Consolidated Aircraft factory in San Diego, it was a C-87, converted for modern executive accommodations.

Nothing less than a luxury line transport considered better to "kept overseas lest it draw adverse attention," and it was "out of this world. Enormous clear windows, an ice box, a galley, an office, card tables, venetian blinds, seating for sixteen or sleep eleven, the interior was in yellow and grey."[220]

A trial run was scheduled for the next day, and David got a free ride to New York on April 27th, 1945. From there David would stay at their family home in Westchester.

Before the end of the month, Meiklejohn became engaged to be married. He took his mother and his fiancée to New York where he shopped for an appropriate engagement ring, Kathleen as advisor. A few days of rest and recreation followed, including dancing for all of them at the New York Biltmore Hotel.

On May 2nd, Kathleen called Meiklejohn to inform him that her father was returning to in two days. He would be needing Meiklejohn in Washington.

Harriman's return was delayed. For his staff, the days of waiting in Washington were passed with general office duties and social evening outings.

On May 7th, 1945 Germany surrendered. Stalin would argue for a surrender in Berlin. Next day, Harriman sent word that he would spend two days in Washington, then go to New York.

The news that came back with Harriman from San Francisco was not good.

In his Memorandum of Conversations attended by Secretary of State Stettinius; Molotov; Ambassador Gromyko; Pavlov and Bohlen at San Francisco, Harriman reported that Molotov had come to see the Secretary of State to raise a number of points. Also, that he wished to be directly informed on all developments and arrangements affecting the Conference.

At hand would also be the final Amendments to the Dumbarton Oaks Agreements.

Molotov's issues rested on the question of the four Chairmen of the UN Conference [China, plus Allies] "since his government felt that this would establish before the other nations the principle of equality of the sponsoring powers".[221]

It was the held position of the Soviets that Allied superiority over other nations should steer the missions of the post-war United Nations.

Roosevelt's vision, on the contrary, was to establish an open and democratic representation by all nations being equal.

To the Soviets, this squandered their political capital as an Ally.

The situation in Moscow had not been alleviated at all. Molotov and Chip Bohlen travelled back together and discussed the option of having Harry Hopkins go to Moscow to talk with Stalin "to arrest the deterioration in the Soviet-

American relationships since the Yalta Conference."

Truman agreed, and though in delicate health, Hopkins agreed to accompany them back to Moscow. Further, Harriman urged the President to hold another Conference of the three heads of state as soon as possible. "Potsdam" was to take effect in July 1945.

Kathleen was returning to Moscow with her father.

Mrs. Harriman, Mary Fisk (Harriman's eldest daughter; General Ira Eaker and others came to see them off again to Moscow in their new plane. Travelling on the new plane bound for Moscow were Harriman, Kathleen, Colonel Kirkendall (AUS), David Henry (Embassy Third Secretary,) and Lt. Cdr. Meiklejohn.

They took off. The modern marvel of the B-24 bomber roared into altitude, ambient cabin pressure unfaltering.

In flight it was a fabulously outfitted plane for Ministers of State. Having endured travel for four years over dangerous territory in older crafts; dingy airports; unscheduled quarters and bug-infested trains with little regard to comfort or clock, these accommodations were worth savoring. They marveled at windows ports that gave them a bird's eye view of places they recognized - including the USS CANBERRA spotted in dry dock at Boston by Meiklejohn.

By the time they were over Newfoundland, Kathleen, Meiklejohn and Wright were unpacking equipment for the office; making bunks from leather drop-down couches and private cabins with newly provisioned sheets, blankets and pillows!

Crossing high above the Atlantic, they discovered that they had wash rooms and a kitchen. "It was a new experience to lie in a comfortable bed reading a magazine and watching the world roll by below" wrote Meiklejohn.

This being May, and with short-duration nights at northern latitudes eastward, they enjoyed eggs, oranges and milk for breakfast...

Kathleen, Wright and Meiklejohn helped with the chores. Of course, there was no steward "but we have considerable fun doing the housekeeping ourselves and will probably keep at it."

The improvement signified the new political world of their next mission. When attaining 1400 feet altitude, they flew south to avoid icing, and they reached Bovingdon, England in luxury and safety.

At landing, they were greeting by Pam Churchill, citing the English people as being in mourning over the loss of President Roosevelt.

Harriman and Kathleen were driven by their driver Smith directly to the Prime Minister's House for dinner with Winston Churchill and his wife, Clementine. The mood was somber.

While officially presenting their nation's condolences, Churchill had decided against attending the Roosevelt funeral, his absence a reflection of the deterioration of the friendship between the two leaders. Roosevelt, he thought privately, had been cavalier.

Harriman observed that all was not well. Not only was Churchill's health impaired, but the world was awaking to the destitution of Europe; the atrocities of the holocaust; the spread of communism; the awful damages inflicted upon Germany and now even some internal government disquiet.

Winston Churchill had worked hard. Less the apologist, he was disappointed, and with lingering sores. Especially with Roosevelt as recently as Yalta when Roosevelt made the mistake of informing Stalin that he planned to withdraw all troops from Europe, leaving Churchill to speak for the remnants - and who "fought like a tiger" to gain for France dominance in a post-war Europe. Plus, Roosevelt had been disingenuous with his remarks about Poland as someone "'coming from America'"

Thus, it was left to Harriman to deliver to Churchill the message, from Roosevelt's successor Harry Truman, of "how greatly he would personally value the opportunity" of meeting with him at Potsdam.

The next morning, Harriman and his party took off from Bovingdon Airport for Paris, adding Joe Evans of *NEWSWEEK* to the party.

When landing at Paris, the plane had superseded the notice of its arrival, such that Harriman got on the phone and made his own schedule of appointments for the afternoon. He discovered that he could use his new plane as he had used his railcar, as a working depot.

A car arrived to take them to the Ritz on the Place Vendome, and the party was joined by Harry Hopkins and his wife; Chip Bohlen, and Lovett, Assistant Secretary of War for Air.

Harriman and Hopkins lunched with General Eisenhower May 25, 1945; had tours and dinners out while also packing to proceed to Moscow the next morning. One passenger, Colonel Kirkendall, failed to appear in time for the flight. Harriman was not impressed by tardiness.

They flew directly to Moscow over Reims in France by way of Luxembourg, a new flight plan. However, when Harriman and Hopkins began querying the navigator Brodsky for city names, it became clear they were lost. The navigator said they were over Poznan, Poland. Harriman said they were over Berlin.

They were flying low enough to observe the ruins of Berlin, a city devastated. They landed near Warsaw at Torun, picked up a signal from a Russian navigator that oriented them north to the Neris River, and flew over snow-covered terrain to land at Moscow. Vishinski and other Foreign Service personnel had come out to greet them.

They drove straight to Spaso House and rediscovered a beautiful budding of Spring in Moscow. The Hopkins, Harrimans, Bohlen, Ed Page and Meiklejohn were the only residents of Spaso House.

* * *

Kathleen was glad to be back. On their return to Moscow it was clear that Kathleen Harriman's position in Moscow was established as a significant contributor.

She received a letter from General Ismay, who had delivered for Kathleen a letter to Pam "Yours of February 13th, enclosing a letter for Pam, only reached me last week, as I did not accompany the Prime Minister to Cairo…. I saw all too little of you and Averell in the Crimea. It was maddening that we lived so far apart and were so pre-occupied with Conference business."[222]

Harry Hopkins and his new wife remained in Moscow until June 7th during which time he and Harriman had evening meetings with Stalin, six in all. They were working sessions. Dinners included Kathleen and Mrs. Hopkins.

Kathleen found Mrs. Hopkins easy to entertain since she was a nurse, and she visited multiple Russian hospitals. "We had 3 days of concentrated sightseeing – hospitals etc., and since then have done mild motoring, sightseeing, sitting in the sun and then of course going to the theater come evening."[223]–

Harriman took the time to write about the meetings. A number of issues were covered for the end of the war, including the termination of the Lend-Lease program to the USSR. They argued on many occasions, but mainly they negotiated on topics needing resolution, including reparations from Germany and its allies, and the Allied Control Council in Berlin.

Also the political aspects of China as Russia entered the war against Japan. Here, Stalin set a date, August 8th for entering the Pacific war. Peaceful arrangements were to be made with Chiang Kai-Shek's government regarding crossing their territories in Manchuria to do so.

Hopkins however, could not move Stalin on decisions that reversed Soviet agreements made in Yalta. There would be no coalition government for the people of Poland. The matter was discussed at length in Harriman's book.

The matter of Japan was becoming critical. Previously, the Americans had agreed to supply and provision Russian troops in Manchuria in their effort against Japan.

In his cable to the President, Hopkins reported "Last night Harriman and I saw Stalin and Molotov for the third time. By August 8 the Soviet Army will be properly deployed on the Manchurian positions." And, "The Marshall repeated his statement made at Yalta that the Russian people must have a good reason for going to war [against Japan] and that depended on China's willingness to agree to the proposals made at Yalta."[224]

The matter of China's willingness to agree to the proposals made at Yalta required the Chinese to allow Russian troops on their soil, over a million Russian troops, on their way to fight the Japanese.

Stalin had stated his willingness to meet directly with Soong, and to take the matter up with Chaing Kai-Shek. He backed the Generalissimo [Chaing Kai-Shek] as China's new leader to provide for a unified China. "He [Stalin] stated categorically that he had no territorial claims against China and mentioned specifically Manchuria and Sinkiang and that it in all areas his troops entered to fight the Japanese he would respect Chinese sovereignty."

Further, in his cable of May 30th Hopkins reported on a sensitive issue about returning soldiers and prisoners of war. Stalin agreed to appoint Marshal Zhukov to the Control Council for Germany, a matter of interest to the Americans arranging for the disbanding of Germany. "[225]

On June 7th 1945, Harriman sent his cable. "The subject of the Far East came up again last night in our talk with Stalin. While he reaffirmed his intention to carry out his part of the Yalta Agreement on this subject he again stated that the Generalissimo must first agree to that part involving China. He said that when T. V. Soong came to Moscow he would take this up with him, but he had not yet as yet heard when he would arrive."

Harriman offered a schedule. "It is Harry's [Hopkins] and my strong opinion that Soong should be told of the importance we place on his reaching Moscow before the end of June…"[226]

Mr. T. Soong, China's Foreign Minister, would sign his Agreement on his return from San Francisco.

If Harriman had feelings of disquiet, he showed none and remained focused. With Japan's untold allegiances in China; a groundswell of revolutionary socialism growing, and Soviet troops crossing Manchuria, the situation was increasingly worrying.

During all this, said Meiklejohn, Kathleen was attending to the needs of Hopkins and Harriman walking about Spaso House in their bathrobes until noon dictating cables; their focus on matters of diplomacy and policy positions of the United States to be delivered at the evening's meetings with Stalin - followed by mad dashes to the Embassy through traffic of side-streets and detours by Meiklejohn to deliver those cables for dispatch.

The city was filling with people and preparing for festivities, and the Harriman team were beginning to relax. However, on the 27th of May, a cable came in from Sofia that alarmed them.

The American representative to Bulgaria, Mr. Barns had his country home surrounded by Communist Militia. Apparently, he was giving refuge to Dimitrov, a Bulgarian agrarian leader who opposed the Soviet dictatorship of his country.

The following day the British Ambassador Archibald Clark Kerr returned to Moscow, just as Moscow erupted in celebration for Victory in Europe. Muscovites besieged the Embassy with happy celebration.

At Spaso House, the evenings passed in quiet entertainment with others, a few invited by Kathleen for cocktails to meet their house guests. By the end of May, Molotov gave a reception for them all. Said Kathleen "One evening Molotov had a huge sort of victory reception – pleasant, sober affair with the invariable concert, food and dancing afterwards. "My feet suffered most having gotten stepped on by Litvinov and 2 Soviet generals." [227]

Stalin offered dinner at the Kremlin. "The following night Stalin gave a dinner to which Louie and I were invited '…if we wanted to come.' Probably the Soviets hoped we'd not, as women haven't ever been included in Kremlin dinners before."[228]

Kathleen later reported that many at that meal were NKVD officials, including Beria. "The most interesting thing of all really was seeing, for me the 1st time, all the more sinister members of the government" Still, the ladies took the edge off ""After dinner we adjourned next door and had coffee at little tables. Then came movies – 3 newsreels – May Day parade, the capture of Vienna and Berlin. Averell commented to Stalin about the horse the Chief of Staff rode. It was a beautifully trained animal…" [229]

Harry Hopkins's health took a turn for the worse and Harriman was fatiguing. The Navy physician Dr. Parker kept them going, and the meetings with Stalin proceeded.

The noose of Communism was tightening.

The American Representative at Sofia reported that Dimitrov was still in refuge – his young secretary found dead and badly tortured.

On June 5th 1945 Harriman was handed a message given him by the British Ambassador written by Churchill to Truman.

"I view with profound misgivings the retreat of the American Army to our line of occupation in the central sector, thus bringing Soviet power into the heart of Western Europe, and *the decent of an Iron Curtain between us and everything to the East.*"[230]

Next day, reports came in for Hopkins from Red Cross officials. They had been fired for making enquiries on Poland. They witnessed Soviet atrocities and persecutions by the Soviet-sponsored Lublin government. Jews in Poland, for fear of retribution, had joined as enthusiastic supporters. The picture was grim.

Then suddenly, in early June, an unexpected call came from the Russian General Kutuzov. He was requesting a meeting with the Ambassador at Spaso House.

General Deane was summoned to be with Harriman, and they received their visitor mid-morning. General Kutuzov and his colonel were holding a leather-bound folder.

It turned out that Stalin wanted to present to the Ambassador and Kathleen a gift of two fine horses. He had heard that Harriman had noted the fine mount ridden by General Antonov in a newsreel of the Mayday Parade. The red leather binder contained the papers of their pedigrees. General Kutuzov was here to deliver the gift.

Kathleen was delighted. It was an unexpected surprise, and she accepted the gift graciously.

The war over in Europe, Spaso House was now saying farewells. A party for departing British Mission heads was generated, and others followed.

They took Harry Hopkins and his wife out to the ballet "Lola" at the Stanislavski Theater, stopping on the way home for a social gathering at Mr. Kennan's apartment. As Minister Counselor, he was residing in the Finn House where diplomatic accommodations - borrowed from the Finns for American staff for a short duration - allowed for extra space.

* * *

With the war over, a time of bitter introspection and deep regret descended upon them. Kennan, following a survey of Europe for President Truman, reported on his findings. An assessment was necessary before the daunting task of reconstruction could begin.

Included in his account were the previous administration's omissions, gaps and intelligence leaks that might well have jeopardized the integrity of the European conferences and negotiations. He cited it as "New Deal neglect of sensitive and serious material engaging American forces."

In the fray, the British had also been compromised.

Clearly, the cost of socialist thinking in America had added immeasurable harm to the cause of liberation.

To the utter dismay of Washington, they discovered that, in addition to covert spies, Roosevelt's administration had been so sloppy as not even to provide Embassies abroad with fresh portraits of their Commander in Chief - most missions still delivering documents under Hoover's pictures…

The previous Administration's White House, in an effort to compensate for wholesale lack of security, had brought in special translators for secret negotiations between Roosevelt and Molotov to avoid internal leaks. Unfortunately, the Harvard-trained man recommended by Sumner Welles got drunk in Boston and revealed all that was transpiring between Molotov and Roosevelt. That, plus the secret itinerary of Churchill and his Advance Agreements were public knowledge before Churchill arrived at his destination! For the most part, they decided, Roosevelt had been most of the time without a clue and severely hampered as a statesman.

As it was, Roosevelt's New Deal agenda had been considered by many as misplaced ambition that bordered on the ridiculous. Hopkins, sadly now, had more to add to Kennan's report.

"Hopkins said he came into the White House signal office late one Sunday night and saw the operator typing out a message to Churchill and Stalin from Roosevelt saying, in substance, that the United States had no interest in European matters once Germany was defeated, and for

Churchill and Stalin to go ahead and make any kind of a deal they wanted to. Hopkins couldn't talk the operator into stopping the message as it was already signed by Roosevelt, so Hopkins phoned Prexy [Roosevelt] from the signal office and got him to tell the operator to hold the message till Hopkins had a chance to talk to the President about it. Ten minutes later Hopkins returned to the signal office with another message, signed by the President, saying that the United States was intensely interested in anything that Churchill and Stalin discussed and wanted no commitments made without its knowledge." [231]

It turned out that Roosevelt had to depend on Advisors that offered diametrically opposed views on any decisions he made, many of them seeking their own agenda, and disallowing decisive action from the President. Thus, two message-signals would appear that were in direct conflict. When asked, Roosevelt rarely knew which directive it was he wanted to advance, said Hopkins.

It had been a difficult century. The conversation was a sad indictment of a divided Presidency over a conflicted nation. Neither had individualism been recognized by organized socialism, nor had capitalism offered demonstrable opportunity. Enduring were the sacrifices, including those of a President who held the line. For his efforts, he remained nothing less than heroic.

Harriman doubtless felt redeemed for his diligence over the past four years. Harriman's knowledge as an Industrialist railroad man, and by dint of his hard work on the Lend Lease, enabled a victory that showed America's production capability at its finest. He had done his best, his security was the finest, thanks to Meiklejohn.

But now other leading Americans saw their newfound relationship with the Soviets as an opportunity to show off politically.

It was a popular visit, arriving on the Russians without checking with their official representatives in Moscow first. In his report on the Mission to Moscow, Harriman declared "It is believed that in all important matters the United States was able to obtain the essential information from Soviet authorities. The Soviet authorities were free in giving any information they had concerning the enemy [to us]" And while Eisenhower was satisfied with their cooperation "Many requests were received from home asking that [other] American representatives be allowed to come to Moscow or to visit the Soviet front line headquarters to familiarize themselves with Soviet methods…There was no chance of such requests being approved and the transmission of them to Soviet officials served only as an irritant…"[232]

It was at this point that the Americans felt that they should abandon their expectations for the Soviets as an ally. Hopkins advised them against pressing the Soviets on positions that they found they could not adhere to. "He…saw little value in any kind of agreement, signed or otherwise, with the Soviets which calls upon them to do something which is different from what they would naturally do in any event, of which is in conflict with the basic philosophy and way of doing things."

To deal with Soviet policy, it was now to be at "arm's length" manner of conducting business. Kennan pointed out that the Soviets would never negotiate on anything outside their autocratic directives issued from the top authority. Nor would they go beyond "a simple statement of decision"

The Great Alliance was disintegrating. On May 11, 1945, three days after the end of hostilities against Germany, President Truman ordered an immediate cessation of lend-lease aide to Russia. "The following day, civilian and military officials, zealously executing the directive, halted loadings in port and even recalled several ships at sea bound for Russia."

It was viewed, in retrospect, as Truman's "strategy of an immediate showdown" with the Soviets, [whereby] Truman abandoned Franklin D. Roosevelt's policy of friendship and conciliation toward the Russians and embarked upon a "powerful foreign policy initiative aimed at reducing or eliminating Soviet influence from Europe." [233]

Some considered this to be the beginning of the Cold War.

* * *

At Spaso House, there were duties.
Kathleen entertained new arrivals for lunch, such as the new British Air Attaché Air vice Marshal Thorold. Also invited were those of the Red Cross reporting on Poland. To Harriman they claimed that the Polish Underground Army "that fought the Germans is still underground fighting the Soviets."

Harriman was occupied with the Allied Reparations Committee which was set up in Moscow to determine the overall amount of reparations to be exacted from Germany.

In keeping with the assertion that those who bore the greatest burden should receive the most, the Russians proposed 20 billion dollars from Germany, half of which should go to the USSR. The sum had been first cited at Yalta.

Some arriving to serve on Allied Reparations Committee were political appointees and landed in Moscow on C-54s on June 11, 1945. Amongst them was a major financial contributor to the Democratic Party, Mr. Pauley. Others exiting Moscow on the same planes were Generals Spalding, Roberts and Colonel Bogart.

Spaso House saw U.S. Scientists invited to Russia for the 20th Anniversary session of the Soviet Academy of Sciences. With the assistance of Harriman, they were to meet with the Soviets.

Still, small infractions occurred that frayed nerves. In mid-June, the Soviets took umbrage at the Swiss for not recognizing them. They overran the Swiss Consulate in Berlin, treated them disrespectfully and brought them to Moscow instead of repatriating them across American lines.

The Americans were disconcerted that in the round up, the Russians brought in "non-Swiss individuals, including some with claims to American citizenship who had worked in the Swiss Embassy.

At Moscow, they carefully separated out those with Swiss passports. The rest, according to Meiklejohn's record, including "men, women and children, disappeared."[234]

Still, victory was in the air.

The Polish question continued with the London Poles arriving to parlay with the Lublinites; and the British and American Ambassadors mediating. It took up a lot of time, even as the arrest of 16 Polish Ministers was now proceeding with trial prosecutions.

* * *

Kathleen was thrilled with her new horses. An able rider, she exercised them herself whenever she could. "We went riding again today, first time in about five days. The Poles are taking up a great deal of Averell's time. I just fooled around and enjoyed myself and did a moderate amount of schooling, which annoyed Averell no end. His idea of fun riding is getting into a big sweat over whether or not the figure 8 comes out right..."[235]

Moscow was preparing for parades for returning troops, tanks, half-tracks and heavy artillery, showing large and impressive forces arranged to resemble a military campaign for effect. The parades went on for weeks, followed by marches of supporters – workers induced to "to turn out" at morning assembly points and furnished with large banners and placards.

Red Square was the viewing stand for official parades, and though only the heads of certain missions were given tickets to attend, the Americans had tickets for the Ambassador, Kathleen, Mr. and Mrs. Pauley, Dr. Lubin and members of the British Reparations Commission. Also invited were visiting British and American scientists in Moscow for the session of the USSR Academy of Sciences. Only top designated Soviet military and top civil officials attended.

On June 30th 1945, the Chinese Foreign Minister T. V. Soong arrived in Moscow in an American C-54 to negotiate some changes to the Yalta decisions made by Roosevelt and Stalin. For Harriman, there was still work to do.

The next day, Kathleen and Harriman went to Colonel Brinkman's datcha in the country. They had a Jeep, and as followed by their retinue of NKVD security guards - nicknamed the "boys," they had fun with them, giving flowers for their families.

If under pressure, the Americans were still smiling.

The formal resignations of Hopkins and Stettinius from the government was released, both citing poor health. Stettinius would be succeeded by James F. Byrnes to serve President Harry Truman as Secretary of State.

Kathleen remained busy.

The Americans hosted a Fourth of July Independence Day boat-trip, followed by a picnic; buffet supper and dancing at Spaso House. Sensing the end of their tour nearing, it was the biggest party yet given at Spaso House. Over five hundred people came, including Molotov. It cost some ten thousand dollars - "almost twice the year's allowance" - but served the Ambassador's purposes of showing solidarity amongst all Americans in Moscow.

Still outstanding was the conference at Potsdam to deal with Germany and her reparations.

Kathleen left Moscow. First, she was to stop in London, then on to Stockholm where she was to be joined by the others following the conference of Potsdam.

* * *

The war was not entirely over.

In the Pacific, Japanese dominance stretched across the entire Asian Pacific rim, from the Sea of Okhotsk to the Indian Ocean, including parts of mainland China, Indochina, Thailand and Korea and down through Burma.

A U.S. government assessment of the enemy force in the Pacific dated July 1945, identified the extent of this threat to America. For one thing, Japan was not a centralized economy.

Without Russia declaring against Japan, the State Department knew that defeating the Japanese might take longer than America could sustain. The Japanese culture could not entertain defeat or closure "…The Japanese believe…that unconditional surrender would be the equivalent of national extinction."

The report, later assembled as a book, made assertions that when calculated as a whole, the gravity of the situation was a clear and present danger. Especially considering America's present condition.

While the Japanese economic position had deteriorated considerably during the past year, it was considered insufficient to stop them. "Important raw materials from the southern areas, such as non-ferrous metals, high grade iron ore, bauxite, oil and rubber are no longer available. The severe cut in the size of the Japanese merchant marine, rail transportation difficulties on the continent….have reduced the potential…below levels of a year ago."

While infrastructure was badly damaged, the rate of production was only 25% lower than before. "The Japanese have received assistance from the Germans in the form of techniques, devices, and weapons, the employment of which might have a bearing on the war …electronics, ordnance, rockets, guided missiles, submarines, aircraft and jet propulsion…."

"The ground component of the Japanese armed forces remains …some 110 infantry and four armored divisions in the Army, 4.600,000 men. Increasing by 30 division by the end of the year…About 1,000,000 men within the Japanese Inner Zone. The remainder, some 95 divisions and over 4,000,000 men will be disposed in the main Japanese islands, Korea, Manchuria, and in China north of the Yangtze`

"We estimate that by late 1945 there will be available in the Japanese home island and their outposts in the Ryukyus, Izu-Bonins and Kuriles more than 35 active divisions and 14 depot divisions, which, plus army troops, will total over 2,000,000 men…

"Korea, Manchuria, and North China the Japanese ground forces in this area now total of 1,200,000 men, 24 active divisions and 5 depot divisions. These forces will be augmented once Russia enters the war by the end of the year.

"Central and South China and Formosa. The Japanese now have about 20 division in central and South China another 190,000. However, the Japanese will shift strength in China northward and abandon all holdings in China south of the Yellow River, leaving a force of about 125,000…"

"While the Japanese still find unconditional surrender unacceptable, but they are becoming increasingly desired of a compromise. Fully aware of the growing weakness of Japan's position, her leaders will make desperate attempts to keep the Soviet Union at least neutral, to sow civil strife in China, and to win the support of conquered peoples. In their present dilemma they are playing for time in the hope that Allied war weariness, jealousies, and conflicts of aims, or some "miracle" will present a method of extricating them from their admitted critical situation. "[236]

President Truman read the report going into the Potsdam Conference.

* * *

The Potsdam Conference was to take priority in Harriman's work. This was the third and last Conference meetings of the Heads of State of the United States; Great Britain and the Soviet Union. It was to open July 17th 1945, Stalin arriving one day later.

Vishinski had recommended the location at Potsdam since Berlin was so totally destroyed. Truman, Churchill and Stalin would stay at Babelsberg, not far from Cecilienhof Palace.

The Harriman party left for the Potsdam Conference on their new plane July 13th, 1945. However, he had been busy until the very last minute, securing from the Chinese Foreign Minister the necessary arrangements to have the Soviets enter the war against the Japanese.

Harriman's team consisted of Page, Meiklejohn, Edwin Pauley, and an American representative to the Allied Reparations Commission in Moscow, Robert Murphy, Eisenhower's political advisor.

His group, and that of President Truman were accommodated on Lake Griebnitz in a three story stucco villa.

A bus tour of Berlin showed the destruction of the city. They heard tales of plunder; destruction and wanton rape by Russian troops - behavior punishable by death for GIs in the U.S. Army. Russian troops had hauled away loot by the train-loads.

The German population, quiet and resigned, were in lines waiting for food and provisions. Post war clean-up had begun, but only in small measures.

Churchill was lodged not far away, and a few peaceful days of rest and introductions occurred prior to the official conference.

Suddenly, Churchill had to leave the Conference and he excused himself from the group: He returned to London where the British had cast their ballot and held public elections. Winston

Churchill was no longer the Prime Minister of England. In Britain, there were no transition periods for change of leadership.

Clement Atlee was the newly elected British leader, and he went directly to Potsdam with his new Foreign Secretary, Ernest Bevin, July 28th, 1945.

This totally threw the Allied negotiators. Already dealing with a new American leader following the death of Roosevelt, his new Vice President Harry Truman, now the British were to replace Churchill with an unknown politician. It was not easy for those who had worked so long and so hard to bring the war to an end.

"Averell reported that the British elections really did come as a surprise to the British politicians" said Kathleen in her letter written after her return to Moscow. In Stockholm we got English papers 3 or 4 days late. They certainly showed what a nasty mud-slinging election it was." But all was not lost. "The big hero of the meeting I gather was Bevin. He stood up to our friends [the Soviets] at every turn and racked down hard when 'twas needed. Unlike all others, he didn't go through a teething process" [237]

On July 20th, 1945, Harriman's nephew Ebby Gerry joined him in Berlin along with Colonel Boothe, Commander at Tempelhof Airport.

On July 24th, President Berut, Vice Premier Wladyslaw Gomulka and Stanislaw Mikolajczyk of Poland arrived in Berlin to lobby for the British and American support of their Oder-Neisse frontier between Poland and East Germany.

The next day, alarmed by more reports of unmitigated looting by the Soviets, Harriman and Mr. Pauley took a tour of the factories and railroad yards to witness that all American owned properties had been "stripped bare of anything movable."

The conference went less than smoothly.

At Potsdam, Harriman had himself been displaced by Byrnes, the new Secretary of State who "played his cards very close to his vest" and did seldom consult with Harriman. [238]

Harriman said that both he and Stimson "had plenty of free time. So we sat in the sun together outside his villa talking about when and how the Japanese might be brought to surrender, and how to deal the Russians after the war.' Neither was Harriman given a copy of the Agreements"[239]

Of course, for Harriman not to have a copy of the Potsdam Agreements was a ridiculous dilemma since he would need to proceed with the negotiations once he returned to Moscow. They received a copy from the British, who laughed. The explanation came later.

Meiklejohn was dismayed for he had produced the documents of all previous war conferences. "As it was, Truman and his staff had to deny Harriman a copy of the Agreements in order to deny them to all, especially one Joseph E. Davies, "a singularly stupid blabbermouth and former Ambassador to the Soviet Union under Roosevelt, a hanger-on at the Potsdam Conference, had demanded a copy of the conference as a privilege of his rank. In order to avoid having to give Davies a copy, it was decided that none of our ambassadors should receive copies." [240]

As the Potsdam report showed, the first Agreement was the establishment of a Council of Foreign Ministers that would begin the task of peacemaking. France and China would be admitted; and the Council would draft peace treaties for Italy, Rumania, Bulgaria, Hungary and Finland. Peace with Germany would be delayed until appropriate conditions were created.

This framework provided for the meetings, locations, members and mechanisms by which such decisions would be made. Byrnes proposed to Molotov that each of the occupying powers should be free to take whatever it wanted from its own zone. Further, the Russians could get additional reparations from the Western zones in exchange for food and coal from the east. Europe was in a deplorable state of need.

Dissolving the European Advisory Commission, they created a coordinated Allied policy for the control of Germany and Austria to come under the Allied Control Council at Berlin and the Allied Commission at Vienna. [241]

The terms were sweeping. On Germany they stated "German militarism and Nazism will be extirpated and the Allies will take in agreement together, now and in the future, the other measures necessary to assure that Germany never again will threaten her neighbors or the peace of the world."

Further, in the written Agreement of Potsdam is was asserted that "…It is not the intention of the Allies to destroy or enslave the German people. It is the intention of the Allies that the German people be given the opportunity to prepare for the eventual reconstruction of their life on a democratic and peaceful basis. If their own efforts are steadily directed to this end, it will be possible for them in due course to take their place among the free and peaceful peoples of the world."[242]

Other provisions included "Political and Economic Principles to Government the Treatment of Germany in the Initial Control Period included the complete disarmament and demilitarization of Germany and the elimination or control of all German industry used for military production."

"..To destroy the National Socialist Party and its affiliated and supervised organizations…'

"To prepare for the eventual reconstruction of German political life on democratic basis..."

"All Nazi laws which provided for the discrimination on grounds of race, creed, or political option shall be abolished."

"War criminals shall be arrested and brought to judgment"

"All Nazi Party members shall be removed from public office"

"The educational, judicial and administrative processes of government was to provide for the decentralization of the political structure and development of local responsibility"[243]

Amongst other principles, the Potsdam principles called for the "freedom of speech, press, and religion." And, "Subject likewise to the maintenance of military security, the formation of free trade unions shall be permitted"

On economic mandates, the Germans were to organize their economy for peaceful purposes and would be treated as a single economic unit. The Control Council was to exercise the power of disposition over German-owned external assets, and the payment of reparations was to leave sufficient resources to enable the German people to subsist without external assistance…"

There were still some outstanding matters.

The Soviets wanted to keep her provisional government over Austria. The Allies agreed to examine the question. As to Poland, the nation was at the Potsdam Conference considered a matter accomplished as an open and free coalition government. [244]

Stalin returned to Moscow August 2nd 1945. No longer looking at the familiar faces of his allies Roosevelt, Churchill, Hopkins or Harriman, he knew the end of German oppression had been achieved. What remained of concern for him now, was Russia's share of Europe.

The Conference of the formal plenary sessions went on until August 2nd 1945, with Truman returning to the US on the USS AUGUSTA, and Harriman to Moscow via a stop at London for a consolatory meeting with Churchill.

* * *

For the Americans, Potsdam had a far deeper dimension.

During the Potsdam Conference, the Japanese informed the still "neutral" Soviets of their interest to negotiate for peace. But it failed to meet the terms of an unconditional surrender.

In July, developments occurred that showed the Americans preparing for the use of an Atom Bomb. It was tested in New Mexico, and Stalin was informed by Truman of those intentions. Stalin showed support, but was clearly already informed through spies both in London and the United States. He knew that he had mobilized his troops in Manchuria.

According to Harriman's reports, on July 26th 1945, President Truman issued a public ultimatum to the Japanese to surrender unconditionally, warning that their refusal would mean the country's "prompt and utter destruction."

Meiklejohn noted the response from the Japanese "On July 28th, in a press conference, the Japanese Premier, Admiral Baron Kantaro Suzuki, appeared to dismiss or reject the ultimatum. Truman, thereupon ordered that the atom bomb be dropped on Japan as soon as possible after August 3rd 1945."

* * *

The Harriman party left Berlin for London August 2nd, and booked into Claridges for a brief stop.

The next day, at the Harriman Mission of Economic Affairs, they received word that General Eisenhower accepted Stalin's invitation to go to Moscow on August 11th. Also, that that the Chinese delegate Soong would be in Moscow to meet with them.

They left London for Stockholm and stayed at the Grand Hotel, observing a city in full operation - if fueled entirely by wood piles stacked everywhere for the lack of oil supply. Others were to join them, clerical staff transporting to Moscow.

The Harriman group grasped for some brief touring, shopping, socializing, dancing and even a swim the bathing resort of Saltsjobaden.

Harriman was searching for newspapers at every corner. They were days old, and he was without news. Had there been any changes? What was happening?

Kathleen, who had left Moscow antecedently for a vacation, was joined in Stockholm. She was focused on buying gifts and supplies and loading up on baggage for their return to Moscow.

The rest of the staff were quickly performing duties before leaving for the Airport, collecting classified documents and courier papers from their Embassy; changing money-currency and closing accounts. Their plane, named "Grand pappy," was waiting to fly them back to Moscow.

The plane was full of passengers including Captain Richardson, an Australian; the Harriman's staff; the Davies'; Arnold Smith; Mrs. Edenberg, wife of him Swedish Naval Attaché and her two children. They were seen off by Brigadier General Kessler, scheduled to fly over Leningrad for Moscow.

The flight brought them home safely and promptly. That night, they had dinner in their familiar surroundings at Spaso House. It had been a protracted and stressful excursion.

Kathleen wrote to her Sister saying "My two week vacation got stretched considerably thanks to Potsdam (Babblesberg as Averell calls it) and Averell's stay in Stockholm got considerably cut thanks to T.V. Soon arriving here." [245]

By the time Harriman went to pick up T.V. Soong on Monday morning, the news had reached them that the atomic bomb had been dropped on Hiroshima. At the Airport, Harriman asked Molotov what news he had from Japan about the effect of the atomic bomb.

On August 8th, the Soviets declared war on Japan. On August 9[t] 1945, the Japanese naval base of Nagasaki received the second atomic bomb.

The next day, Kathleen came through the house in some agitation to say that the radio had just made an announcement that it would be delivering news.

Midafternoon, Mrs. Pauley heard the broadcast. The Japanese had agreed to the terms of the July 26 Potsdam surrender ultimatum on the condition that no foreign troops occupy the mainland of Japan, or that the Emperor's status be affected.

Harriman engaged all day with cable traffic. The Japanese delivered their surrender to the American government via the Swiss government on August 10th, 1945.

To her sister Mary, Kathleen said "…Yesterday was a big day for great news. First the atomic bomb story…" She added "Ave's just returned with the news that Russia's at war with Japan! I wonder how many people will attribute it to the atomic bomb. I'm going off on the town to see reaction. There will be no joy…"[246]

The Americans had turned the corner on this war.

* * *

That evening, Harriman went out riding with Kathleen. He visited the Chinese Minister on the way home, and that night, at midnight, Molotov asked to see both Harriman and the British Ambassador. Russia had troops now stationed in Manchuria.

Harriman was engrossed in a series of cables; meetings with the Soviets and negotiations over the next twenty four hours relating to the terms of surrender, their conditions and frameworks.

The Japanese Emperor would have to take orders from the Supreme Allied Commander. The Soviets argued that since China was in the picture, that there should be four principal allies in the Pacific war, with more than one Supreme Commander. Harriman told Molotov that it was unthinkable that there should be more than one Supreme Command, or that it should any other than an American.

* * *

"…Ave does not know his plans," wrote Kathleen on August 14th "but the job he came to do is done, so presumably, he'll not be here through the winter…."[247]

Kathleen was busy, it was August 11th, 1945. General of the Armies Eisenhower and his party was coming to Moscow by Stalin's official invitation. Harriman's party met him at the airport. They would be staying at Spaso House.

The following day, Harriman received a message from the President to deliver to Stalin. They would appoint General Douglas MacArthur as Supreme Commander in Japan. By noon, it was arranged that everyone should go off to Red Square to see the Annual Sports Parade – all of them to attend by special invitation.

Mokhovoya, where the Embassy was located, was thronged with people, the mood festive. Unlike the previous military parades, this event comprised of "youth groups" from all over the Soviet Union, including "girls in bathing suits, sunburned men in shorts and others in white and colored suits"

It was a show of competition and support by the younger generation of Russians. Kathleen enjoyed it. "Averell and the General and Russ stood with U.J. [Stalin] and all the boys on top of Lenin's tomb – something which no foreigner's been asked to do ever."[248]

The parade took an hour and a half. It was followed by exhibitions and contests of athletic events including foot races, jumping, pile vaults, tumbling, wrestling and other races. A float appeared bearing two ice skaters. Everyone was impressed, including General Eisenhower.

Kathleen had her hands full. For dinner at Spaso House there was General Eisenhower and his staff including General Davis, his ADC, and General Clay. Plus the Harriman "family" as he called them including Ed Page, Dr. Michel and Meiklejohn. Also present was Lt Eisenhower, the General's twenty-two year old son just graduated from West Point.

General Eisenhower, his party and Harriman were invited for dinner at the Kremlin the evening of the 13th, August.

Meantime, the staff at the Embassy noticed subtle differences of administration from Washington. Mail deliveries from home, now weeks old, were no longer delivered by the military missions. Bureaucratic regulations were taking over.

* * *

Normally, Ambassadors would be expected to welcome new arrivals on the Embassy staff for lunch as guests. Harriman had done no such thing since his table at Spaso House was full of wartime officials dealing with the crisis of the moment.

Mr. Kennan recommended that Harriman comply with Department regulations. He told Harriman's staff as much with a scheduled welcome for their Vice Consul at Vladivostok. There were others on the Embassy staff. Of course, the burden would fall upon Kathleen.

The next day became hectic at Spaso House for Kathleen. Meiklejohn had passed along the Kennan recommendation and Harriman agreed to have them all to lunch at 1.30 pm. But by 1.00 PM, one party had gone missing, and a substitute invitation was sent out to another. Suddenly a relay of arriving guests appeared at the front door. A second dinning space, the Blue room at Spaso House, was set up and a second lunch was arranged by Kathleen.

A Soviet Marshall appeared, and Kathleen realized that he had mistaken the time for an evening reception being held for Eisenhower at Spaso House. She sent him away, only to be faced with a returning General Eisenhower and staff with a Marshal Zhukov - twelve in number, all of them coming to Spaso House, and famished. Their sightseeing tour had been shortened!

"They had to be divided into 2 bunches for eating purposes and for conversation. Our own luncheon just got started when Soong called up and Averell dashed over to see him. Just then the cook sent up a hurried call – She'd run out of vanilla for the ice-cream for tonight, would I provide immediately. Fun Fun."[249]

Kathleen managed beautifully. She rearranged all the fresh and cold food left over from the first dining room, had the kitchen refresh the servings, create new platters and sent it all up to the suite of General Eisenhower for a buffet style luncheon; the others lunched in the Blue Room, as scheduled. Later, when the lost party (train-delayed) guests arrived, they were served elsewhere, all three dinning groups having a wonderful luncheon at Spaso House. Kathleen received cards, flowers and letters of thanks for days.

* * *

On August 14th 1945, Harriman met with the Chinese Embassy, and was summoned for a simultaneously-delivered transmittal at the signal room, a "teletype conference" with Secretary of State Byrnes in Washington. It was an elaborate effort at timing and failed to produce the desired results. Instead, the BBC news announced the Japanese surrender as the Emperor addressed his people. Still, the American conference calling effort was a first.

Kathleen remained busy. At 8.00 P.M. a formal evening reception was held at Spaso House for General Eisenhower and guests that included all the top levels of the diplomatic corps in Moscow, including Marshal Georgi Zhukov; Marshall Budeny and General Alexei Antonov. The event was followed by a casual gathering when invited to the movie room to see "To the Shores of Iwo Jima."

Suddenly, Harriman was summoned for another teletype conference where he, Secretary Byrnes, Ambassador Hurley in Chungking and Bevin in England were all on simultaneously, talking in code. The Japanese had accepted the surrender terms and that the official declaration would be made in two hours. Harriman went back to the party, and with translators, read the cable from the President. They cheered, and the party ended.

Kathleen had to be flexible. "Just seen Averell for a moment, I'm not going off with Eisenhower tomorrow. "Twill have to be postponed."[250]

Harriman dictated an official letter to Molotov relating to the victory in the Pacific, and he delivered it himself at 1.00 in the morning of the 15th, August, 1945. This, while special arrangements were made to prepare the plane for General Eisenhower to return to the United States at sunrise.

A second formal message came in for Molotov at 3.15 AM which was signed by Harriman, and then sent on to the British Foreign Office at 4.00 AM.

Following an early breakfast arranged by Kathleen, General Eisenhower and his staff left on his plane. One hour later, the Chinese Foreign Minister left for London and Washington in Harriman's plane. Then Ambassador Pauley and the staff of the Reparations Commission left on the C-47.

That evening, exhaustion and hangovers notwithstanding, Spaso House was to hold a Victory Party for all Americans. "Fortunately, there was considerable food left over from the Eisenhower party." As usual, it was a stunning success with much food, drink and dancing to Kathleen's victrola.

Arriving at this time for the party were several Congressmen and Senators touring Europe. The Wickersham Committee enjoyed food and circulated amongst the guests, many of them asking for constituents from their state as they roamed about. Meiklejohn noted that the GIs at the party wanted their celebration at Spaso House as their own, Congressmen or not.

The next day, Harriman was invited to their official "America House" on the Moscow River, mess for GIs. He arrived announcing that he could stay only half an hour. However, with a three piece band; reporters from LIFE interviewing and a publicity victory campaign underway, Harriman stayed and partied for hours.

Kathleen took the Wickersham Committee to the theater.

However, as they carried on with their own touring, it was later reported that their behavior of drunkenness and bad manners were so appalling as to induce Mr. Kennan, the career diplomat, to complain to Washington.

* * *

Harriman, while preparing to fly out of town for an event mid-August, received a worrisome report from the Russians. They claimed that Japan was continuing combat offenses against Russian troops.

Later Stalin discovered that the troops had not been informed to stand-down. Neither in Manchuria, nor in Manila.

It was August 16, 1945 and Harriman and Kathleen flew with the Red Cross to Smolensk to dedicate a hospital.

The event lasted four hours. However, in true Harriman style, the Americans made an effective and lasting impression on the locals. A reporter in their company passed a note to Harriman via Kathleen's hands "It took Napoleon months to conquer Smolensk, the Germans three weeks, and Averell 4 hours. He did a good job" [251]

The following day the staffs got a chance to rest and recuperate at the British country Datcha - a country farming lodge redolent with the style of the Russian Empire. They swam in the lake; picnicked and strolled through the woods for the day. Here they could talk and share informal sentiments.

Certainly, the world had changed. The war was mercifully over. But politically, there might be yet deeper concerns lurking.

The first Council of Foreign Ministers was scheduled to take place in London, September 10th. 1945.

For the present, Harriman knew his mission was concluding, and he was talking of resigning his post as Ambassador. Further, for Harriman there was an issue outstanding.

That evening, Spaso House was to entertain the Dutch and English Ministers, again with movies afterwards.
The following day he and Kathleen were invited to an airplane show at the airport for the Red Air Force Day, but on account of the weather it was postponed.

It rained. Kathleen wrote "It's a rainy Sunday – so for the first time since we got back there' nothing urgent to do – 6 of us are playing bridge - my rubber out. There was to have an air show…." [252]

Spaso House was showing some wear. The roof leaked. Kathleen managed to get jars out to contain the dripping until the roof was repaired. There were puddle buckets and slippery spots to step over.

Gradually information came in that the Japanese Emperor effected his peace. The Embassy was relieved.

However, Harriman now saw older haunts surface. The Chinese Communists wanted the Japanese to surrender to them. Their intent was to acquire their weapons for use against Chiang Kai-shek. This was worrisome to the Americans who had just provisioned the Russians for their deployment of some 30 Army Divisions in Manchuria.

* * *

12

Neither Soviet soldiers returning, nor prisoners of war found much quarter.

American diplomats in Vladivostok were treated with suspicion. On the 27th of August, 1945, Harriman was called in to see Stalin at 10.00 PM to talk about things.

Meantime, the Japanese signed the formal surrender document in Tokyo on the battleship USS MISSOURI. Present Truman announced V-J Day.

Labor Day was celebrated in Washington and V-J Day in Moscow.

By early September 1945, a second Congressional committee was scheduled to be arriving in Moscow consisting of the House Foreign Affairs Committee and some military personnel. The Colmar Committee was to have its own agenda with their own independent itinerary.

Spaso House was outfitted with a few more Embassy luxuries, including safes for documents and other operating equipment. So far, they had managed without them.

The evenings at Spaso House resumed to lesser activities, if an Opera to which the ladies were escorted by Meiklejohn, followed by a party given by the clerical staffs sharing housing arrangements.

Summer was coming to an end, and the heater at Spaso House was turned on - Harriman muttering while sitting in the warmed room.

Their time at Spaso House was coming to a close, they knew, even as signs of their domestic occupation flourished everywhere.

Corn crops planted by Kathleen erupted from the soil and produced corn stalks all over the grounds. They grew to eight feet, and Kathleen wondered if the ears would be ripe enough to eat before they returned to London for the first Council of Foreign Ministers on September 10, 1945.

* * *

Harriman had decided to resign.

On August 30th 1945, Harriman wired President Truman saying that he wished to resign since he had "fulfilled his obligation to Roosevelt for getting Russia into the war against Japan, and now that the Pacific war was over and the Chinese-Soviet agreement was signed."[253]

The reply was a poorly phrased form-typed letter from the Assistant Secretary of State (Byrnes' office) saying that the President accepted his resignation.

As described by Meiklejohn, the cable was carried into the room by Kathleen in a sealed envelope while he was writing to Harry Hopkins. When Harriman read it, he howled with laughter.

Following the Potsdam Conference, Harriman had informed Secretary of State Byrnes that he wished to resign, and that the details could be ironed out in London while working out the peace treaties for satellite countries. Byrnes said that he would be too busy to discuss it during the Conference scheduled to begin September 10, and that Harriman could arrive on the 20th September to do so.

Byrnes' response was an affront to Harriman, the date implying that he was not needed for the Peace Treaties.

Kathleen had Spaso House being prepared for an event.

On Friday 7th September, 1945, a reception and movie at Spaso House was being arranged for the celebrated winners of the recent Soviet-American Chess contest. Kathleen arranged the invitations to include their wives, and asked them to wear informal dress.

The next day came a surprise reward. Eisenhower invited them all for a week at Cannes on the French Riviera before going to London for the Council of Ministers. Eisenhower would send his personal C-54 to pick them up!

Suddenly, a guest appeared. It was Mrs. Roosevelt, the former President's wife.

Mrs. Roosevelt invited herself to Moscow as a correspondent for United Features Syndicate "to see what the Soviets plan to do for women and children in the social field. Education, hospitals, etc..."

The Americans at the Embassy viewed it as a publicity stunt and gave it little time. Kathleen however, hosted her at Spaso House with graciousness.

The excitement for travel was still on. Eisenhower's plane, which was to take them to Cannes, arrived with passengers that included the Colmar Committee. Harriman apprised them of the present status with the Russians before he left for the south of France.

The Harrimans stayed at Eisenhower's villa and at local hotels. It was time to enjoy a break!

Variously assembled and casually dressed, they played in Cannes. They toured the islands, sunned by the sea, shopped, went aboard cruises and swam in their new bathing suits bought in Stockholm. Evenings they dined, saw movies and night-clubbed at the Cannes Casinos, and saw the show "The Copacabana Revue."

The place was teeming with US Army troops on leave at the Riviera, and the atmosphere was vibrant.

It did wonders for Kathleen and Meiklejohn, and repaired things for Harriman.

On the 19th September, they took off from Nice in General Eisenhower's C-47 for Frankfurt and London and stayed at Claridges Hotel.

Harriman joined the ongoing Conference of Ministers working on the Treaties on the 20th September, 1945 while his staff caught up with old friends and acquaintances in London.

Kathleen and some friends went out on the town, taking the staff with them to see the play "The First Gentleman" followed by dinner at a London night club. At Reynold they met movie personalities in London and enjoyed some celebrations.

Also arriving in London on the QUEEN MARY at this time was Ray Morris, a Senior Partner in the New York investment banking company of Brown Brothers Ltd. Harriman, an industrialist with a commercial mission of his own, had options to return to his business.

The conference in London closed empty handed on October 4th, 1945.

Unfortunately for Byrnes, the meetings had deteriorated to such a point that a follow-up was cancelled altogether. The Russians refused to parley with the French and Chinese.

Secretary Byrnes, finding the Council of Foreign Ministers hard to handle and needing to follow-up with another meeting in Moscow at the end of the year, asked Harriman to stay on as Ambassador there.

Harriman had announced he was leaving Moscow in October, 1945. But he agreed to stay on.

* * *

"Grand pappy" their plane took them to Frankfurt from where they drove to Eisenhower's Residence at Bad Homburg.

Harriman and Eisenhower went fishing together. If poorly baited up, they caught five trout for dinner.

Eisenhower was impressed by Kathleen, and seated her and Meiklejohn to his right and left for dinner at his villa. It was a special day. "In my later years I will probably be telling how I had a General of the Army Eisenhower, the Assistant Secretary of War, and the Ambassador to the USSAR to my birthday party" she wrote.

Dinner, as explained Meiklejohn, progressed with Scotty the dog climbing on the guests.

Attending also was Zhukov whose travel arrangements with the Americans were scuttled once the conference went sour.

There was talk of Germans who might well be mounting another offensive in the mountains, something their captured documents revealed. This had once caught the Russians by surprise, they found, leaving Zhukov to explain.

The dinner was greatly appreciated by Kathleen. For the rest, it was a chance to be away from their station and able to reflect amongst friends their circumstances and the state of affairs now.

Later, they discussed the French treatment of prisoners, and then turned to the topic of the atomic bomb - something which they wished they did not have to use to end the war.

More significantly, the Americans knew they had opened a new era. Whereas the technology was now important for defense and wartime tactics, they understood the implications of unleashing such an arsenal.

Harriman and Eisenhower worked on papers together while Kathleen and Meiklejohn enjoyed a quiet evening as guests. At dawn they would be taking off to Berlin in "Grand pappy" - a trip lasting one and half hours.

Harriman, who was to take his ride on Mr. McCloy's C-54, would join them later.

At Berlin, they stayed at Eisenhower's quarters in the city. The gathering included Glay, McCloy, Murphy, and the Harriman party, and a full reception party was put on for them.

Kathleen met Summersby - Eisenhower's driver, and together with Meiklejohn toured the Lake.

The evening of that day in October was occupied in private conversation about War Criminals trials to be held at Nuremburg.

Harriman's party flew on to Vienna on the 7th October and were met by Brigadier General Snavely.

They stayed at a hotel still respectably intact, and enjoyed a formal reception held for the resident British, French, Russian and American commanders in Berlin. Kathleen met them all.

Harriman took an informal tour of the war damage. At the Danube they observed from a Fortress-like tower the bombarded ruins. It was a grim sight.

The following day, Harriman toured again to review other damage to the region. He returned from Budapest that evening to join the party going to the Hofburg Theatre for a performance.

The theater was remodeled, if war-damaged, but accommodated the audiences with a spirit of rejuvenation.

The next morning, after a "luscious" Viennese breakfast, they were driven to the airport for their flight back to Moscow. For Kathleen the respite was needed. For Harriman, an informative trip on Hungary was necessary. Either way, here was the first step to moving forward.

Using the diplomatic energy that propelled them through to end the war, Harriman knew they must keep moving onward for repairs and a new reconstructed Europe.

* * *

The infrastructure of the war was winding down.

The Harrimans returned to Spaso House on October 14th 1945 and entertained key New Yorkers touring Europe following their Trade Union Conference in Paris. They had been hosted by the Russians also, and for reasons of his own, Harriman kept them away from his staff who were now winding down the mission at Spaso House.

The crew of the "Grand pappy" plane was gradually disbanding for rotation. Her service was to be replaced. Thus Mrs. Summersby left with another plane out of Moscow, her celebrated affair with Eisenhower revealed as being rooted in wishful thinking rather than reality, noted Meiklejohn.

Kathleen was still writing home.

The following day the Greek Ambassador Mr. Politis came to dinner and regaled Kathleen with a story of poetic Russian affairs-of-the-boudoir. This, she noted with some humor was "before the wife and children arrived."

It was 17th September, 1945 and snow fell upon Moscow, leaving them to wonder if this was to be a heavy winter weather, perhaps with a touch of remorse after all that they had been through together here.

On Wednesday October 24th 1945, Ambassador Harriman and Page, as interpreter, left in a Soviet DC-3 to visit Stalin at Sochi on the Black Sea coast. They were to deliver a message from Truman in an effort to disentangle the mess made by Byrnes at the Foreign Minister's Council.

During Harriman's absence, several of the administrative staffs of the British and American Embassies had gone on a visit to a Russian monastery and toy museum at Zagorsk. The excursion was a show of interest in Russian history neglected by the war, and they viewed a past of Russia before the socialist revolutions and the communist regime.

The toy museum was a disappointment, it had been ignored as a Russian legacy of artisan crafts. But a lady attendant, seeing their interest, showed them the collection of dolls and toys used by previous Czars. The monastery dazzled them. They reported that the legendary Troitskaya Monastery was a structure of medieval splendor founded in 1340 by Abbot Sergius, son of an impoverished Boyar of Rostove. The story was told that after the Tartars invaded, Sergius the Abbot was found by his successor Nikon who preserved his body on the grounds of the monastery. Russia, in the end was still Russia. For the visitors, she was a vast territory with a remarkably resilient people.

By the 25th October 1945, the team was back at Spaso House, Meiklejohn checking on the plane – a B-17 that was the stand-in for "Grand pappy".

Spaso House was welcoming in General Roberts as Military Attaché who had arrived in a B-17 piloted by the few remaining crew from "Grand pappy."

Also being celebrated was Navy Day – an event widely attended by Soviet officials and their wives. Kathleen and her father had long encouraged them to be comfortable about playing host to diplomatic missions in Moscow. It opened a new world for them, and they embraced the Harrimans.

October 31st marked the last day of Harriman's combined Military Mission in Moscow. The Embassy was now to resume under separate auspices of Army and Navy Attaches. Meiklejohn was to be the Assistant Naval Attaché and Assistant Naval Attaché for Air.

General Roberts made a delivery of all military war files now going back to the U.S.

The snow melted on November 3rd, 1945. With Kathleen out, Harriman attempted to catch up on some social obligations. He invited to dinner at Spaso House the Ambassadors and their wives of Norway, Holland, Mexico and Venezuela.

The winter closed in with darkness at 4.00 P.M., and they passed the time calmly for several weeks at Spaso House, finally taking the time to "get haircuts" and enjoy some personal time off.

Kathleen was back at home at Spaso House with family, it seemed, enjoying the comforts that she had become accustomed to in Moscow. Informal, carefree and less encumbered, they knew they were in a period of waiting for transition.

They "raided the ice box in the middle of the night; had tea in the Day office room upstairs, played badminton in the afternoons."

Since the heater operating best in the Day room, they had their breakfasts upstairs. The "girls" – Arlene their secretary since Yalta and Kathleen painted their fingernails and toenails in Meiklejohn office Day room, drying their hair. The Ambassador, noted Meiklejohn, become increasingly casual and "human."

Still, the coldness was tested in relations with Moscow. Harriman stayed on at Spaso House safely enough. Only worse was the frostiness from Washington DC.

A cautionary note came in from an old friend informing them that their Dictaphones in both the British and American missions should be checked for bugs. It was a sad legacy to a relationship.

On the 20th Anniversary of the Soviet October Revolution a parade was arranged which Kathleen and Harriman attended.

That evening, the Military and Naval heads came to Spaso to accompany the Ambassador to the British Foreign Office reception.

Clearly, the Soviet Union was changing complexion. Affairs of the war were still filtering in. Dismal reports of soldiers denied repatriation were relayed. Especially vulnerable were those countries whose boundaries were being changed or reorganized by the new post-war peace, even as propaganda for the communist regime augmented.

Mark Etheridge, sent by Truman to investigate the Balkan States, stayed at Spaso House.

* * *

Kathleen found levity with much of her daily life. She and Page had a problem getting anti-freeze for their car. They solved the situation by pouring four bottles of vodka in the radiator and one bottle of Vermouth "to make it smell better when it got hot." They laughed for days and were still having fun.

Harriman turned 50. November 15th was Harriman's birthday. Kathleen arranged for it, and

Admiral Olson got him out of the house for the set up. It was a close gathering of familiar friends, including a birthday cake of nine layers and fifty candles. What began as a simple gathering turning into a harmonizing song party, to which was added a troupe of Gypsy Theatre players procured by Kathleen. They played on until passed midnight.

Mr. Kennan was due back at Moscow, bringing needed provisions, if more red tape from a bureaucratic Washington. He was delayed by the plane "Grand pappy." Considered no longer need for the Moscow mission, the plane was diverted and grounded.

The Soviets were showing less interest in the American mission's social accommodations. A Red Cross dance attended by many diplomats lost most of its permitted orchestra players. With the end of the war and returning troops showing disenchantment, fewer local permits were issued for workers; and less invitations were forthcoming.

General Kay and his party returned from Hungary. As the Allies found more to complain about, the Soviets demonstrated resistance.

By now it was abundantly clear that they were not on the same side. The Soviets were now competitors, if not adversaries.

The Soviets were stirring up revolt in northern Iran; Rumania was falling under Russian control; Hungary was going next, and the messages coming out of Moscow were not encouraging. An official disruption occurred amongst the Bulgarian Communists who made remonstrance about the American Atomic Bomb.

Increasingly, there was a serious pall descending upon Russia, everywhere a baleful feeling of resentment.

Moscow itself was seeing changes after the war. The city was filled reports of looting and disorderly conduct by troops unable to transition to civil life. A crime wave hit the city and unrest filtered through society. Kids were robbing Soviet officials; NKVD Generals had their houses robbed as they slept.

The government militia took to the streets for protection, and citizens withdrew in fear of the lawlessness.

The Harriman team was longing to be home for Christmas.

Kathleen came home to Spaso House reporting that the Dutch Ambassador's wife, who knew Kathleen, had a masseuse who was being questioned about more than looks of beauty to be emulated by Russian women. The interrogation was not considered friendly.

The year was closing, and by early December the Harrimans and General Ritchie, who went out to the Datcha for lunch to alleviate the lull that settled upon them, finally heard from Byrns. Pending instruction on the upcoming Minister's Meetings, affairs remained vague since Harriman was uninformed of any new directives.

Even as Harriman knew there was much to do, he had to allow for time for resettlement.

Europe had been upended, the demographic of a former world changed forever. The issues of repatriating soldiers and prisoners of war still rankled. Now the immediate needs of survival were staggering; unpredictable and complex. The provision of food, fuel and shelter was paramount. The human losses, migrations and labor management required adjustment. Accountability of assets dislocated and seized was cause for social unrest and anger at this war. It was a dangerous and unpredictable period.

In his interview with Harry Hopkins in May, Stalin confessed to knowing of over 2.5 million prisoners of war, including Germans, Rumanians, Italians, and Hungarians.

Now the Americans wondered how many within populations of Europe, already devastated, had been marched off into Russia's labor camps?

Harriman was to assess.

In America, that great nation represented by a Roosevelt running for elections, families of first and second generation immigrants from Europe were wanting answers.

In Britain, a nation whose costs could never be counted let alone compensated by Reconstruction, feelings of hurt and economic hardship would linger, despite Lend Lease.

In Russia, those returning were angry at the war; angry at the perpetrators, at their own state. In Moscow, nobody felt safe, not even the police.

Stalin had himself admitted to a Russia unable to feed itself, much less expend for an expensive wars. Had the media properly represented the matters of this war, he wondered.

In China, rumors emerged of a sweeping movement of Communism. They observed the demise of Japan - former ally of Germany. They observed Russian Armies, still on Chinese soil and supplied by American Lend Lease aid, still reaping rewards for Stalin from China in territorial acquisitions of warm-weather seaports, Port Arthur and Port Darien.

Harriman immediately recognized the danger of such foment, and he determined to use his tools of diplomacy and public representation, if asked. Nobody was better qualified to understand the Russian nuances, or better informed. Especially if commerce and opportunity should follow.

Meanwhile, Kathleen invited Eisenstein, the Soviet movie director to Spaso House. She kept her composure calm, her spirits high, understanding that hers was the only encouragement for a diplomatic colony in Moscow increasingly concerned about the darkening countenance of the Soviets.

She assisted with light touches of liaison - language difficulties. The Turkish Ambassador had a dilemma. He had received an invitation from the Spanish delegation written in Spanish. How to reply officially? Kathleen encouraged him to reply in his native tongue, Turkish.

* * *

Finally on December 7th, Secretary Byrnes proposed the three Foreign Minister's meeting to be hosted by the Soviets in Moscow. But since the Soviets were not onboard, it was up to Harriman to arrange.

The Byrnes meetings was not without its challenges. The meetings would be conducted while the delegates stayed at Spaso House. Fifteen Americans in all, fifty British, all arriving in four planes.

The Conference took place in Moscow, December 14-27th, 1945.

It was a conference with little merit and many errors of omission - the Soviets now deeply convicted of their own global interests.

Harriman closed the files finally.

* * *

With their tour of duty in Moscow ended, the Harrimans returned to the United States.

In the spring of 1946, Kathleen Harriman was featured in a newspaper article in Washington DC.

She looked glamorous, a sophisticated woman in a fur stole over a buttoned jacket and leather gloves. She was smiling, a close up, her hair swept in waves beneath a stylish hat. She was holding the reins to *Fact*, an English bred bay stallion, the mount of a Field Marshall in the Russian Victory parade. The horse, its coat groomed to glimmering, was one of a pair - the other a sixteen hand golden chestnut gelding *Boston*, a Cavalry hero who had fought through the siege of Stalingrad. They had just made the 6,200 mile sea journey to America, arriving in Baltimore under the care of a Russian major; two lieutenants and two privates. Harriman's groom would assume charge of them now.

The article was titled "Gift from Stalin"[254]

END

1 Robert Pickens Meiklejohn WWII Diary of official calendar events written on duty while serving at London and Moscow March 10, 1941-February 14, 1946, Vol I, Forward P IV, The Harriman Papers, Special Collections, Library of Congress, Washington DC
2 Ibid, page 2
3 Ibid, page 4
4 Ibid, page 8
5 See Meiklejohn Diary, Library of Congress Harriman Collection.
6 Telegram, Letter of May 6, 1941. (Harriman Collection of Papers, Special Collections, Library of Congress, Washington DC).
7 This written office record, dated by calendar day in chronological order was an ongoing contemporary description of their daily activities. As a later published Diary (Vol. 1 and Vol. II) it is today kept in the Collection of the Harriman Papers at the Library of Congress.
8 Roosevelt, when making the official announcement of Harriman's posting to London, failed to give any title to the position, such that when a reporter asked, he responded "we can call him an *Expediter*, if you will" See White House newsreel, March, 1941.
9 Meiklejohn, page 8
10 Kathleen Letter, dated May 17, 1941. (See Kathleen Letters, chronologically intermingled, The Harriman Papers, Special Collections, Library of Congress Washington DC).
11 Kathleen Letter to Marie, March 18, 1941. Harriman Collection, Library of Congress.
12 Kathleen Letter, dated May 17, 1941
13 Report, Harriman Mission, March 1941-October 1943. (Harriman Papers, Special Collections, Library of Congress Washington DC)
14 Kathleen Letter, Dated May 30, 1941
15 Ira Katznelson, "Fear Itself. The New Deal and Origins of Our Time" WW Norton, 2013.
16 Report, Harriman Mission, March 1941-October 1943, p 3. Harriman Papers, Special Collections, Library of Congress Washington DC.
17 Kathleen Letter of June 7th 1941 to Mary.
18 Letter of June 8th, 1941
19 Kathleen to Mary, London, middle of June, 1941
20 Kathleen Letter to Mary, first week in June
21 ibid
22 ibid
23 Kathleen Letter, Dated May 30, 1941
24 ibid
25 ibid
26 Letter of June 8th, 1941
27 Letter of June 7th, 1941
28 ibid
29 Special Envoy to Churchill and Stalin. Page 64. Harriman Papers, Library of Congress.
30 Letter to Mary, June 7th, 1941
31 Meiklejohn Diary, Vol. 1, p92. Harriman Papers, Library of Congress.

32 Conference held on July 31, 1941 between Mr. Stalin, Mr. Hopkins and the Interpreter Mr. Litvinov at the Kremlin in Moscow, 6.30 to 9.30 pm. Part I. Harriman Papers, Special Collections, Library of Congress, Washington DC
33 Ibid.
34 Ibid.
35 ibid
36 Report on Special Mission to the USSR, W.A. Harriman and Party, September and October 1941. P1. Harriman Papers, Special Collections, Library of Congress, Washington DC
37 Letter to Mary of July 30th, 1941.
38 Letter to Mary, August 8, 1941
39 Letter to Mary, July 16th, 1941.
40 Ibid.
41 Letter to Mary, June 27th, 1941
42 Julie Summers, "Jambusters. The Story of the Workmen's Institute in the Second World War" Simon & Schuster, 2013
43 Letter to Mary, July 7th, 1941
44 Harriman Memo regarding the meeting between the President and the Prime Minister August 9th, 1941.
45 Ibid.
46 Ibid.
47 This was revealed by his son Elliot writing about a conversation he had with his father at the time of the Conference.
48 Ibid.
49 Harriman's Memorandum regarding meeting between the President and the Prime Minister August 10, 1941
50 Ibid.
51 Ibid, page 2
52 Ibid.
53 Kathleen to Mary letter, September 16, 1941.
54 Ibid.
55 Kathleen letter to Mary, September 30th, 1941.
56 ibid
57" Notes Regarding dinner the Kremlin – 6pm October 1st, 1941" by W. A. Harriman
58 Ibid.
59 Ibid.
60 Notes Regarding Special Performance of the Moscow ballet October 3, 1941 – For the British and American Missions" by W. A. Harriman.
61 Telegram no. 1757 from Moscow for Hopkins from Mr. Harriman, October 4, 1941. (Franklin Roosevelt Library, Hyde Park, N.Y.)
62 Memo by Hopkins to Secretary of State, to inform Harriman and the US Embassy of London October 7th, 1941. (Franklin D. Roosevelt Library, Hyde Park, N.Y.)
63 Robert Pickens Meiklejohn World War II Diary, At London and Moscow, March 1941-February 14, 1946, Vol. 1, p135
64 Ibid, p 155
65 Kathleen to Mary, September 30th, 1941.
66 Kathleen to Mary letter of October 8th, 1941.
67 Ibid.
68 Kathleen Letter to Mary of October 14th, 1941.

69 Ibid.
70 Ibid.
71 Kathleen letter to Mary, October 23, 1941.
72 Ibid.
73 Kathleen Letter to Mary of October 28th, 1941.
74 Kathleen Letter to Mary, November 6th, 1941.
75 Kathleen Letter to Mary and the rest of the family, November 21st. 1941.
76 ibid
77 Kathleen to Miss Marshall and Mary, December 5th, 1941
78 Ibid.
79 Ibid.
80 Meiklejohn Diary, Chapter IV, pp 164.
81 Letter to Mary, December 16th, 1941
82 Letter to Mary, December 18th, 1941
83 Meiklejohn Diary, Chapter IV, p 167
84 Letter to Mary, London January 1, 1942.
85 Letter to Mary January 11, 1942
86 ibid
87 Kathleen Letter to Mary, February 20th, 1942.
88 ibid
89 Meiklejohn diary, Vol. II, page 179
90 ibid
91 Kathleen to Mary, February 23rd, 1942.
92 Kathleen to Mary, February 25, 1942
93 Meiklejohn Diary, Vol. I, 3 (P 183)
94 ibid
95 Ibid (187)
96 Letter to Mary, date unknown (February or March, 1942) in collection of Harriman Papers.
97 Kathleen Letter to Mary, March 6th, 1942, Harriman Collection of Papers, Library of Congress.
98 Kathleen Letter to Mary, March 6th, 1942, Harriman Collection of Papers, Library of Congress.
99 ibid
100 Stephen Heathorn, (*McMaster University*) Historiographical Review, The Mnemonic turn in the Cultural Historiography of Britain's Great War, *The Historical Journal,* 48, 4, (2005), pp 1103-1124, 2005 Cambridge University Press.
101 ibid
102 Kathleen to Mary, March 24th to April 6th, a continuous letter of added notes. Harriman Collection of Papers, Library of Congress.
103 Kathleen to Mary, March 24th to April 6th, a continuous letter of added notes. Harriman Collection of Papers, Library of Congress.
104 ibid
105 Kathleen Letter to Mary, May 10-12, 1942 Harriman Papers Library of Congress.
106 Ibid.
107 Ibid.
108 Meiklejohn Diary, Vol. 1, p 197. Harriman Papers, Library of Congress.
109 Ibid.
110 Kathleen letter to Mary, London June 27, 1942. Harriman Papers, Library of Congress.

111 ibid
112 Letter to Harriman from Richard E. Myers, New York, July 20th, 1942. Harriman Papers, Library of Congress
113 Kathleen letter to Mary, July 30th, 1942. The Harriman Papers, Library of Congress.
114 Special Envoy to Churchill and Stalin" by W.A. Harriman and Elsie Abel, Harriman Papers, Library of Congress.
115 Meiklejohn Diary, July 17th 1942, Vol. 1, Harriman Papers, Library of Congress.
116 Kathleen Letter to Mary, July 30, 1942. Harriman Papers, Library of Congress.
117 ibid
118 Kathleen letter to Mary, August 10-18, 1942. Harriman Papers, Library of Congress.
119 Ibid.
120 Meiklejohn Diary, Vol. I, age 241. Harriman Papers, Library of Congress
121 Kathleen letter to Mary, August 24, 1942. Harriman Papers, Library of Congress.
122 Kathleen Letter to Mary, September 9th, 1942. Harriman Papers, Library of Congress.
123 Meiklejohn's Diary, Vol. 1, page 245.
124 Kathleen's letter to Mary, September 9th, 1942. Harriman Papers, Library of Congress.
125 Kathleen letter to Mary, September 23rd, 1942. Harriman Papers, Library of Congress.
126126 ibid
127 Kathleen Letter to Mary, October 22, 1942. Harriman Papers, Library of Congress.
128 Meiklejohn Diary, Vol. 1, p 254. Library of Congress.
129 Kathleen Letter to Mary, October 22nd 1942. Harriman Papers, Library of Congress.
130 ibid
131 Ibid.
132 Harriman's book "Special Envoy to Churchill and Stalin" (pages 176-177); Harriman Papers, Library of Congress
133 Kathleen letter to Mary, January 4th, 1943.
134 Kathleen letter to Mary, January 23, 1943. Harriman Papers, Library of Congress.
135 Ibid.
136 Kathleen letter to Mary February 16th 1943. Harriman Papers, Library of Congress.
137 Robert Meiklejohn diary, Vol. I, p 299. Harriman Papers, Library of Congress.
138 Harriman Book on the Mission History of Moscow. Office of the Commanding General, American Embassy, US Military Mission Moscow, USSR. Part I, Para 37, draft copy, dated 30 October, 1945
139 Ibid.
140 ibid
141 Meiklejohn Diary, Vol. 1, page 345A. Harriman Papers, Library of Congress.
142 ibid
143 Ibid
144 Memorandum of August 7th Memorandum of conversation with the Prime Minister at dinner onboard SS QUEEN MARY in route to U.S. Present were The

Prime Minister, Mrs. Churchill, Lord Louis Mountbatten, W.A. Harriman, Kathleen Harriman, Mr. Rowan, Commander Thompson and Brigadier Jacob.

145 Meiklejohn's Diary, Vol. 1 page 363. Harriman Papers, Library of Congress.

146 Kathleen letter to Mary, September 1943, the return voyage.

147 Ibid.

148 Kathleen letter to Mary, September 15-18, 1943. Harriman Collection, Library of Congress.

149 The Harriman Mission Report, pp 216: Relations with the Soviet Union, Harriman Papers, Library of Congress.

150 ibid

151 ibid

152 Letter to Mary, Mid-October 1943. Harriman Collection, Library of Congress.

153 "Special Envoy to Churchill and Stalin" page 267. Harriman Papers, Library of Congress, Washington DC

154 Meiklejohn Diary, Vol. II, page 440. Harriman Papers, Library of Congress, Washington DC

155155 Tehran, Top Secret. J.V. Chamberlin, p 205. Chamberlin Press, 2012. ChamberlinPress.com

155. Yalta Conference, The first Stalin Speech.

156 On February 7th, 1952 a story appeared in the New York News saying that Kathleen Harriman, daughter to Ambassador Averell Harriman serving in Moscow had accompanied a party of newsmen to the Soviet staged demonstration of the Katlyn Forest massacre where 10,000 Poles lost their lives at the hands of the Germans. The article was a recital of the testimony of Henry Cassidy, former AP Press correspondent, to the Select Committee conducting an Investigation of the Facts, Evidence and Circumstances of the Katyn Forest Massacre. Cassidy claimed he was there with Rev Leonard Braun, a catholic priest who was in Moscow at the time. Kathleen, by now married and known by her married name, was cited as being there as a correspondent for the Office of War Information. The investigation deliberated to find that the massacre was done by the Russians.

157 "Special Envoy" pages 296-297

158 Meiklejohn Diary, Vol. II, p 492. Harriman Papers, Library of Congress.

159 Meiklejohn Diary, Vol. II, p 501. Harriman Papers, Library of Congress.

160 "Special Envoy to Churchill and Stalin" report,p.311,"

161 "Special Envoy to Churchill and Stalin" in the parts concerning Wallace's trip. Harriman Collection, Library of Congress

162 Kathleen letter to Mary, Moscow July 3, 1944. Harriman Collection of Papers, Library of Congress.

163 Ibid.

164 ibid

165 "Special Envoy to Churchill and Stalin" by W. A. Harriman and Elsie Abel, Chapter XV. Harriman Papers, Library of Congress.

166 Meiklejohn Diary, Vol. II, p 547. Harriman Papers, Library of Congress.

167 ibid

168 Kathleen Letter to Mary, Moscow, September 1st, 1944. Harriman Collection of Papers, Library of Congress.

169 Ibid

170 Ibid.

171 History of Mission to Moscow, by W.A. Harriman, Page 109. Harriman Papers, Library of Congress.

172 Ibid, p 554

173 This information about the Russians would inform Harriman's career as Advisor to future US Administrations during the cold war.
174 Meiklejohn Diary, Vol. II, page 565. Harriman Collection, Library of Congress,
175 ibid
176 Ibid.
177 "Special Envoy to Churchill & Stalin" p 353, 355, 364. Harriman Collection, Library of Congress.
178 Kathleen Letter to Pam Churchill, October 16, 1944. Harriman Papers, Library of Congress
179 Meiklejohn Diary, Vol. II, p 585. Harriman Papers, Library of Congress.
180 Letter to "Shirley and Larry" Moscow, January "?", 1945. Harriman Papers, Library of Congress.
181 Letter to Mary, December 9th, 1944. Harriman Papers, Library of Congress.
182 ibid
183 ibid
184 ibid
185 Memorandum of the trip to General Eisenhower's Headquarters from Paris, Sunday-Tuesday November *26-28, 1944*. Harriman Papers, Library of Congress.
186 Ibid, p1
187 Ibid, p3
188 Ibid, p4
189 Letter home by Meiklejohn, December 26, 1944. Meiklejohn Diary, Vol. II, page 598. Harriman Papers, Library of Congress.
190 Ibid.
191 Ibid.
192 Meiklejohn's Diary, Vol. II p 603. Harriman Collection of Papers, Library of Congress.
193 Letter of Kathleen home, January – 21st? 1945. Harriman Papers, Library of Congress.
194 Ibid
195 ibid
196 Harriman's book "Special Envoy to Churchill and Stalin" (pages 380-381)
197 Ibid.
198 Letter to Mary, Yalta, February 4-10th, 1945. Harriman Papers, Library of Congress.
199 ibid
200 Kathleen letter to Miss Marshall, Yalta, February 1st, 1945
201 ibid
202 Unaccustomed, Meiklejohn noted in his diary that he neither did salute the quarter deck, nor salute the officer of the deck nor did he "Request permission to come aboard" claiming, apologetically that he didn't know where the quarter deck was, or what it looked like. He saluted the propeller, he said.
203 Kathleen letter to Mary, Yalta, February 4-10th, 1945. Harriman Papers, Library of Congress.
204 ibid
205 ibid
206 Rudy Abramson, *The Life of W. Averell Harriman, 1891-1986*, Wm. Morrow and Co,. 1992 p 391
207 Kathleen letter to Mary, Moscow, February 16th, 1945
208 Kathleen letter to Mary March 8th, 1945
209 Kathleen letter to Mary, February 16th, 1945.

210 Meiklejohn Diary, Vol. II page 643. Harriman Papers, Library of Congress.
211 Letter to Harriman and Kathleen from Frances Balfour, London, February 24th, 1945. Harriman Papers, Library of Congress.
212 Kathleen Letter to Mary, March 8th, 1945. Harriman Papers, Library of Congress.
213 ibid
214 ibid
215 ibid
216 Kathleen to Pam, Moscow, March 20th 1945. Harriman Papers, Library of Congress.
217 Kathleen to Pam, March 20th, 1945.
218 Ibid.
219 Minutes, Secretary's Staff Committee Friday Morning, April 20th, 1945. Harriman Papers, Library of Congress.
220 Meiklejohn Diary, Vol. II page 660. Harriman Papers, Library of Congress.
221 Memorandum of Conversation, April 24th, 1945, San Francisco Conference. Harriman Papers, Library of Congress.
222 Ismay letter to Kathleen, London, April 6th, 1945. Harriman Collection, Library of Congress.
223 Kathleen Letter to Mary, Moscow, June 4, 1945. Harriman Papers, Library of Congress.
224 "Paraphrase of Navy Cable May 29,1945. Top Secret and Personal for the Eyes of the President only from Hopkins" Harriman Papers, Harriman Collection, US Library of Congress (Document Declassified by Department of State, 1986) . See *End of War*, p 227 Documents Edited by J.V.Chamberlin. Chamberlin Press, 2012.
225 Paraphrase of Navy Cable May 30,1945. Top Secret and Personal for the Eyes of the President only from Hopkins" Harriman Papers, Harriman Collection, US Library of Congress (Document Declassified by Department of State, 1986). See *End of War*, p 227. Documents Edited by J.V.Chamberlin. Chamberlin Press, 2012.
226 Paraphrase of Navy Cable June 7, 1945. Top Secret and Personal for the Eyes of the President only from Hopkins" Harriman Papers, Harriman Collection, US Library of Congress (Document Declassified by Department of State, 1986). See *End of War*, p 227 Documents Edited by J.V.Chamberlin. Chamberlin Press, 2012.
227 ibid
228 ibid
229 ibid
230 "The End of War II" by J.V. Chamberlin, page 255. Chamberlin Press, 2013. Text received from the British Ambassador, June 5, 1945. A personal message No. 72, dated June 4, 1945 from the Prime Minister to President Truman.
231 Meiklejohn Diary, Vol. II 682, Harriman Papers, Library of Congress.
232 Harriman Report on Mission to Moscow, p 110. Harriman Papers, Library of Congress.
233 *Lend-Lease to Russia and the Origins of the Cold War,* 1944-1945 GEORGE C. HERRING, JR. *The Journal of American History*, Vol. 56, No. 1 (Jun., 1969), pp. 93-114Published
234 Meiklejohn Diary Vol. II, page 685. Harriman Papers, Library of Congress.
235 Kathleen letter to Mary, June 18th, 1945 Moscow. Harriman Papers, Library of Congress.
236 State Department Report, An Assessment of Japan, July 1945. P 15. Harriman Papers, Library of Congress.
237 Kathleen letter to Mary, August 8th, 1945.

238 Harriman "Special Envoy to Churchill and Stalin" page 488, Harriman Papers, Library of Congress.
239 Ibid.
240 Diary of Meiklejohn, Vol. II, page 695. Harriman Papers, Library of Congress.
241 Document Collection of the Potsdam Conference, Chamberlin & Chamberlin, 2013. Harriman Papers, Library of Congress.
242 ibid
243 ibid
244 Ibid.
245245 Kathleen Letter to Mary, August 8th, 1945, Moscow. Harriman Papers, Library of Congress.
246 ibid
247 Kathleen Letter to Mary, August 14th, 1945. Harriman Papers, Library of Congress.
248 ibid
249 Kathleen letter to Mary, August 14, 1945. Harriman Papers, Library of Congress.
250 Kathleen Letter to Mary, August 19th, 1945, Harriman Papers, Library of Congress
251 Kathleen Letter to Mary, August 19th, 1945, Harriman Papers, Library of Congress.
252 ibid
253 Meiklejohn Diary, Vol. II, page 736. Harriman Papers, Library of Congress.
254 Evening Star, Washington DC April 30th (20th?), 1946. Harriman Papers, Library of Congress.

www.ingramcontent.com/pod-product-compliance
Lightning Source LLC
Chambersburg PA
CBHW020121020526
44111CB00048B/155